The Beach Boys on CD
(an illustrated guide)

Joe Thomas

RisingTide Publications

Dublin - 2003

The Beach Boys on CD: The Beach Boys

© RisingTide Publications/J. Thomas

Cover & Book design by J. Thomas

All disk & CD case images are digitally photographed from private CD collections

Photographs: Redferns, London (annotated throughout)

"Uncover the corn fields" - Smile art, reprinted by kind permission of Frank Holmes, SF

ISBN: 0-9546692-1-5

Also available in hardback: - **ISBN 0-9546692-0-7**

All rights reserved. No part of this book may be reproduced in any form or by any electronic or mechanical means, without permission in writing from the author.

In a couple of cases, the source of a photograph was not established. We would be grateful if the photographer concerned would contact us.

A catalogue record of this book will be lodged at the British Library and at Trinity College, Dublin.

Special thanks to Mártan McDevitt for assisting in the digital print process and to the various 'advance readers'

Digital printing by ProntaPrint, Dun Loaghaire, Co. Dublin, Ireland

10. Fold the top layer downwards along the dotted line and unfold. Turn the paper over and do the same again.

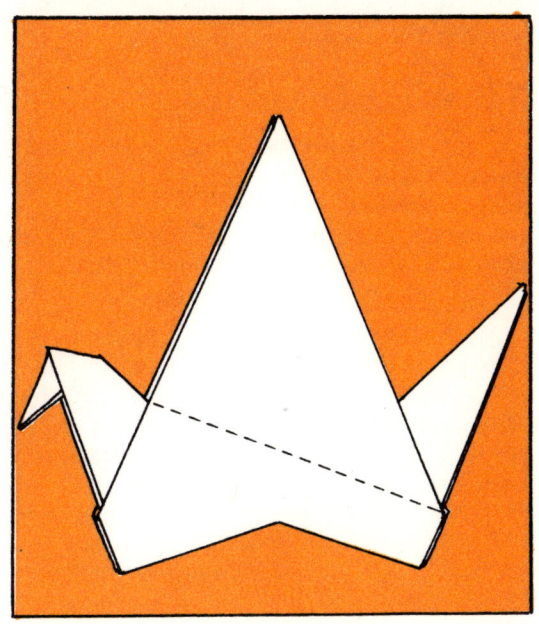

That's it. To make the bird flap its wings, hold it firmly at the front with one hand, and push the tail in and out with the other.

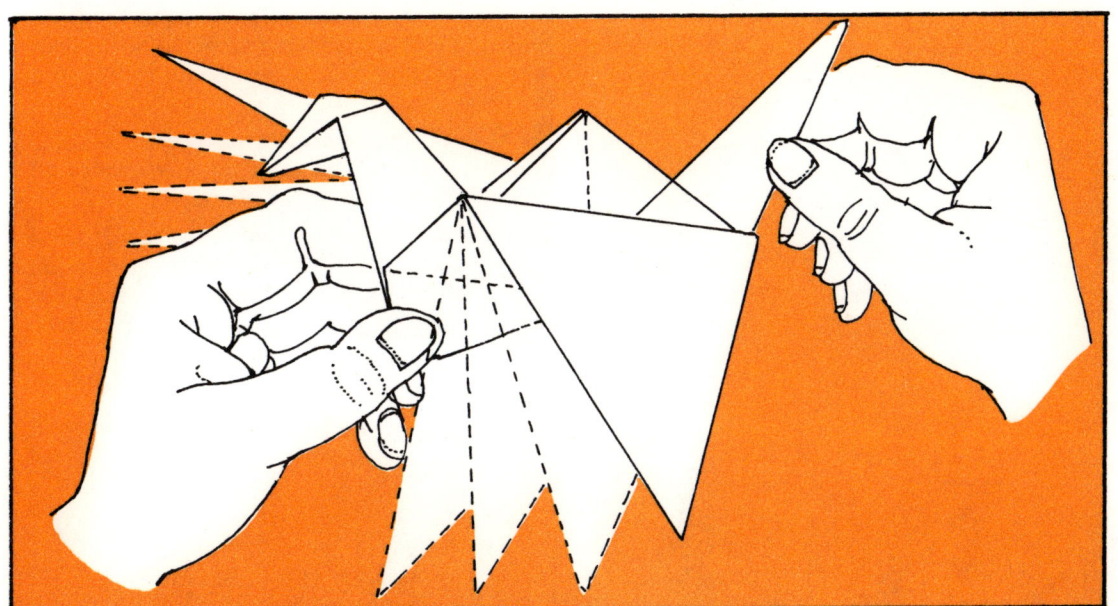

Materials

Adhesives and glues

For many of the toys described in this book you will need a strong glue to fasten the pieces together. But model-making shops and hardware stores sell so many different kinds—in jars, tins and tubes—that it's often difficult to know which to choose.

I suggest that you buy a PVA type adhesive (PVA is short for polyvinyl acetate). The letters PVA don't always appear on the label—manufacturers often give it a simpler name—so be sure to ask the shopkeeper for PVA.

It's thick, like treacle, but very white, and will stick almost anything. More important perhaps—if you spill it, or use a paint brush to apply it, it can be quite easily washed away with cold water. Yet when it dries hard, it is waterproof and transparent.

By mixing it with water (roughly half water and half PVA), you can make a varnish which can be painted over any of the toys described here, to give them a shiny finish, and help keep them clean.

Modelling paste for the Greek doll:
Instead of using ordinary modelling clay (which, as you know, has to be fired in a kiln to make it go hard) buy a packet of modelling paste from your local art or craft shop. Modelling paste looks like clay, and feels like clay, but it has something added to it which makes it set very hard without being fired in a kiln.

Some modelling pastes will set hard after being left on the window-sill for a day or so; others will require baking in the oven—but at a very low heat.

You can buy the paste in small polythene packets—it's quite cheap—and the printed instructions will tell you exactly how to use it.

Papier-maché paste for the Punch and Judy puppets:

1. Tear up two or three newspapers into very small pieces, and leave them to soak in half a bucketful of warm water with a teaspoonful of washing-up liquid, for about a week.

2. Take out the paper pulp, squeezing as much water as possible from it with your hands, and put the squeezed-out pieces into a bowl.

3. Break up the pieces into tiny granules and stir in a cupful of flour and a cupful of thickly mixed wallpaper paste.

4. Knead the mixture with your hands until it is like soft clay. If the mixture is too wet, add some more flour; if too dry, add a little water. Now the papier-maché is ready to use.

The Beach Boys on CD: The Beach Boys

© RisingTide Publications/J. Thomas

Cover & Book design by J. Thomas

All disk & CD case images are digitally photographed from private CD collections

Photographs: Redferns, London (annotated throughout)

"Uncover the corn fields" - Smile art, reprinted by kind permission of Frank Holmes, SF

ISBN: 0-9546692-1-5

Also available in hardback: - **ISBN 0-9546692-0-7**

All rights reserved. No part of this book may be reproduced in any form or by any electronic or mechanical means, without permission in writing from the author.

In a couple of cases, the source of a photograph was not established. We would be grateful if the photographer concerned would contact us.

A catalogue record of this book will be lodged at the British Library and at Trinity College, Dublin.

Special thanks to Mártan McDevitt for assisting in the digital print process and to the various 'advance readers'

Digital printing by ProntaPrint, Dun Loaghaire, Co. Dublin, Ireland

The Beach Boys on CD
(an illustrated guide)

Contents

Introduction
The Beach Boys
    A brief history of The Beach Boys   2
    A profile of The Beach Boys   5
    The Beach Boys recording history   8
        A brief history of the Beach Boys on CD   9
        Beach Boys Studio Recordings (US Releases)   10
    How to use this book   11

Studio Albums
    Single Album CD releases   13

Twofers
    The Twofers   51

Pet Sounds
    The Pet Sounds Chronicle   71

Smile
    Smile (A tragedy in many parts)   85
        Smile Recordings   91
        Smile Artwork   91
        Smile references   92

Compilations & Collections (Pandora's Box)
    Official Compilations   93
    Special Markets & Disky   133
    Licensed Compilations   149
    Christmas albums   169
    Promos   173

Japan, the Land of the Rising Song
    Twofers   180
    PastMasters   183
    CoolPrice   185
    Mini LP CD's   187
    Pet Sounds   189
    Current Set, Best Of, Carl Wilson +   195

Bootlegs - Did I want to do this? There be MONSTERS here!
    Unsurpassed Masters   208
    Rarities   231
    Vigotone   238
    Various   248
    Russia   255

Solo recordings on CD
    I'm a cork on the Ocean   259

Beach Boys Miscellany (Appendices)
    Appendix I: Beach Boys Associates
    Appendix II: Beach Boys Composers, Co-lyricists
    Appendix III: CD Discography (Alpha order)
    Appendix IV: Song listing (Alpha order)
    Appendix V: The Rogues Gallery
    Appendix VI: **STOP!!** the presses
    Appendix VII: References

The Beach Boys on CD: The Beach Boys

Introduction

So why write a book about and catalogue the CD releases of the Beach Boys? Well, there are many reasons, but the most compelling was that no book of this nature currently exists. I thought by writing such a book, Beach Boys fans could navigate and purchase/collect the available CD releases with the assistance of a point of reference. I also had the time and interest to carry out the task. The intention is that the book should serve many purposes: to act as an aid for anyone newly interested in the Beach Boys and for veterans who might wish to recall some facts. It may also help collectors and act as a buyers guide in certain circumstances. Overall, the book is designed to assist, inform, and to augment the collective history of The Beach Boys.

The complete range of 'official' Beach Boys CD's essentially falls in two categories a) CD releases of their studio and live recording, and b), compilation/collections developed from a). 'Bootlegs' or 'unofficial' releases can be isolated as a third category of Beach Boys CD. The complete available collection of Beach Boys CD releases can be further divided into current releases, and releases which are 'out of print' (OOP) but which are still available on the open market via shop (physical/online), internet auction site and various other sources.

In this book, I have presented the CD catalogue in a logical and simple way; CD content has been categorised by type/series and all known information is present in a consistent manner. Introduced first, the studio albums should be taken as the foundation for all other CD categories. Generally, I have presented the CD information in release date order and I have included refined song/track and CD indices to make searching and validation quick and efficient. I have also provided images, notes, background information and occasionally I have provided commentary and other useful data.

Although this is not a history book, I have provided a certain amount of specific foundation and background data at the beginning and throughout. This should enable the novice to get some feel for The Beach Boys, the people involved in the production of their songs, and the CD catalogue.

At the outset, I should point out that although I have identified more than 500 individual CD's, this book and catalogue is not complete - there are hundreds of fans out there with Beach Boys collections, collections which containing other Beach Boys CD releases not listed herein. I have collected my CD library over the past four years and used many different sources, ranging from barrow markets in Glasgow, to Amazon and eBay, to private sellers in Australia, Argentina and all over the world (internet & physical).

The book does not include information on 'single' track CD releases by The Beach Boys, shared compilations, Tribute CD's and is light on the 'promo' CD catalogue; perhaps these areas will be covered more fully in a future revision. Since this book was developed with the fan and collector in mind, I would encourage anyone who can extend and enhance this catalogue to contact me and so contribute to this essential record of one of the greatest bands in the history of 'Rock'n'Roll'; my contact details are provided: rathmich@gofree.indigo.ie

I would like to express my appreciation to the following people for their help and assistance throughout the development & creation of this book: Robert (Robbie) Thomas (my ever-present research assistant, devils advocate, eldest son and Beach Boys encyclopaedia, Sean Courtney (Dauber), Beach Boys Britain, Bill (www.vigotone.com), and to Sibeal, for her patience and support.

The Beach Boys on CD: The Beach Boys

The Beach Boys

A brief history of the Beach Boys

The Beach Boys came out of Hawthorne, a suburb of Los Angeles in Southern California. Formed in 1961, The Beach Boys consisted of the three Wilson brothers (Brian, Carl, and Dennis) their cousin Mike Love and Brian's friend Al Jardine. In mid 1961, The Beach Boys recorded their first record, 'Surfin'' for the Candix record label. The group took the name The Beach Boys and had their first regional hit in LA in Dec. 1961. The single reached the No.75 spot on the National Billboard chart in early 1962.

Candix records went bust in the spring of 1962, the Beach Boys were free to find a new record Company, and recording deal. Murry Wilson, the father of the Wilson brothers and The Beach Boys manager, eventually secured a recording contract with Capitol Records in early summer 1962. In early 1962 and prior to the Capitol deal, Brian and Gary Usher started to write songs together, some of these song were recorded for demo and acted as the catalyst in securing the Capitol deal.

Between the years 1962 – 1969 the Beach Boys would record 20(21) albums for Capitol and release numerous successful singles in the US and across the world. The Beach Boys recording career with Capitol spanned the years 1962 - 1969. The first Beach Boys album was 'Surfin' Safari'; released in late November 1962, it reached No.32 on the US chart. The single, 'Surfin' Safari', had preceded the album and reached number No.14. The following nine album releases (recorded in just three and a half years) would all achieve gold status, and spend over 450 cumulative weeks on the US charts. During this time Brian Wilson, the bands primary composer and leader also composed and produced numerous recordings for other artists.

The years 1962-1964 brought remarkable chart success and World fame, but were not problem-free; well-documented struggles between Brian/the band and his father led to Murry Wilson being sacked in early 1964. Touring pressure, corporate-recording pressure and personal problems also took their toll on Brian Wilson and in Dec. 1964 Brian Wilson had a breakdown. In 1965 and into the future, The Beach Boys would tour without Brian, who would stay at home, writing, recording and producing. The Beach Boys would fill the gaps in tour duty with spells at the studio recording the vocal parts that Brian had ready and prepared. Glen Campbell initially took up Brian's place in the touring Beach Boys, he was in turn replaced by touring member and subsequently fully-fledged Beach Boy, Bruce Johnston. Johnston would stay with band for the next seven years and become the sixth Beach Boy.

In 1965, Brian started to experiment with drugs and with new themes in his songs, The 'TODAY!' album included songs which provided a new insight into Brian Wilson's new direction, his growing maturity and with hindsight its content pointed the direction for the album 'Pet Sounds', which was released in 1966. Gone was the surf, sand and cars and in came mature themes of adult love, love lost, change and uncertainty; an introspective Brian Wilson was starting to bear his soul, wear his heart on his sleeve and leave himself wide open to the world. The songs of 'Pet Sounds' were a collaboration between Brian Wilson and lyricist Tony Asher, when it was released in May 1966 it was greeted with a mixed reaction and performed poorly in the US charts (Pet Sound was not officially certified as US 'gold' until its thirtieth anniversary re-release in 1997). Perplexed by its poor showing, Brian Wilson was wounded, Tony Asher "crestfallen". By contrast 'Pet Sounds' was successful overseas, particularly the UK. After the perceived failure on Pet Sounds in the US, Brian Wilson bounced back with the gigantic worldwide success of the single 'Good Vibrations' (Nov 1966), the

A brief history of the Beach Boys

Beach Boys had achieved their biggest selling single record to date and were arguably Britain's top band heading into 1967. If you can imagine The Beach Boys' career as twin humps on a rollercoaster, then 1966 was the US peak with the UK/World peak about 2/3 years away. The failure to release the 'Smile' album in early 1967, Brian's drug habit and various other issues/problems took a heavy toll on the Beach Boys and on Brian Wilson; American 'taste' was changing and the Beach Boys would quickly be perceived as dated. In the following years, Brian Wilson would spend less and less time composing/recording and producing

At home in the US, the years 1967 to 1969 bore little fruit for the Beach Boys and although they released some very special recordings during that time, the contract with Capitol would wither in mid 1969 without any substantial post 1966 US chart successes. In late 1969, The Beach Boys as a corporate entity (Brother Records, created in 1966) was 'broke' and the new decade began with The Beach Boys 'out of contract'. Around 1970 and without Brian's and the band's knowledge, Murry Wilson, who still published The Beach Boys music via 'Sea of Tunes Publishing' sold all of Brian's compositions to A&M Records. The 60's ended painfully for the Beach Boys.

The Beach Boys fortunes recovered somewhat when in early 1970 the band secured a contract with Warner Music. Brian returned to the studio and even performed live with The Beach Boys at the Whisky-a-Go-Go club in 1970. The first album for Warner, 'Sunflower' was a chart failure (although a great album). In late 1970, Jack Reilly took up the position of business manager; The Beach Boys would gradually recover some lost support and end 1971 with the release of 'Surf's Up' and relative chart success. In spring 1972, Bruce Johnston was out of The Beach Boys and Brian Wilson who was only partially involved with 'Surf's Up' was some way into a full blown mental and physical decline which would last until 1976 ('15 Big Ones') and well beyond. In 1972, Brian Wilson co-produced 'Spring….plus' for American Spring - his wife Marilyn Rovell and her Sister Diane (ex Honeys). Ricky Fataar and Blondie Chaplin had augmented The Beach Boys in the early 1972 and the band continued to tour/perform successfully to large audiences

and would release the albums 'Carl & The Passions' and 'Holland'. The 1973 live album, 'In Concert', charted in the US and achieved gold status. Relatively speaking however, The Beach Boys new creative output in the mid seventies was ignored in favour of the older 'Surf and Cars' music of the early 60's. The release and success of the compilations 'Endless Summer' and 'Spirit of America' crushed any hope that The Beach Boys would have had that their new output would be successful and appreciated once more. The 'live' Beach Boys would ponder over the concert set-list - 'old or new' and how to get the mix right was the dilemma of the mid seventies. Wasted by drug and alcohol abuse, in 1975, Brian began his first period of treatment with Dr. Eugene Landy; his 'treatment' would last until December 1976. In the spring of 1976 and with Steve Love at the helm, Brian Wilson "was back" and '15 Big Ones' was a US top ten hit - the album would achieve gold status. The success of '15 Big Ones' was short-lived though and any real chart success would elude the band afterwards and throughout the late seventies as drugs and alcohol took their toll on the Wilson Brothers. In the UK, the old songs were blasting to the top of the charts as Capitol Records/EMI mercilessly pumped out the old stuff on compilation while the Reprise output of the seventies struggled. Internal managerial problems had dogged the Beach Boys throughout the 70's; in 1972, Nick Grillo was dismissed as manager while his successor Jack Reilly, promoted only six months earlier to band manager, was dumped in late 1972 and prior to the release of the Holland album.

A brief history of the Beach Boys

Rieley's successor (after a short stint by Stan Love), James Guercio, managed the Beach Boys until he too was sacked in early 1976. Stan and Steve Love, brothers of Mike Love, came and went as part the Beach Boys 'management team'; Steve allegedly taking a few dollars in his back pocket in the process for which he was later convicted; the conviction was later overturned on appeal.

In 1978, the Beach Boys signed to CBS and produced three albums that provided little commercial success. Bruce Johnston returned to The Beach Boys in 1978 to help produce/complete L.A. (the first CBS-Caribou album), Brian Wilson was once again 'resurrected' for contractual reason, but the album was a commercial dud. By the late 1970's all three Wilson brothers were suffering ill health, brought about by drug and alcohol abuse.

Tragically, in 1983 Dennis Wilson died in a drowning accident and in late 1983, Brian Wilson (sacked by The Beach Boys the previous year) was handed over to Dr. Eugene Landy (for the second time) and would spend the rest of the decade and beyond under Landy's 'care and attention'. Brian Wilson would not be released from Landy's control until the end of 1992. In January 1988, The Beach Boys were initiated into the Rock'n'Roll 'Hall of Fame' and in August that year a still recovering recovered Brian Wilson released his first solo album, the self-title 'Brian Wilson'. There was no shortage of irony in the fact that The Beach Boys' penultimate album, 'Still Cruisin' (1989) was released by Capitol Records and achieved gold status. Spawned by the success of the world hit single 'Kokomo', taken from the soundtrack of the Tom Cruise film Cocktail, 'Still Cruisin' included soundtracks, a few new songs and the 'Fat Boys' single. The Beach Boys (without Brian Wilson) released their last studio album 'Summer In Paradise' in 1992.

In 1998, Carl Wilson died of after succumbing to lung Cancer and The Beach Boys were effectively no more. Today, Brian Wilson continues to tour and record, Mike Love and Bruce Johnston still tour as The Beach Boys, Al Jardine performs with his band. In early 2004, Brian Wilson will release his latest CD and will tour Europe with the music of 'Smile'.

The Beach Boys

A profile of the Beach Boys

Brian Wilson   (born: 20th June 1942, Hawthorne, CA)

Brian Wilson founded the Beach Boys in 1961 and was the bands leader, composer and producer. Brian Wilson also wrote and produced songs for many other artists (early/mid sixties). Taking influence from Chuck Berry, The Four Freshman and Phil Spector, Brian Wilson (along with Cousin, Mike Love) wrote and produced the majority of the Beach Boys output from 1961 to 1967. Brian Wilson along with lyricist Tony Asher created Pet Sounds in 1965 and although greeted with mixed reaction at the time, it is now recognised as one of the greatest productions in the history of popular music. A combination of drugs, personal problems, changing tastes in music, pressure and poor advice pushed Brian Wilson into decline in 1967, and although he continued to write (about 60% of the Beach Boys musical output until 1993), he would not recreate/repeat the volume of chart success and high quality output set in the early and mid sixties. In the 1970's and beyond, Brian Wilson descended into ill health, suffered marital breakdown, isolation and virtual poverty. In the mid eighties Brian Wilson emerged from the darkness and began recording; to positive reviews he released his first solo album in 1988. Since 1988, Brian Wilson has released a number of CD's and toured extensively since 1999. In June 2000, he was initiated into the Songwriters, Hall of Fame and received an 'Ivor Novello' award in 2003. In 2004, Brian Wilson will release his 6th CD and will tour Europe and America with SMILE live. Brian Wilson remains one of the most influential and creative forces in the history of popular music.
Further information:- http://www.brianwilson.com/brian/

Dennis Wilson   (born: 4th Dec. 1944, Inglewood, CA. died 28th Dec. 1983)

Dennis Wilson was the only real surfer in the Beach Boys and it was at his initiation that Brian Wilson started to write surf music. Dennis Wilson was the slow burner and developed from the kid who could not play the drums in 1961 to the Beach Boy with the most creative output in the late 70's. The 'pin-up' of the band, Dennis Wilson was a free spirit who often found himself on the wrong end of the law or a fist; he became an alcoholic and abused himself with drugs throughout the 70's and early 80's until his premature death (by drowning) in 1983. Crying out to be re-released, his only solo recording 'Pacific Ocean Blue' is a superior record.
Further reading:- http://www.cabinessence.com/dennis/

Carl Wilson   (born: 21st Dec. 1946, Hawthorne, CA. died 6th Feb. 1998)

The youngest of the Wilson brothers, Carl Wilson was a gifted vocalist and sang lead voice on Brian Wilson's finest compositions; he was an accomplished guitar player and a great songwriter, although he composed too few songs. His vocals on 'Pet Sounds' are unequalled; listen to this and his other recordings, 'Full Sail', 'This Whole World', 'Darlin'', 'Long Promised Road', 'She believes in Love Again' and the stunning live performance of 'Only with You' (Chicago 1972)…the list is endless and now demands full recognition by EMI/Capitol and Brother by way of a more substantial tribute release. Carl sang lead on 'Good Vibrations' and was the effective bandleader when the Beach Boys were on the road and after Brian Wilson abandoned touring in 1965. In 1980, Carl Wilson left The Beach Boys for a short while and recorded two solo albums 'Carl Wilson' (1981) and 'Youngblood' (1983). In 1998, he succumbed to complications brought about by cancer; Carl Wilson died on the 6th of Feb, 1998 and the world of popular music lost one of its finest voices.
Further information:- http://www.tildens.net/occ/

A profile of the Beach Boys

Mike Love   (born: 15th Mar. 1941, Los Angeles, CA)

Mike love is a founding member of The Beach Boys and the bands lead singer. He co-wrote a number of the Beach Boys' most popular songs but rarely fulfilled any promise as a solo writer with the exception of 'Big Sur', which he penned in the early 70's. Mike Love continues to tour as part of the remnants of the Beach Boys, he still performs with energy and provides an entertaining show. Mike Love release one solo album 'Looking Back With Love' in 1981 and in a recent interview stated that he was looking forward to many more summer tours with The Beach Boys. Mike Love currently has the sole rights to tour under the name 'The Beach Boys'. Further information:- http://www.mikelovefanclub.com/index.html

Al Jardine   (born: 3rd Sept. 1942, Lima, OH)

A founding member of the Beach Boys, Al Jardine left the Beach Boys between early 1962 until his return a year and a half later in 1963. Al Jardine and Brian Wilson formed the genesis of the Beach Boys when they sang together at college in the early sixties. Al Jardine contribution to The Beach Boys catalogue is limited but significant; he sang lead vocals on 'Help Me Rhonda', 'Heroes and Villains' – live and 'Cottonfields' he also provided a number of album tracks and co-produced the failed M.I.U. album of 1987. A major legal decision (taken by Brother Records against Al Jardine 2003) bars him from using the word 'Beach' in the name of his band. No longer a part of The Beach Boys, he now tours as 'Al Jardine's Family and Friends (his sons and Brian Wilson's daughters, Carnie and Wendy). For further information:- http://www.aljardine.com

Bruce Johnston   (born: 24th June 1944, Chicago, IL)

Bruce Johnston (the 6th Beach Boy) joined the band in 1965, His first studio contribution was on 'California Girls' and Bruce provided substantial vocal input to the album 'Pet Sounds'. He was 'pushed out' of the band in 1972; Bruce Johnston himself claims that he left. In 1977, he released his solo album 'Going Public'. Bruce Johnston returned to The Beach Boys in 1978 to contribute to and complete the L.A (Light album) and has been a member since that time. He has written some fine songs for The Beach Boys; 'Deirdre' (with BW), 'Tears in Morning' and 'Disney Girls'. Bruce Johnston wrote 'I Write the Songs' made famous by Barry Manilow which received a Grammy Award for the 'Best Song' composition in 1976. He has worked with Elton John and Pink Floyd; he continues to tour (with vigour) with the Beach Boys, surf's as often as he can, carries an Irish Passport and is a regular poster on the 'Beach Boys Britain' web site. Further reading:- http://www.allmusic.com/ (search 'Bruce Johnston')

A profile of the Beach Boys

David Marks   (born: Newcastle, PA)

David Marks joined the Beach Boys when Al Jardine left in early 1962. It is not clear, but David Marks seems to have contributed/recorded on the first four Beach Boys albums; he left the Beach Boys in late 1963 after the 'Little Deuce Coupe' and before the release of 'Shut Down Vol. 2'. In 1990, David Marks worked with Brian Wilson on the unreleased album 'Sweet Insanity'. In August 1997, he returned to the touring with the remnants of The Beach Boys but left in 1999. For further information:-

http://www.davidleemarks.com/

Blondie Chaplin   (born: South Africa)

Blondie Chaplin was a member of the South African band The Flames. Al Jardine and Carl heard the band in London in 1969; they signed the band to Brother Records. Renamed The Flame, Carl Wilson produced their debut album 'The Flame' in 1971. In the early 70's The Flame played support for The Beach Boys. In 1972, The Flame broke up and Blondie Chaplin and Ricky Fataar joined the Beach Boys as full band members. Blondie Chaplin recorded on three Beach Boys albums: 'Carl and The Passions, 'Holland' and 'In Concert'. His contribution to the Beach Boys includes: 'Hear She Comes' (co-wrote/vocal), 'He Come Down' (co-vocal), 'Leaving This Down' (co-wrote/vocal), 'Sail On, Sailor' (vocal), 'Hold On Dear Brother' (co-wrote/vocal). Blondie Chaplin left the Beach Boys in Dec. 1973.
Further reading:- http://www.the-flames.com/

Ricky Fataar   (born: South Africa)

Drummer with The Flame, Ricky Fataar joined the Beach Boys with Blondie Chaplin in 1972. He recorded on three Beach Boys albums: 'Carl and The Passions, 'Holland' and 'In Concert'. He co-wrote a few Beach Boys songs with Blondie Chaplin. Ricky Fataar left The Beach Boys in late 1974 but played drums on 'It's OK' (15 Big Ones), 'Pacific Ocean Blue' (Dennis Wilson's solo album) and 'Keepin' the Summer Alive'. He was(is) an original member of The Rutles (The Beatles parody band). He co-produced two of Tim Finn's solo albums 'Escapade' and 'Before and After' and played drums on the brilliant 'Woodface' by Crowded House. He currently plays with Bonnie Raitt's band.
Further reading:- http://www.the-flames.com/

Beach Boys Recording History

The Beach Boys began their 'professional' recording career with Candix records, a small record company based in Los Angeles. Their first single 'Surfin' was released on Dec. 1961 and became a regional hit in LA and southern California and reached no. 75 on Billboard, the US national chart register, Candix collapsed shortly afterwards. Murry Wilson secured a record deal with Capitol records in mid 1962 and The Beach Boys went on to record/release eighteen albums (twenty-one counting the compilations releases) over the following seven years until they finally split with Capitol in mid 1969. Outside of the US, The Beach Boys albums/Singles were marketed and released by EMI (EMI now owns Capitol Records). The first Capitol album was Surfin' Safari which was released in Oct. 1962; the last Beach Boys album recorded for Capitol was 20/20, released in Feb. 1969. The last album, the Beach Boys 21st album for Capitol, was the live album 'Live in London'; recorded in Dec. 1968 it was released in the UK in May 1970 and in the US in 1976.

In 1966, The Beach Boys created Brother Records; this new company was independent of Capitol. And was created as an outlet for other artists and for Brian's non-Capitol works, Brother would also operate as The Beach Boys corporate entity. The contractual arrangement with Capitol Records was concluded with the release of the single 'Breakaway' in June 1969. In early 1970, the Beach Boys signed to Warner Music and future recordings would be released through the Warner Music subsidiary, Reprise, and under license from Brother Records. The Beach boys released eight studio albums for Warner beginning with Sunflower in Aug. 1970 and ending with M.I.U. album in late 1978.

In mid 1978, the Beach Boys signed to CBS, they released their first album for Caribou (the CBS subsidiary) in March 1979. The album was L.A. (Light Album) and The Beach Boys would go on to record a further two albums for the Caribou label; 'Keepin' The Summer Alive' (1980) and 'The Beach Boys' (1985). Dennis Wilson released the solo album 'Pacific Ocean Blue' in 1977 on Caribou (CBS) and during the Caribou years, Carl would release two solo albums 'Carl Wilson' (1981) & 'Youngblood' (1983). In August 1989, having left CBS, The Beach Boys released 'Still Cruisin' (1988) on the Capitol label and in Aug. 1992 the US version of the Beach Boys last album, 'Summer in Paradise' was released by Brother Entertainment; the UK version was released by EMI the following year in May 1993. Throughout the years from 1966 to the present day, Capitol and Brother Records have continued to release various compilations, collections and variants of the original studio albums. Compilations have also been released by numerous specialty companies and special markets ventures. The most recent Capitol/EMI release is 'Sounds of Summer'; a thirty track Beach Boys collection released in May 2003 - the CD peaked at No.16 on the Billboard charts. The Beach Boys first appear on CD in 1985 with the dual releases of 'The Beach Boys', the first major release of the Beach Boys catalogue came with the release of the US/UK/Japan twofer releases in 1990. Since then, all of the studio recordings have been re-produced/re-engineered in CD format. Replaced by newer/variant compilations, most of the original collections and compilation have not made it onto CD. The most recent album re-release is the superb re-engineered version of Pet Sounds, produced in DVD audio format and providing Dolby 5.1 Surround Sound. On the following page I have provided a chronological list of Beach Boys US recordings (1962-1993), this should orientate the reader and provide background for the rest of the book.

Beach Boys Studio Recordings (US Releases)

Title	Release Date	Artist	Label/Serial No
Surfin' Safari	Oct. 1962	The Beach Boys	Capitol T/DT1808
Surfin' USA	Mar. 1963	The Beach Boys	Capitol T/ST1890
Surfer Girl	Sep. 1993	The Beach Boys	Capitol T/ST1981
Little Deuce Coupe	Oct. 1963	The Beach Boys	Capitol T/ST1998
Shut Down Vol.2	Mar. 1994	The Beach Boys	Capitol T/ST2027
All Summer Long	Jul. 1994	The Beach Boys	Capitol T/ST2110
The Beach Boys Xmas Album	Oct. 1964	The Beach Boys	Capitol T/ST2164
Beach Boys Concert	Oct. 1964	The Beach Boys	Capitol TA/STAO2198
The Beach Boys Today!	Mar. 1965	The Beach Boys	Capitol T/DT2269
Summer Days (and Summer Nights!!)	Jul. 1965	The Beach Boys	Capitol T/DT2354
Beach Boys Party	Nov. 1965	The Beach Boys	Capitol MAS/DMAS/SMAS2398
Pet Sounds	May. 1966	The Beach Boys	Capitol T/DT2458
Smiley Smile	Sep. 1967	The Beach Boys	Brother T/ST9001
Wild Honey	Dec. 1967	The Beach Boys	Capitol T/ST2859
Friends	Jun. 1968	The Beach Boys	Capitol ST2895
Stack O' Tracks	Aug. 1968	The Beach Boys	Capitol DKAO2893
20/20	Feb. 1969	The Beach Boys	Capitol SKAO133
Sunflower	Aug. 1970	The Beach Boys	Brother-Reprise RS6382
Surf's Up	Aug. 1971	The Beach Boys	Brother-Reprise RS6453
Carl And The Passions "So Tough"	May. 1972	The Beach Boys	Brother-Reprise 2MS 2083
Holland & Mount Vernon EP	Jan. 1973	The Beach Boys	Brother-Reprise MS 2118
The Beach Boys in Concert	Nov. 1973	The Beach Boys	Brother-Reprise 2MS 6484
15 Big Ones	Jul. 1976	The Beach Boys	Brother-Reprise MS 2251
The Beach Boys '69 - Live in London	Nov. 1976	The Beach Boys	Capitol ST11584
The Beach Boys Love You	Apr. 1977	The Beach Boys	Brother-Reprise MSK2258
Going Public	1977	Bruce Johnston	Edsel (UK) EDCD697
Pacific Ocean Blue	Sep. 1977	Dennis Wilson	Caribou ZK 34353
M.I.U. Album	Oct. 1978	The Beach Boys	Brother-Reprise MSK 2268
L.A. (Light Album)	Mar. 1979	The Beach Boys	Caribou-Brother JZ 35752
Keepin' The Summer Alive	Mar. 1980	The Beach Boys	Caribou-Brother FZ 36283
Carl Wilson	Mar. 1981	Carl Wilson	Caribou NJZ 37010
Lookin' Back With Love	Oct. 1981	Mike Love	Boardwalk 33242
Youngblood	Feb. 1983	Carl Wilson	Caribou BFZ 37970
The Beach Boys	May 1985	The Beach Boys	Caribou-Brother ZK 39946
Brian Wilson	Aug. 1988	Brian Wilson	Rhino R2 79960
Still Cruisin'	Aug. 1989	The Beach Boys	Capitol CDP 7 92639
Summer in Paradise	Aug. 1992	The Beach Boys	BBR 727-2
Bamboo (unreleased)		Dennis Wilson	
I Just Wasn't Made For These Times	Aug. 1995	Brian Wilson	MCD 111 270 2
Imagination	Jul. 1998	Brian Wilson	Giant 9 24703 2
Like a Brother	Jun. 2000	Carl Wilson	Transparent 1221829
Live at The Roxy	Jun. 2001	Brian Wilson	BriMel SANDD 107
Live in Las Vegas	Aug. 2001	Al Jardine	Jardine Tours 2019
Pet Sounds Live (UK)	Jun. 2002	Brian Wilson	BriMel SANCD118
Good Timin': Live at Knebworth	Mar. 2003	The Beach Boys	Eagle Records

Note on Prefixes: [T] - mono [ST] - stereo [DT] - duophonic

A brief history of the Beach Boys on CD

The production of Beach Boys' studio albums spanned the years 1962-1992; Brian Wilson continues to write, produce and record. The Beach Boys were signed to different record companies throughout this period and a number of producers were involved in the recordings. The Beach Boys albums have been marketed in many different forms: vinyl; mono, duo phonic, stereo, 8 track, reel-to-reel tape, cassette tape and finally CD & mini CD. The first Beach Boys recording to appear on CD was the 1985 album 'The Beach Boys, this was followed by CD versions of 'The Best of The Beach Boys', 'Made in USA, '20 Golden Greats', 'Still Cruisin'' and a few other compilations. The first CD's versions of the Beach Boys back catalogue appeared in 1990 with the release by Capitol records of the *twofer* releases (two albums on one CD). This was followed by the release of the post Capitol albums on CD - the Reprise/Caribou/Brother Records recordings. Capitol Records released single albums on CD format in 1994 having discontinuing the 1990 twofers.

The Brother Records and Capitol single album CD releases were skeletal in nature; they were not accompanied with liner notes, had no additional bonus tracks and save for some of the Caribou CD's had no lyric sheets. Similar to Capitol and the original *twofer* 'releases, Caribou also release the single albums in a 'longbox' version; no meat on the bone here, just a fancy box with the single CD inside. The single album CD's (Capitol and Caribou) were discontinued in the 90's and were eventually replaced by the HDCD re-mastered *twofer*s released in mid 2000 and early 2001 (Note: The post Capitol *twofer*s are not HDCD products but are 24 bit). The Capitol and Caribou-Brother single albums CD's are now out of print (OOP). The only single album CD's that remain 'in print' are the 'higher fidelity sound quality' versions released through Toshiba-EMI. The current versions of the Japanese single album CD's were themselves originally released in 1990 as the 'Past Masters' series (16 bit); these can be found for sale on the internet, but are quite rare and appear less and less often. Yet another Japanese set of 'mini-album' sleeve CD's of the Capitol releases were produced; these too can be found for sale on the internet but are also rare and hard to obtain. Finally, 'Pet Sounds' 'The Christmas Album', 'In Concert', 'Still Cruisin' and 'Summer in Paradise' remain single CD products. The original non-Japanese versions of the single album CD's are available on the internet via eBay, Amazon and many online sites; a list of the most useful internet sources is provided at the back of the book. In summary, the single album CD's and *twofer*s were released as sets in the following chronological order

Out of Print series:-

Capitol (16 bit) Twofer Series (Capitol albums only) + Pet Sounds + Christmas album	May-Aug 1990
(Versions released in the UK, Canada & Japan)	
Toshiba-EMI release single album CD's - Pastmasters series (Capitol albums only)	July 1990
Caribou-Epic (Brother Licence) release of post Capitol albums	Oct 1990-Feb 1991
Capitol release of Single album CD's (Capitol albums only)	June-July 1994
Toshiba-EMI release single album CD's - Coolprice (Capitol only/Still Cruisin/Rarities)	Sept. 1997
Toshiba-EMI release single album CD's – Mini LP CD's (+ Endless Summer/Made in the USA)	July 1998/2000

The current series:-

Capitol release post Capitol albums twofer sets (24 bit, not HDCD)	July-Aug 2000
Capitol release of HDCD (24 bit) twofers (Capitol recordings only)	Mar 2001
Toshiba-EMI release single album CD's (all album 1962 to 'Still Cruisin' + bonus tacks)	June 2001

The Appendices provides the chronological list of all known CD releases, associated tracks, and information on composers and Beach Boys associates.

How to use this book

The information in this book is presented in a consistent way. Each page provides an image of the CD cover back and front; the CD track listing appears in the top left hand corner. Relevant CD details are provided and historical information is detailed where applicable. Album and general track notes provide information about the CD content and any important information relating to the CD or original vinyl 'parent' release. The figure below illustrates the general layout of each page. Some CD's will require more than one page of information.

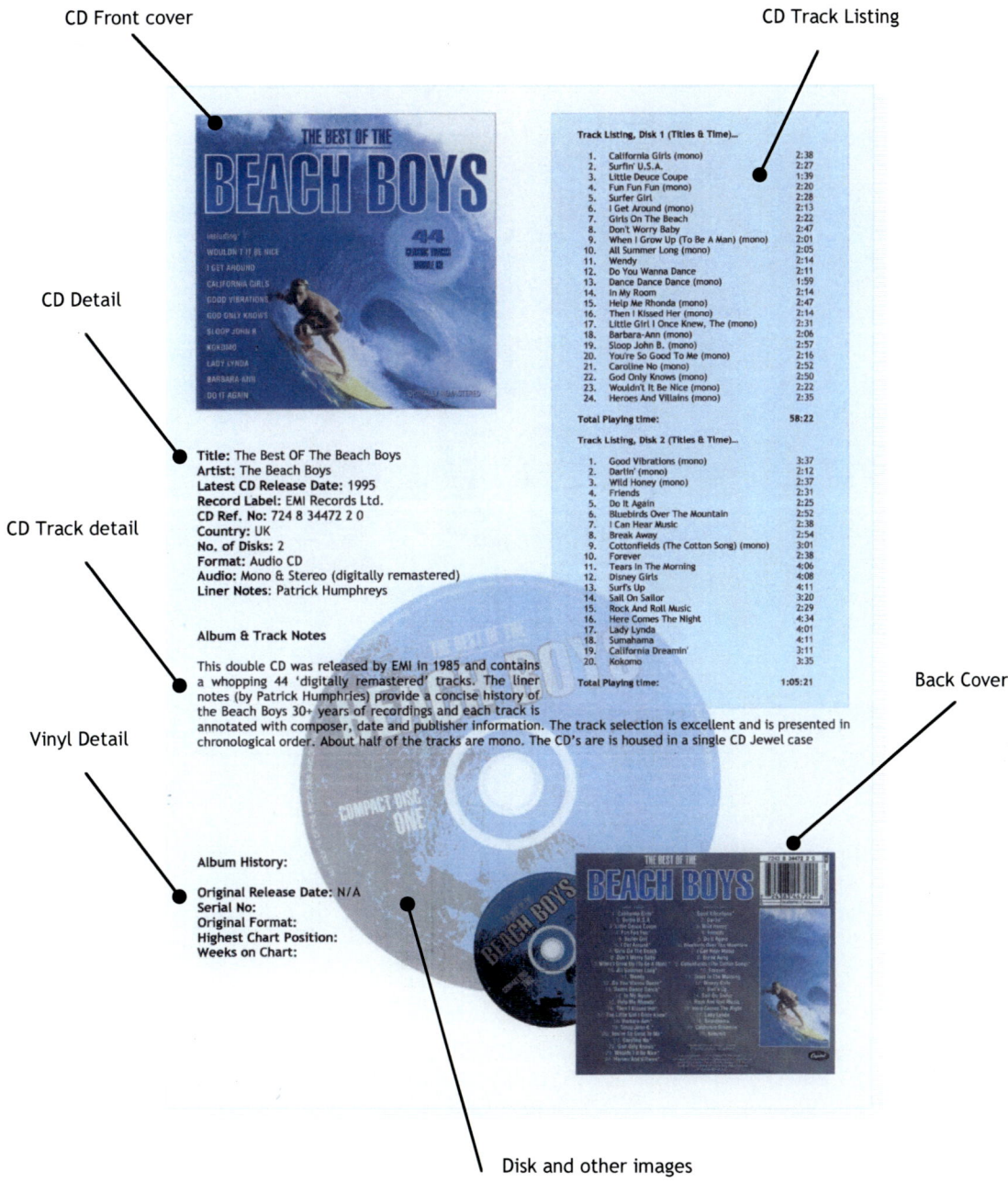

Redferns

Single album CD releases

The first Beach Boys album released on CD format was 'The Beach Boys' released in 1985. Prior to the release of the 1990 twofers, only a few Beach boys recordings appeared on CD - 'Still Cruisin' (1987), The Christmas album (1988), 'Pet Sounds' (Greenline, Japan, 1988)) and a few CD compilations; 'Endless Summer (1987) and 'Made in USA' (1986). In 1990 Caribou-Brother Records released the Beach Boys' Post Capitol back catalogue on CD (US & UK, different serial No's). Brian Wilson, referring to 'Surf's Up' in his 'autobiography' states - "….I played it non stop for several days and then put it away until it was re-released in 1990…". In 1994, after discontinuing the original 1990 twofers, Capitol records released 'emaciated' versions of the Beach Boys album back catalogue on single album CD (The Capitol albums only, including Smiley Smile). In the early 90's, analog to digital technology was inferior, and all of these original remastered versions have subsequently been re-mastered and transferred to CD via 24 bit technology. The only single album CD versions currently available (in print) are the Japanese versions (Toshiba-EMI). The Japanese CD's utilize the same tracks which appear on the Capitol 2001 twofers and the 2000 Brother Twofers (released by Capitol). These CD's also include the twofer bonus tracks.

Within the category of single album CD releases a number of anomalies exist, these are listed below.

1) Brother, Caribou, Epic released 'longbox' products; essentially CD's packaged within a longbox
2) BMG Music directly marketed a number of Beach Boys single CD albums
3) A ten track version of 'All Summer Long' was released by CEMA – Capitol-Emi Special Markets
4) A ten track abridgement version of Summer Days (and Summer Nights!!) exists
5) A CBS collector editions of certain CD's exist; notably L.A. (Light Album) & the Beach Boys
6) In the UK, the Brother albums were released as part of the Epic 'NICE PRICE' series - **EPC** xxxxxxx.
7) In Canada, the Brother albums were also release as 'Nice Price or Joli Priz series - **W**ZK xxxxx

The following pages provide detail of the single album CD's releases: Capitol, Brother Records, Warner and CBS. Detail is also provided of other Beach Boys' single album CD releases. The current Japanese series of the single album CD's is detailed in a separate chapter - 'The Land of the Rising Song'. At the end of this chapter, I have provided some information on 'unusual' single album CD releases. I have also provided detail on the notable 7" US/UK single releases associated with each of the original Capitol albums. Please note that the single version was sometimes a different/variant version of the recording that appeared on the parent album. For background, I have detailed some history of the chart success (or not) of all of the original album releases. For further information on Beach Boys chart history, you might consult the following:

Top Pop Albums 1955-2001: Joel Whitburn, Recor Reasearch Inc. ISBN 0-89820 147 0

The Warner Guide to UK & US Singles 1954 – present: Dave McAleer, Carlton ISBN 0-316-91076-7

The Complete Book of the British Charts: Tony Brown/Jon Kutner/Neil Warwick, Omnibus ISBN 0-7119-9075-1

The Billboard Book of Top 40 Hits: Joel Whitburn, Billboard Books ISBN 0-8230-7690-3

The MOJO collection (The Ultimate companion): Jim Irvin/Colin McLear, Canongate ISBN 1-84195-438-1

The Great Rock Doscography: Martin C. Strong, Canongate ISBN 1 84195 3121

http://www.angelfire.com/la/Beachboysbritain/   'Beach Boys Britain'

Track Listing (Titles & Time)...

1. Surfin' Safari — 2:07
2. County Fair — 2:17
3. Ten Little Indians — 1:29
4. Chug-A-Lug) — 2:01
5. Little Miss America — 2:06
6. 409 — 2:01
7. Surfin' — 2:13
8. Heads You Win, Tails I Lose — 2:20
9. Summertime Blues — 2:10
10. Cuckoo Clock — 2:11
11. Moon Dawg — 2:03
12. Shift" — 1:52

Total Playing time: 24:56

Title: Surfin' Safari
Artist: The Beach Boys
Latest CD Release Date: June 28th, 1994
Record Label: Capitol/EMI Records
CD Ref. No: CDP 7243 8 29661 2 8
Country: US
No. of Disks: 1
Format: Audio CD (re-mastered, 16 bit)
Audio: mono/duophonic

Album & Track Notes:

The seminal Beach Boys album this CD was transferred from analog tape to digital format in 1990. Transferred 16-bit density, the 'No noise' system was applied during the remastering process to eliminate 'noise'. The CD product was skeletal in nature; no liner notes, no additional pictures and no re-mastering notes or track details.

Album History:

This album was never released in the UK, The US release entered the chart on 24/11/62, peaked in 1963 at No. 32 and spent a total of 37 weeks on the Billboard' chart. Capitol released two singles in the US; 'Surfin' Safari (release before the album) reached No. 14 in 1962, 'Ten Little Indians' peaked at No. 49, again in 1962

Original Release Date: US - 10/62
Serial No: US - Capitol T/DT 1808
Original Format: Vinyl
Chart Performance/Weeks: US - #32 (37)

The Beach Boys on CD: Single album CD's

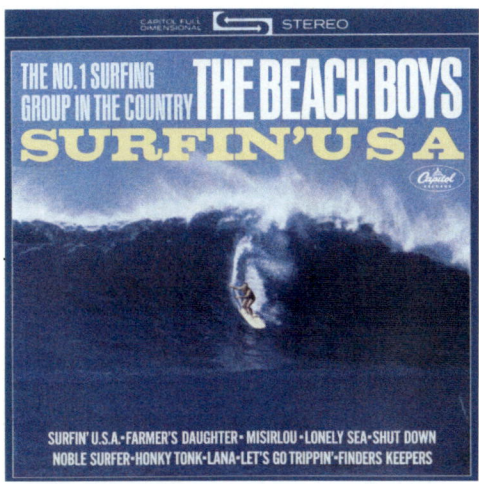

Track Listing (Titles & Time)...

1.	Surfin' U.S.A.	2:30
2.	The Farmer's Daughter	1:52
3.	Miselou	2:05
4.	Stoked	2:02
5.	Lonely Sea	2:24
6.	Shut Down	1:52
7.	Noble Surfer	1:54
8.	Honky Tonk	2:05
9.	Lana	1:43
10.	Surf Jam	2:14
11.	Let's Go Trippin'	2:00
12.	Finders Keepers	1:40

Total Playing time: 24:26

Title: Surfin' U.S.A.
Artist: The Beach Boys
Latest CD Release Date: June 28th, 1994
Record Label: Capitol/EMI Records
CD Ref. No: CDP 0777 7 48422 2 8
Country: US
No. of Disks: 1
Format: Audio CD (re-mastered, 16 bit)
Audio: mono/stereo

Album & Track Notes

The Beach Boys second US album and their first UK album release.

Album History:

The album was released in March, 1963, entered the US charts in April '63, reached the No.2 position (for two weeks), and spent 78 weeks in total on the Billboard chart. It was the Beach Boys first Gold Album. In the UK, the album entered the charts in Sept. '65, reached no.17 and spent seven weeks in the charts. Only one single was released in the US; 'Surfin USA', reached No.3 and sold over 1 million copies (gold). In the UK the single reached No.34 and spent 7 weeks on the chart

Original Release Date: US - 3/63, UK - 4/63
Serial No: US - Capitol T/ST 1890, UK - Capitol T/ST1890
Original Format: Vinyl
Highest Chart Position/Weeks: US - #2(78), UK #17(7)

The Beach Boys on CD: Single album CD's

Track Listing (Titles & Time)...

1.	Surfer Girl	2:29
2.	Catch a Wave	2:11
3.	The Surfer Moon	2:15
4.	South bay Surfer	1:48
5.	The Rocking Surfer	2:03
6.	Little Deuce Coupe	1:40
7.	In My Room	2:16
8.	Hawaii	2:01
9.	Surfer's Rule	1:56
10.	Our Car Club	2:24
11.	Your Summer Dream	2:30
12.	Boogie Woodie	1:56

Total Playing time: 25:31

Title: Surfer Girl
Artist: The Beach Boys
Latest CD Release Date: June 28th, 1994
Record Label: Capitol/EMI Records
CD Ref. No: CDP 7243 8 29628 2 3
Country: US
No. of Disks: 1
Format: Audio CD (re-mastered, 16 bit)
Audio: mono/stereo

Album & Track Notes

The Beach Boys third US album and their seventh in the UK. Surfer Girl was released in the UK in 1967 after TODAY! and Pet Sounds. It seems to have been released after the success of 'The Best of the Beach Boys' compilation, released in the UK in late 1966.

Album History:

The album was released in Sept. 1963 and entered the US chart the following month, it reached the No.7 position and stayed in the chart for 56 weeks. The album sold over 500,000 copies becoming the Beach Boys second gold album of 1963. Again, only one album track was released as a 7" single in the US; 'Surfer Girl' (with 'Little Deuce Coupe' as the B side), reached No.7. In the UK, the album reached the No.13 spot in the spring of 1967

Original Release Date: US - 9/63, UK - 3/67
Serial No: US - Capitol T/ST 1981, UK T/ST1981
Original Format: Vinyl
Highest Chart Position/Weeks: US - #7(56), UK - #13(14)

The Beach Boys on CD: Single album CD's

Track Listing (Titles & Time)...

1.	Little Deuce Coupe	1:41
2.	Ballad of Ole' Betsy	2:17
3.	Be True To Your School	2:08
4.	Car Crazy Cutie	2:49
5.	Cherry, Cherry Coupe	1:50
6.	409	2:01
7.	Shut Down	1:50
8.	Spirit of America	2:26
9.	Our Car Club	2:23
10.	No-Go Showboat	1:56
11.	A Young Man is Gone, A	2:18
12.	Custom Machine	1:42

Total Playing time: 25:21

Title: Little Deuce Coupe
Artist: The Beach Boys
Latest CD Release Date: June 28th, 1994
Record Label: Capitol/EMI Records
CD Ref. No: CDP 7243 8 29661 2 8
           CEMA S21-57682-2 (Canada)
Country: US
No. of Disks: 1
Format: Audio CD (re-mastered, 16 bit)
Audio: mono/stereo

CEMA version

Album & Track Notes

The Beach Boys 4th US album and their 7th UK album release. A CEMA version of LDC was released in 1992 (Canada) prior to the Capitol 1994 releases.

Album History:

In the US, the album was released in October, 1963 and entered the US chart the following month, it reached the No.4 in 1964, and spent 46 weeks on the chart - it would become the Beach boys 1st US platinum album. Released in the UK in October 1965, the album did not chart. Once again, only one album track was released as a 7" single; in the US, 'Be True To Your School' (with 'In my Room' as the B side), reached No.6...The Singing Nun (Soeur Sourire) was topping the US charts at the time

Original Release Date: US - 10/63, UK - 10/65
Serial No: US - Capitol T/ST 1998, UK - Capitol T/ST1998
Original Format: Vinyl
Highest Chart Position/Weeks: US - #4(46), UK - DNC

Track Listing (Titles & Time)...		
1.	Fun, Fun, Fun	2:06
2.	Don't Worry Baby	2:50
3.	In The Parkin' Lot	2:04
4.	"Cassius" Love Vs. "Sonn..."	3:31
5.	The Warmth of the Sun	2:56
6.	This Car of Mine	1:39
7.	Why Do Fools Fall in Love	2:00
8.	Pom Pom Play Girl	1:32
9.	Keep an Eye on Summer	2:23
10.	Shut Down, Pt.2	2:11
11.	Louie, Louie	2:20
12.	Denny's Drums	1:55
Total Playing time:		27:28

Title: Shut Down Volume 2
Artist: The Beach Boys
Latest CD Release Date: June 28th, 1994
Record Label: Capitol/EMI Records
CD Ref. No: CDP 7243 8 29629 2 2
Country: US
No. of Disks: 1
Format: Audio CD (re-mastered, 16 bit)
Audio: mono/stereo

Album & Track Notes

Shut Down Vol. II was the Beach Boys' 5th US album release. It was tagged 'Vol. II' because Capitol had already released a 'car' album named 'Shut Down' (which contained two Beach Boys tracks). The album was released in the UK, the Beach Boys 2nd UK album, it did not chart.

Album History:

The album was released in March 1964 and entered the chart in April, it reached the No.13 position, and would spend 38 weeks on the Billboard chart. It would become the Beach Boys' fourth gold album in a row. Only one album track was released as a 7" 'A' side; 'Fun, Fun, Fun' (with 'Why Do Fools Fall In Love' as the B side), reached No.5 prior to the release of the album, in Feb. '64 - The Beatles had five chart topping singles in the US charts around this time.

Original Release Date: US - 3/64, UK - 7/64
Serial No: US - Capitol T/ST 2027, UK – T/ST2027
Original Format: Vinyl
Highest Chart Position/Weeks: US - #13(38)

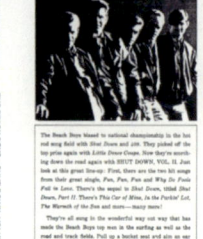

The Beach Boys on CD: Single album CD's

Track Listing (Titles & Time)...

1.	I Get Around	2:14
2.	All Summer Long	2:09
3.	Hushabye	2:42
4.	Little Honda	1:54
5.	We'll Run Away	2:02
6.	Carl's Big Chance	2:27
7.	Wendy	2:18
8.	Do You Remember	1:40
9.	Girls on the Beach	2:26
10.	Drive-In	1:53
11.	Our Favorite Recording...	1:59
12.	Don't Back Down	1:47

Total Playing time: 21:23

Title: All Summer Long
Artist: The Beach Boys
Latest CD Release Date: June 28th, 1994
Record Label: Capitol/EMI Records
CD Ref. No: CDP 7243 8 29631 2 7
Country: US
No. of Disks: 1
Format: Audio CD (re-mastered, 16 bit)
Audio: mono/stereo

Album & Track Notes

The Beach Boys' 6th US release; a year later, their 5th UK album.

Album History:

Released in March 1964, 'All Summer Long' entered the Billboard chart in August 1964, it reached the No.4 position, and would spend 49 weeks on the Billboard chart; the Beach Boys' 5th gold album. The album failed to chart in the UK. 'I Get Around' was released as a 7" single and became the Beach Boys' first US No.1 hit. At the same time (July '64), 'I Get Around' became a top ten hit in the UK (No.7) and spent 13 weeks on the UK singles charts

Original Release Date: US - 7/64, UK - 6/65
Serial No: US - Capitol T/ST 2110,
                  UK - Capitol T/ST 2110
Original Format: Vinyl
Highest Chart Position/Weeks: US - #4(49), UK - DNC

The Beach Boys on CD: Single album CD's

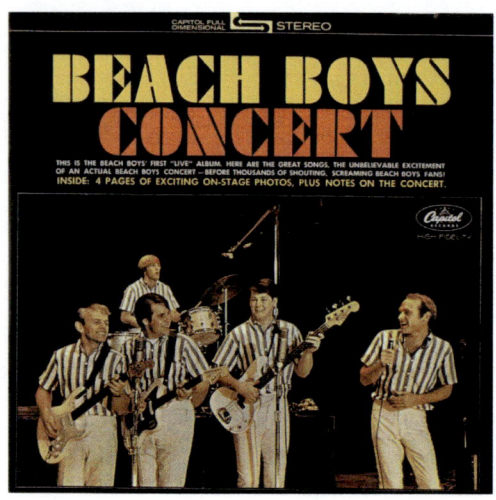

Track Listing (Titles & Time)…

1.	Fun, Fun, Fun	2:25
2.	The Little Old Lady from Pasadena	3:01
3.	Little Deuce Coupe	2:27
4.	Long Tall Texan	2:32
5.	In My Room	2:24
6.	Monster Mash	2:27
7.	Let's Go Trippin'	2:34
8.	Papa-Oom-Mow-Mow	2:18
9.	The Wanderer	1:59
10.	Hawaii	1:51
11.	Graduation Day	3:28
12.	I Get Around	2:42
13.	Johnny B. Gode	1:55

Total Playing time: 32:08

Title: Concert
Artist: The Beach Boys
Latest CD Release Date: July 26th, 1994
Record Label: Capitol/EMI Records
CD Ref. No: CDP 0777 7 90427 2 2
Country: US
No. of Disks: 1
Format: Audio CD (re-mastered, 16 bit)
Audio: mono/stereo

Album & Track Notes

The 7th US release and the 4th UK release. The album was recorded at the Civic Auditorium, Sacramento, California on the 1st Aug. 1964.

Album History:

Released in Oct. 1964, 'Concert' was the Beach Boys' 7th US album release in two years. The album entered the US charts in the first week of Nov. 1964; it reached the No.1 position, and would spend 62 weeks on the Billboard chart, holding the No.1 spot for 4 weeks - the Beach Boys' 6th gold album in a row and their 1st US chart topping album release. Incredibly, the album failed to chart in the UK.

Original Release Date: US - 10/64, UK - 2/65
Serial No: US - Capitol TA/STA 2198 UK - Capitol T2198
Original Format: Vinyl
Highest Chart Position/Weeks: US - #1(62), UK – #4(22)

THE
BEACH BOYS'
CHRISTMAS ALBUM

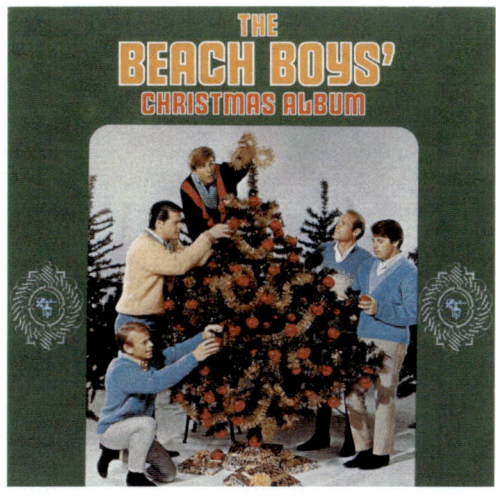

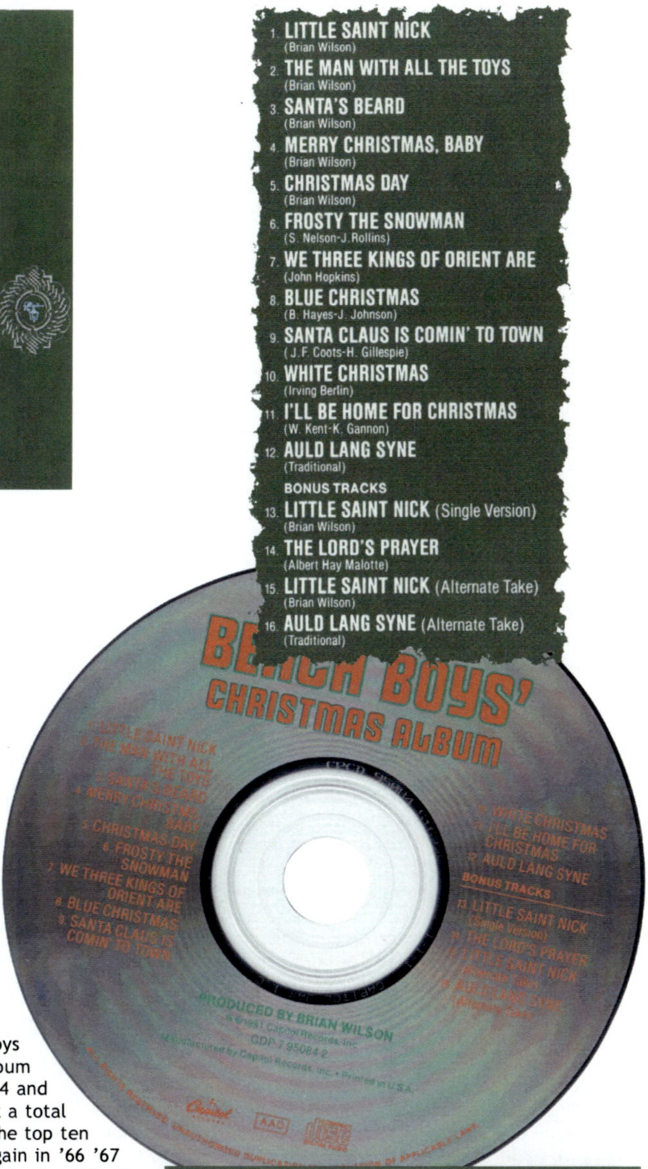
1. LITTLE SAINT NICK
(Brian Wilson)
2. THE MAN WITH ALL THE TOYS
(Brian Wilson)
3. SANTA'S BEARD
(Brian Wilson)
4. MERRY CHRISTMAS, BABY
(Brian Wilson)
5. CHRISTMAS DAY
(Brian Wilson)
6. FROSTY THE SNOWMAN
(S. Nelson-J. Rollins)
7. WE THREE KINGS OF ORIENT ARE
(John Hopkins)
8. BLUE CHRISTMAS
(B. Hayes-J. Johnson)
9. SANTA CLAUS IS COMIN' TO TOWN
(J.F. Coots-H. Gillespie)
10. WHITE CHRISTMAS
(Irving Berlin)
11. I'LL BE HOME FOR CHRISTMAS
(W. Kent-K. Gannon)
12. AULD LANG SYNE
(Traditional)
BONUS TRACKS
13. LITTLE SAINT NICK (Single Version)
(Brian Wilson)
14. THE LORD'S PRAYER
(Albert Hay Malotte)
15. LITTLE SAINT NICK (Alternate Take)
(Brian Wilson)
16. AULD LANG SYNE (Alternate Take)
(Traditional)
BEACH BOYS'
CHRISTMAS ALBUM
PRODUCED BY BRIAN WILSON

Title: Beach Boys' Christmas Album
Artist: The Beach Boys
Latest CD Release Date: 1994
Record Label: Capitol/EMI Records
CD Ref. No: CDP 07777910082 - 1988
CDP 7 95084 2 - 1992
7243 8 30729 2 7 - 1994
D 133854 (BMG)
Country: US
No. of Disks: 1
Format: Audio CD (re-mastered, 16 bit)
Audio: mono/stereo

Album & Track Notes

The Beach Boys' 8th album to enter the US chart and 3rd album release in the UK.

Album History:

The 'Christmas album' was the eighth Beach Boys album to enter the Billboard chart. The album entered the chart in the first week of Dec. 1964 and reach No.6 on the Billboard Xmas chart; it spent a total of 13 weeks on the charts. The album entered the top ten on the Christmas charts in the US in 1965 and again in '66 '67 and '68; the Beach Boys' seventh gold album. In the UK, the album was released in Nov. 1964; it failed to chart. The 7" single, 'Little St. Nick had been released in the US in 1963 and peaked at No.3 on the Christmas chart. 'The Man with All the Toys' reached No.3 on the US Christmas chart of 1964. This album is now updated as 'The Ultimate Christmas Album' - see the Christmas chapter. The first CD release was in 1988 and was a replica of the album (no bonus tracks). The 1992 version included bonus tracks; the 1994 CD version had no bonus tracks.

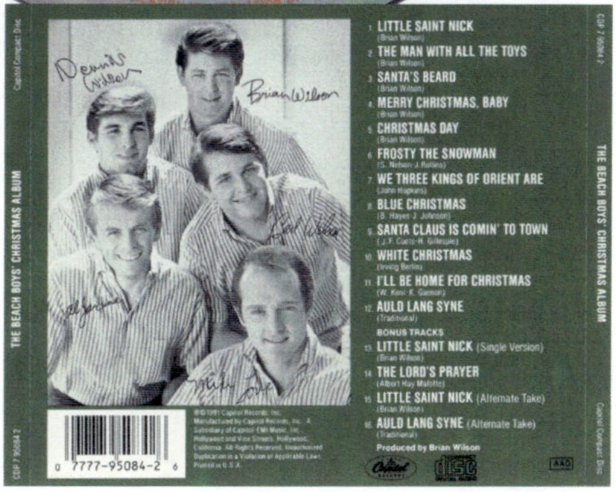
THE BEACH BOYS' CHRISTMAS ALBUM
Produced by Brian Wilson

Original Release Date: US - 10/64, UK - 11/64
Serial No: US - Capitol T/ST 2164, UK - Capitol T2164
Original Format: Vinyl
Highest Chart Position/Weeks: US - #6(13), UK - DNC

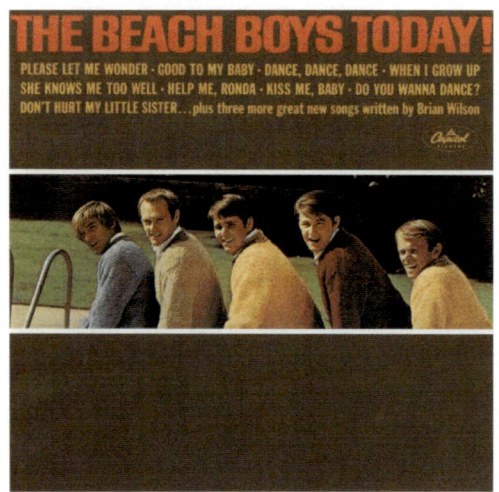

Track Listing (Titles & Time)...

#	Title	Time
1.	Do You Wanna Dance	2:19
2.	Good to My Baby	2:17
3.	Don't Hurt My Little Sister	2:08
4.	When I Grow Up (To Be a Man)	2:03
5.	Help Me, Ronda	3:10
6.	Dance, Dance, Dance	2:00
7.	Please Let Me Wonder	2:47
8.	I'm So Young	2:32
9.	Kiss Me, Baby	2:36
10.	She Knows Me Too Well	2:30
11.	In the Back of My Mind	2:10
12.	Bull Session with the "Big Daddy"	2:11

Total Playing time: 28:47

Title: TODAY!
Artist: The Beach Boys
Latest CD Release Date: June 28th, 1994
Record Label: Capitol/EMI Records
CD Ref. No: CDP 7243 8 29632 2 6
Country: US/UK/World
No. of Disks: 1
Format: Audio CD (re-mastered, 16 bit)
Audio: mono/duophonic

Album & Track Notes

The 9th Beach Boys album in the US, also the 9th UK release.

Album History:

TODAY! was released in March 1965 in the US and in April 1966 in the UK. The album entered the Billboard chart in the same month in the US, reached the No.4 position, and would spend 50 weeks on the Billboard chart, it become the Beach Boys' 8th gold album. In the UK, TODAY! reached the No.6 position and stayed in the charts for 25 weeks. The PARTY! album had preceded this success two months earlier by reaching the No.3 position in Feb. '66. The US single 'Do You Wanna Dance' reached No.8 in Feb. '65. In the UK (in advance of the album release), The Beach Boys had single success with 'Dance, Dance, Dance', No.24 Jan, 1965.

Original Release Date: US - 3/65, UK - 4/66
Serial No: US - Capitol T/DT2269, UK - Capitol T2269
Original Format: Vinyl
Highest Chart Position/Weeks: US - #4(50), UK - #6(25)

Track Listing (Titles & Time)...

1.	The Girl from New York City	1:56
2.	Amusement Parks, U.S.A.	2:30
3.	Then I Kissed Her	2:17
4.	Salt Lake City	2:01
5.	Girl Don't Tell Me	2:20
6.	Help Me, Rhonda	2:49
7.	California Girls	2:38
8.	Let Him Run Wild	2:23
9.	You're So Good To Me	2:16
10.	Summer Means New Love	2:01
11.	I'm Bugged At My Ol' Man	2:18
12.	And Your Dream Comes True	1:03

Total Playing time: 26:37

Title: Summer Days (and Summer Nights!!)
Artist: The Beach Boys
Latest CD Release Date: June 28th, 1994
Record Label: Capitol/EMI Records
CD Ref. No: CDP 7243 8 29633 2 5
Country: US
No. of Disks: 1
Format: Audio CD (re-mastered, 16 bit)
Audio: mono/stereo

Album & Track Notes

Album No.10 in the States, release No.11 in the UK.

Album History:

The album entered the US chart in late July 1965 and reached the No.2 position. It spent 33 weeks on the chart and became the Beach Boys' ninth gold selling album in the US. One year later the album climbed to the No.4 spot in the UK and spent a total of 25 weeks on the chart. The US 7" release 'California Girls' reached No.3 in July 1965 and in the UK the same single reached the No.26 spot in Sept. '65 (again, in advance of the UK release of the album). Prior to appearing on the album, 'Help Me, Rhonda' became the Beach Boys' second US No.1 hit, in April '65. Also in the UK, 'Help Me, Rhonda' reached No.27 in June 1965.

Original Release Date: US - 7/65, UK - 6/66
Serial No: US - Capitol T2354, UK - Capitol T2354
Original Format: Vinyl
Highest Chart Position/Weeks: US - #2(33), UK - #4(22)

The Beach Boys on CD: Single album CD's

Track Listing (Titles & Time)...	
1. Hully Gully	2:22
2. I Should Have Known Better	1:40
3. Tell Me Why	1:46
4. Papa-Oom-Mow-Mow	2:14
5. Mountain of Love	2:47
6. You've Got To Hide Your Love Away	2:57
7. Devoted To You	2:17
8. Alley-Oop	2:55
9. There's No Other (Like My Baby)	3:05
10. Medley: I Get Around/Little Deuce Coupe	3:12
11. The Times They Are A-Changin'	2:39
12. Barbara Ann	3:06
Total Playing time:	31:05

Title: Beach Boys' Party!
Artist: The Beach Boys
Latest CD Release Date: July 26th, 1994
Record Label: Capitol/EMI Records
CD Ref. No: CDP 7243 8 296340 2 5
Country: US/UK/World
No. of Disks: 1
Format: Audio CD (re-mastered, 16 bit)
Audio: mono

Album & Track Notes

The Beach Boys 11th album and the 3rd album release in the UK. The US release preceded the UK issue by a few months. Although PARTY! is a studio album, Brian Wilson does a great job in providing the 'illusion' of a live party recording; a great album!

Album History:

The album entered the UK charts in Feb. 1966, reached No.3 and spent 14 weeks on the UK chart. In the US, the album entered the charts in late July 1965 and peaked at No.6 in early 1966, it spent 24 weeks on the US chart. PARTY! did not reach gold status and so the run of nine consecutive gold records came to an end. In the US the single 'Barbara Ann' got to No.2 in Dec. 1965, in the UK the single reached the No.3 spot in Feb. 1966.

Original Release Date: US - 11/65, UK - 2/66
Serial No: US - Capitol SM/DM/SMAS2398, UK - Capitol T2398
Original Format: Vinyl
Highest Chart Position/Weeks: US - #6(24), UK - #3(14)

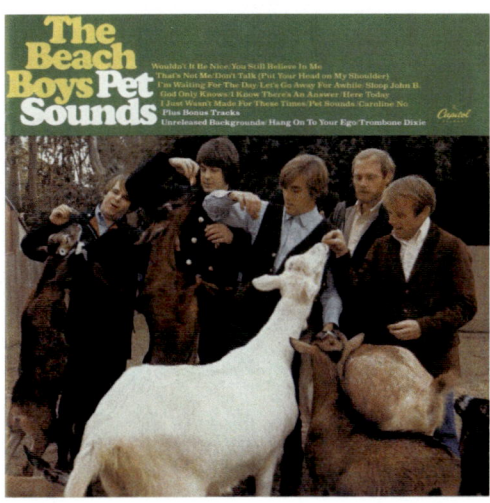

Track Listing...

1. Wouldn't It Be Nice
2. You Still Believe In Me
3. That's Not Me
4. Don't Talk (Put Your Head On My Shoulder)
5. I'm Waiting For The Day
6. Let's Go Away For Awhile
7. Sloop John B
8. God Only Knows
9. I Know There's An Answer
10. Here Today
11. I Just Wasn't Made For These Times
12. Pet Sounds
13. Caroline No

14. Unreleased Backgrounds
15. Hang Onto Your Ego
16. Trombone Dixie

Title: Pet Sounds
Release Date: 1990
Record Label: Capitol-EMI
CD Ref. No: CDP 548421 (D 100513...BMG version)
Country: US
No. of Disks: 1
Format: Audio CD
Audio: mono (Re-Mastered)
Liner Notes: David Leaf

Album & Track Notes

The first US release of Pet Sounds on CD; the original tapes were remastered to digital format in 1987 under the direction of the infamous Dr. Eugene Landy, the reissue was coordinated by Mark Linett. The CD contains three bonus tracks and the CD booklet provides liner notes by David Leaf and extensive technical and historic song/track notes. The booklet also includes many pictures of the promo photo shoot at San Diego Zoo including a picture of all six Beach Boys at the elephant pen. The booklet contains a foreword by Brian Wilson and an excellent little 'potted' history of the period by David Leaf. This version of Pet Sounds is still widely available. There is also a version of this CD marketed by BMG direct marketing; the CD number is D100513. Pet Sound eventually reached platinum status in the US, but it took over 30 years. The history of the original album is dealt with in the chapter 'The Pet Sounds Chronicles'

Original Release Date: US - 5/66, UK - 6/66
Serial No: US - Capitol T/TD 2458, UK - Capitol T2458
Original Format: Vinyl
Highest Chart Position/Weeks: US - #10(39), UK - #2(39)

The Beach Boys on CD: Single album CD's

Track Listing (Titles & Time)...

1.	Heroes & Villains	3:41
2.	Vegetables	2:10
3.	Fall Breaks and Back to Winter	2:19
4.	She's Goin' Bald	2:17
5.	Little Pad	2:32
6.	Good Vibrations	3:39
7.	With Me Tonight	2:20
8.	Wind Chimes	2:39
9.	Getting' Hungry	2:30
10.	Wonderful	2:25
11.	Whistle In	1:04
	Total Playing time:	27:41

Title: Smiley Smile
Artist: The Beach Boys
Latest CD Release Date: July 26th, 1994
Record Label: Capitol/EMI Records
CD Ref. No: CDP 7243 8 29635 2 3
Country: US/UK/World
No. of Disks: 1
Format: Audio CD (re-mastered, 16 bit)
Audio: mono/stereo

Album & Track Notes

The Beach Boys 15th US album and released on the Beach Boys own records company, Brother Records. The album was also the 15th release in the UK. Prior to the release of Smiley Smile, Capitol records released the first two Beach Boys compilations; 'The Best of The Beach Boys' and 'The Best of The Beach Boys Vol.2'. Smiley Smile was the 'Red Haired Orphan' of the ill-fated (and spinningly wonderful) SMiLE album. 'Smiley Smile' should not be underestimated; it is a fantastic album!

Album History:

The album entered the US chart in Sept. 1967 and reached the lowly position of No. 41, it spent 21 weeks on the charts.
The album reached No.9 in the UK. The tide had turned for the Beach Boys; their popularity was declining in the US and on the increase in the UK. In late '66/early'67 The Beach Boys had 7" single success in the US (notably 'Good Vibrations'; No.1- US & UK ('Good Vibrations' was a massive success all over the World) & Heroes and Villains; US No.12 & UK No.8) Future album/single success would be found oversees particularly in the UK. History can provide 20/20 vision; the divide in the Beach Boys fortunes pre 1967 and post 1967 is clear. In late 1966, The Beach Boys were voted the UK's top band (according to 'Melody Maker' readers). Post 1967, The Beach Boys record success in the US would not achieve the highs of the early/mid 60's, although 'The Beach Boys in Concert', '15 Big Ones' and 'Still Cruisin'' would achieve gold status.

Original Release Date: US - 9/67, UK - 11/67
Serial No: US – Brother T/ST9001, UK - Capitol T9001
Original Format: Vinyl
Highest Chart Position/Weeks: US - #41(21), UK - #9(8)

The Beach Boys on CD: Single album CD's

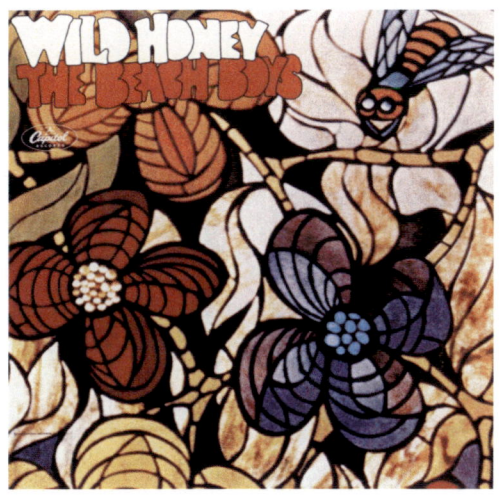

Track Listing (Titles & Time)...		
1.	Wild Honey	2:40
2.	Aren't You Glad	2:18
3.	I Was Made To Love Her	2:07
4.	Country Air	2:22
5.	A Thing or Two	2:42
6.	Darlin'	2:14
7.	I'd Love Just Once To See You	1:50
8.	Here Comes The Night	2:43
9.	Let The Wind Blow	2:21
10.	How She Boogalooed It	1:58
10.	She Knows Me Too Well	2:30
11.	Mama Says	1:04
	Total Playing time:	24:24

Title: Wild Honey
Artist: The Beach Boys
Latest CD Release Date: July 26th, 1994
Record Label: Capitol/EMI Records
CD Ref. No: CDP 7243 8 29636 2 2
Country: US/UK/World
No. of Disks: 1
Format: Audio CD (re-mastered, 16 bit)
Audio: mono/stereo

Album & Track Notes

The Beach Boys 16th US album, also their 16th in the UK.

Album History:

The album entered the US charts in late Dec. 1967, reached No.24 in early '68 and spent only 15 weeks on the chart. In the UK, the album reached No.7 in the spring of 1968 and spent 15 weeks on the UK chart. The tracks 'Wild Honey' and 'Darlin'' were both UK & US single successes; 'Wild Honey' reached No.29 (Nov '67(UK)/No.31 (Oct '67 (US)) and 'Darlin'' hit the No.11 spot (Jan '68(UK)/Dec. '67(US)) - (both UK singles prior to the album release).

Original Release Date: US - 12/67, UK - 3/68
Serial No: US - Capitol T/ST2859, UK- Capitol T2859
Original Format: Vinyl
Highest Chart Position/Weeks: US - #24(15), UK - #7(15)

The Beach Boys on CD: Single album CD's

Track Listing (Titles & Time)...

1.	Meant For You	0.39
2.	Friends	2:33
3.	Wake The World	1:30
4.	Be Here In The Morning	2:18
5.	When A Man Needs A Woman	2:08
6.	Passing By	2:26
7.	Anna Lee, The Healer	1:53
8.	Little Bird	1:59
9.	Be Still	1:24
10.	Busy Doin' Nothin'	3:05
11.	Diamond Head	3:39
12.	Transendental Meditation	1:52
	Total Playing time:	25:00

Title: Friends
Artist: The Beach Boys
Latest CD Release Date: July 26th, 1994
Record Label: Capitol/EMI Records
CD Ref. No: CDP 7243 8 29637 2 1
Country: US/UK/World
No. of Disks: 1
Format: Audio CD (re-mastered, 16 bit)
Audio: mono/stereo

Album & Track Notes

The Beach Boys' 17th US & UK albums.

Album History:

The album entered the US charts in July 1968 reached No.126 and spent only 10 weeks on the chart. In the UK, the album reached No.13 in late Sept. 1968 spent 8 weeks on the UK chart. In May 1968, the track 'Friends' reached No.25 in the UK chart (No.47 in the US, the previous April). 'Do It Again' (eventually released on 20/20) made No.1 in the UK in July '68 and No.20 in the US the same month.

Original Release Date: US - 6/68, UK - 9/68
Serial No: US - Capitol T/ST2895, UK- Capitol ST2895
Original Format: Vinyl
Highest Chart Position/Weeks: US - #126(10), UK - #13(8)

The Beach Boys on CD: Single album CD's

Track Listing...

1. Darlin'
2. Salt Lake City
3. Sloop John B
4. In My Room
5. Catch A Wave
6. Wild Honey
7. Little Saint Nick
8. Do It Again
9. Wouldn't It Be Nice
10. God Only Knows
11. Surfer Girl
12. Little Honda
13. Here Today
14. You're So Good To Me
15. Let Him Run Wild

Artist: The Beach Boys
Latest CD Release Date: July 26th, 1994
Record Label: Capitol/EMI Records
CD Ref. No: CDP 7243 8 29641 2 4
Country: US/UK/World
No. of Disks: 1
Format: Audio CD (re-mastered, 16 bit)
Audio: mono

Album & Track Notes

The Beach Boys 19th US album, 'Stack-O-Tracks' was not released in the UK until Dec. 1976 and was preceded in the US by the release of 'The Best of the Beach Boys, Vol. 3'. The album contains no vocals and was in effect an early Karaoke offering; a kind of sing-along, play-along concept.

Album History:

The album did not chart in the US nor did it chart in the UK

Original Release Date: US - 8/68, UK - 12/76
Serial No: US - Capitol DKAO2893, UK EAST24009
Original Format: Vinyl
Highest Chart Position/Weeks: US – DNC, UK - DNC

The Beach Boys on CD: Single album CD's

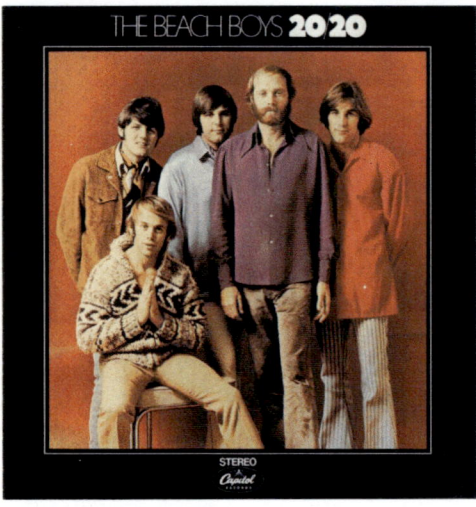

Track Listing...
1. Do It Again
2. I Can Hear Music
3. Bluebirds Over The Mountain
4. Be With Me
5. All I Want To Do
6. Nearest Faraway Place, The
7. Cotton Fields (Cotton Song)
8. I Went To Sleep
9. Time To Get Alone
10. Never Learn Not To Love
11. Our Prayer
12. Cabinessence

Artist: 20/20
Latest CD Release Date: July 26th, 1994
Record Label: Capitol/EMI Records
CD Ref. No: CDP 7243 8 29638 2 0
Country: US/UK/World
No. of Disks: 1
Format: Audio CD (re-mastered, 16 bit)
Audio: mono/stereo

Album & Track Notes

The Beach Boys' 20th US (ergo 20/20) album, the 19th in the UK.

Album History:

The album entered the US charts in March 1969, reached No.68 and spent only 11 weeks on the chart. In the UK, the album reached No.3 in Nov. 1969 and spent 10 weeks on the chart. Three singles were released in the US; 'Do it again' (released before 20/20, reached No.20, Jul '68, 'Bluebirds over the Mountain' reached No. 61, Dec '68 (again. Prior to the release of 20/20) and 'I Can Hear Music' reached No.24 in Jun '69. In the UK, Bluebirds reached No.33 and 'I Can Hear Music' reached the No.10 spot in Feb. 69 (prior to the UK album release). 20/20 was the last studio album recorded for Capitol records. Capitol would however continue to release Beach Boys compilations albums and released 'Live in London' album in 1976 in the US.

Original Release Date: US - 2/69, UK - 3/69
Serial No: US - Capitol SKAO133, UK- Capitol EST133
Original Format: Vinyl
Highest Chart Position/Weeks: US - #68(11), UK - 3(10)

The Beach Boys on CD: Single album CD's

Track Listing...

1. Darlin'
2. Wouldn't It Be Nice
3. Sloop John B.
4. California Girls
5. Do It Again
6. Wake The World
7. Aren't You Glad
8. Bluebirds Over The Mountains
9. Their Hearts Were Full of Spring
10. Good Vibrations
11. God Only Knows
12. Barbara Ann

Total Time: 34:00

Title: Live In London
Artist: The Beach Boys
Latest CD Release Date: July 26th, 1994
Record Label: Capitol/EMI Records
CD Ref. No: CDP 7243 8 29634 2 4
Country: US/UK/World
No. of Disks: 1
Format: Audio CD (re-mastered, 16 bit)
Audio: stereo

Album & Track Notes

The Beach Boys' 20th UK release. The album was not released in the US until 1976.

Album History:

The album did not chart in the UK and reached the No.75 spot in the US in 1976. The concert was recorded in 1969 and was not released in the US until 1976 and was the 24th album release (Including the three 'Best of..' albums) for Capitol Records.

Original Release Date: US - 11/76, UK - 5/70
Serial No: US - Capitol ST11584, UK- Capitol ST21715
Original Format: Vinyl
Highest Chart Position/Weeks: US - #75(10), UK – DNC

The Beach Boys on CD: Single album CD's

Title: Sunflower
Artist: The Beach Boys
Latest CD Release Date: Oct. 23rd, 1990
Record Label: Caribou-Epic
CD Ref. No: US: ZK 46950
UK: EPC 4678362 (Nice Price)
Country: US/UK/World
No. of Disks: 1
Format: Audio CD (re-mastered, 16 bit)
Audio: stereo

Album & Track Notes

In early 1970, The Beach Boys sign to Warner Brothers and the first album released by Brother-Reprise (a division of Warner) is 'Sunflower'

Album History:

The album entered the US chart in Sept. 1970 and reached a peak at No. 151, it spent a total of 4 weeks on the chart – The Beach Boys worst album to date. In the UK, the album did a little better, reaching No.29 in Dec. 1970 and staying on the chart for six weeks. Interesting, the track 'Cottonfields' was included on the original vinyl UK album.

Original Release Date: US - 8/70, UK - 11/70
Serial No: US – Bro-Rep 6382, UK- Stateside SSLA8251
Original Format: Vinyl
High Chart Pos/Weeks: US - #151(4), UK - #29(6)

32

Title: Surf's Up
Artist: The Beach Boys
Latest CD Release Date: Oct 3rd, 1990
Record Label: Caribou-Epic
CD Ref. No: US: ZK 46951
    Canada: WZK 46951
    UK: EPC 4678352
Country: US/UK/World
No. of Disks: 1
Format: Audio CD (re-mastered, 16 bit)
Audio: stereo

Album & Track Notes

A year after 'Sunflower', The Beach Boys release the album 'Surf's Up, it reaches the highest point in the US album charts for four years and contains the beautiful 'Surf's Up' (albeit a re-recorded version of the original SMiLE version)). The Brother CD's were released in Canada with a 'W' prefix and were distributed by SONY Music. SONY bought CBS Records for $2bn in 1988.

Album History:

Surf's Up' entered the US chart in Sept. 1971, reached a peak at No.29 and spent a total of 17 weeks on the chart. In the UK, the album reached No.15 and spent 7 week on the chart.

Original Release Date: US - 8/71, UK - 10/71
Serial No: US – Bro-Rep 6453, UK- Stateside SSL10313
Original Format: Vinyl
High Chart Pos/Weeks: US - #29(17), UK - #15(7)

1. YOU NEED A MESS OF HELP TO STAND ALONE
2. HERE SHE COMES
3. HE COME DOWN
4. MARCELLA
5. HOLD ON DEAR BROTHER
6. MAKE IT GOOD
7. ALL THIS IS THAT
8. CUDDLE UP

Title: Carl & The Passions (So Tough!!)
Artist: The Beach Boys
Latest CD Release Date: Feb 26th, 1991
Record Label: Caribou-Epic
CD Ref. No: US: ZK 46953
                  UK: EPC 4683492
Country: US/UK/World
No. of Disks: 1
Format: Audio CD (re-mastered, 16 bit)
Audio: stereo

Album & Track Notes

In the summer of 1971, The Beach Boys added Ricky Fataar and Blondie Chaplin to their line-up. Bruce Johnston left the band in April 1972 and in May 1972, 'Carl & The Passions' was released in the US and the UK as a double album along with re-released 'Pet Sounds'.

Album History:

The album entered the US chart in June 1972, peaked at No.50 and spent a total of 20 weeks on the chart. In the UK, the album bombed, it reached No.25 and spent 1 week on the UK chart. The 45 single 'Marcella' failed to chart.

Original Release Date: US - 5/72, UK - 5/72
Serial No: US - Bro-Rep 2MS2083, UK- Reprise K441184
Original Format: Vinyl
High Chart Pos/Weeks: US - #50(20), UK - #25(1)

The Beach Boys on CD: Single album CD's

1. SAIL ON SAILOR**
2. STEAMBOAT
3. CALIFORNIA SAGA/BIG SUR
4. CALIFORNIA SAGA/THE BEAKS OF EAGLES
5. CALIFORNIA SAGA/CALIFORNIA
6. TRADER
7. LEAVING THIS TOWN*
8. ONLY WITH YOU
9. FUNKY PRETTY
MOUNT VERNON AND FAIRWAY (A Fairy Tale):
10. MT. VERNON AND FAIRWAY – THEME
11. I'M THE PIED PIPER
12. BETTER GET BACK IN BED
13. MAGIC TRANSISTOR RADIO
14. I'M THE PIED PIPER
15. RADIO KING DOM

Title: Holland
Artist: The Beach Boys
Latest CD Release Date: Oct 23rd, 1990
Record Label: Caribou-Epic
CD Ref. No: US: ZK 46952
UK: EPC 467837 2
Country: US/UK/World
No. of Disks: 1
Format: Audio CD (re-mastered, 16 bit)
Audio: stereo

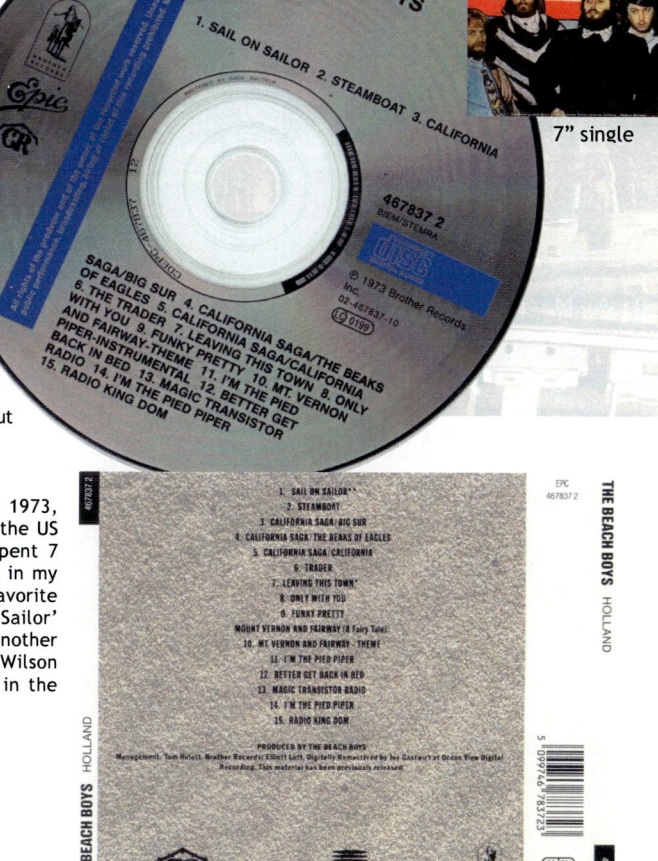

7" single

Album & Track Notes

Holland was released in Jan. 1973. The album was partially recorded in Holland in the summer of 1972. The original album was released with an accompanying EP: Mount Vernon & Fairway (A Fairy Tale): A fairy tale in several parts - a skit about a young prince and his magic radio; apparently a parable about Brian Wilson in his younger years and times spent at cousin Mike Love's house; a charming little piece, but completely nuts!.

Album History:

'Holland' entered the US chart in late January 1973, peaked at No.36 and spent a total of 30 weeks on the US chart. In the UK, the album reached No.20 and spent 7 weeks on the UK chart. Holland is a superb album, in my opinion the last great Beach Boys album and my favorite Beach Boys album cover. The 7" single 'Sail on, Sailor' failed to chart. The Beach Boys would not release another album for another three and a half years, Brian Wilson drifted into a serious physical and mental decline in the years that followed Holland.

Original Release Date: US - 1/73, UK - 1/73
Serial No: US – Bro-Rep MS2118, UK- Reprise K54008
Original Format: Vinyl
High Chart Pos/Weeks: US - #36(30), UK - #20(7)

35

The Beach Boys on CD: Single album CD's

Track Listing

1. Sail On Sailor
2. Sloop John B.
3. Trader, The
4. You Still Believe In Me
5. California Girls
6. Darlin'
7. Marcella
8. Caroline, No
9. Leaving This Town
10. Heroes And Villains
11. Funky Pretty
12. Let The Wind Blow
13. Help Me Rhonda
14. Surfer Girl
15. Wouldn't It Be Nice
16. We Got Love
17. Don't Worry Baby
18. Surfin' U.S.A.
19. Good Vibrations
20. Fun, Fun, Fun

Title: In Concert
Artist: The Beach Boys
Latest CD Release Date: July 18th, 2000
Record Label: Capitol/EMI Records
Caribou-Epic (1990)
CD Ref. No: US: ZGK 46954
UK: EPC 4683452
CDP 724382 963226

Country: US/UK/World
No. of Disks: 1
Format: Audio CD (re-mastered, 16 bit)
Audio: stereo

Album & Track Notes

Recorded in 1972, the 'In Concert', was released in late 1973

Album History:

The album was released in Nov. 1973, entered the US charts the following month, reached a high point of No.25 and spent 24 weeks in the chart. 'In Concert' was the Beach Boys first gold selling 'non compilation' album for eight years. The album did not chart in the UK.

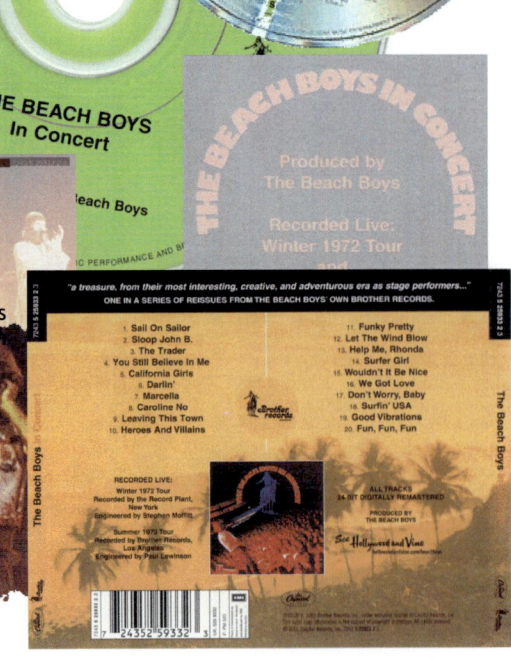

Original Release Date: US - 11/73, UK (not known)
Serial No: US – Bro-Rep 2MS6484, UK- Reprise K84001
Original Format: Vinyl
High Chart Pos/Weeks: US - #25(24), UK - DNC

Artist: 15 Big Ones
Artist: The Beach Boys
Latest CD Release Date: Jan 15th, 1991
Record Label: Caribou-Epic
CD Ref. No: US: ZK 46955
       UK EPC 4638482
Country: US/UK/World
No. of Disks: 1
Format: Audio CD (re-mastered, 16 bit)
Audio: stereo

Album & Track Notes

The 'Brian is back' album, well Brian Wilson was indeed back, but he was still a shadow of his former self. The album was the 6th release for Warner and was release after a three year gap.

Album History:

The album was released in July 1976 in both the US and the UK. It entered the US chart in July and reached the No.8 position; it stayed on the charts for 27 weeks and became the Beach Boys sixteenth gold album (2nd for Warner). In the UK, the album reached No.31 and spent only 3 weeks in the charts. In the years from 1973-76, the Beach Boys enjoyed phenomenal success via the Capitol releases of 'Endless Summer (1974) and Spirit of America (1975). Both compilations (not released in the UK) were huge successes and both achieved gold record status, 'Endless Summer hit the No.1 spot, The Beach Boys 2nd No.1 US album. Warner released 'Good Vibration – Best of the Beach Boys' in June '75 and although not as successful as the Capitol compilations it did reach the No.25 spot on the chart and would eventually spend 23 weeks on the chart. In the UK, the EMI release of July '76, '20 Golden Greats', went to No.1 and would spend 86 weeks on the charts up to 1981. The 7" single 'Rock'n'Roll Music' hit No.5 in the US and No. 36 in the UK.

Original Release Date: US - 7/76, UK - 7/76
Serial No: US - Bro-Rep K54079, UK - Reprise MS2251
Original Format: Vinyl
High Chart Pos/Weeks: US - #8(27), UK - #31(3)

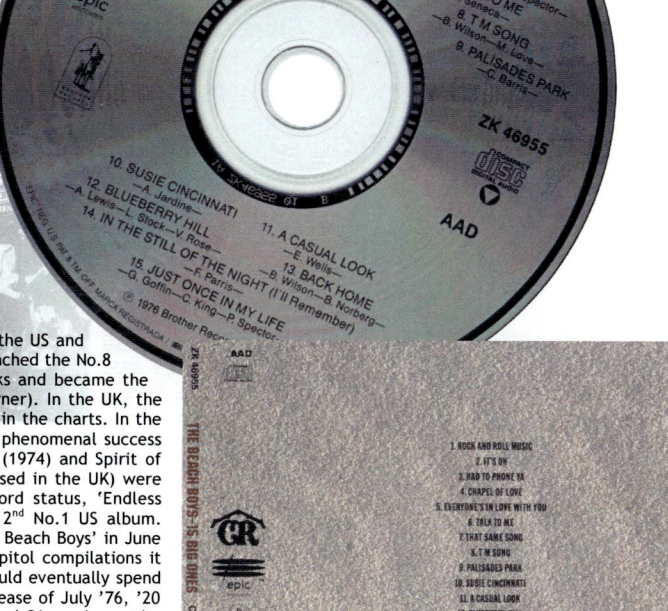

Title: Love You
Artist: The Beach Boys
Latest CD Release Date: Jan 15th, 1991
Record Label: Caribou-Epic
CD Ref. No: US: ZK 46956
UK: 4638472
Country: US/UK/World
No. of Disks: 1
Format: Audio CD (re-mastered, 16 bit)
Audio: stereo

LET US GO ON THIS WAY
(Brian Wilson, Michael Love)
ROLLER SKATING CHILD
(Brian Wilson)
MONA
(Brian Wilson)
JOHNNY CARSON
(Brian Wilson)
GOOD TIME *
(Brian Wilson, Alan Jardine)
HONKIN' DOWN THE HIGHWAY
(Brian Wilson)
DING DANG
(Brian Wilson, Roger McGuinn)
SOLAR SYSTEM
(Brian Wilson)
THE NIGHT WAS SO YOUNG
(Brian Wilson)
I'LL BET HE'S NICE
(Brian Wilson)
LET'S PUT OUR HEARTS TOGETHER
(Brian Wilson)
I WANNA PICK YOU UP
(Brian Wilson)
AIRPLANE
(Brian Wilson)
LOVE IS A WOMAN
(Brian Wilson)

Album & Track Notes

The 'Love You' album was the last album the Beach Boys recorded before signing to their new record company CBS in April 1977. The Beach Boys still at this point still owe Warner one last album.

Album History:

Released in April 1977, the album entered the charts the same month; it reached the No.53 spot and spent just seven weeks on the chart. In the UK, it charted at No.28 and lasted one week on the chart in May.

Original Release Date: US - 4/77, UK - 5/77
Serial No: US – Bro-Rep MSK2258, UK- Reprise K54087
Original Format: Vinyl
High Chart Pos/Weeks: US - #53(7)), UK - #28(1)

The Beach Boys on CD: Single album CD's

Track Listing

1. She's Got Rhythm
2. Come Go With Me
3. Hey Little Tomboy
4. Kona Coast
5. Peggy Sue
6. Wontcha Come Out Tonight
7. Sweet Sunday Kinda Love
8. Belles Of Paris
9. Pitter Patter
10. My Diana
11. Match Point Of Our Love
12. Winds Of Change

Title: M.I.U. Album
Artist: The Beach Boys
Latest CD Release Date: Feb 26th, 1991
Record Label: Caribou
CD Ref. No: US: ZK 46957
UK:
Country: US/UK/World
No. of Disks: 1
Format: Audio CD (re-mastered, 16 bit)
Audio: stereo

Album & Track Notes

MIU was the last album recorded for Warner (Reprise) and fulfilled and completed their contractual arrangement. The album was a giant flop although 'Come Go With Me' would be a 'minor' hit single in 1981 in the US.

Album History:

Released in Oct. 1978, M.I.U. went to No.151 in the US, stayed for 4 weeks and disappeared without a trace...enough said, TAXI!

Original Release Date: US - 10/78, UK - 9/78
Serial No: US – Bro-Rep MS2268, UK- Reprise K54102
Original Format: Vinyl
High Chart Pos/Weeks: US - #151(4), UK – DNC

39

Track Listing ...

1. Good Timin'
2. Lady Lynda
3. Full Sail
4. Angel Come Home
5. Love Surrounds Me
6. Sumahama
7. Here Comes The Night
8. Baby Blue
9. Goin' South
10. Shortenin' Bread

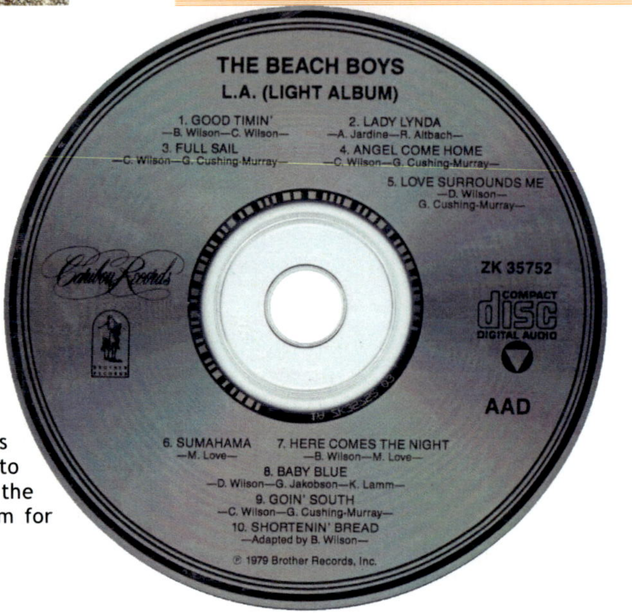

Title: L.A. (light Album)
Artist: The Beach Boys
Latest CD Release Date: Oct 24th, 1989
Record Label: Caribou (CBS)
CD Ref. No: ZK 35752 (original 1989)
ZK 46958 (1990)
CBS 902 127 2
Country: US/UK/World
No. of Disks: 1
Format: Audio CD (re-mastered, 16 bit)
Audio: stereo

Album & Track Notes

Bruce Johnston re-joined the Beach Boys after a long absence but the album fails to light a sparks and failed miserably in the charts. This is the first Beach Boys album for CBS

Album History:

Released in March 1979, the album went to No.100 in the US. It stayed in the charts for 13 weeks and disappears without trace. The album reached 32 in the UK chart but did not hang around for long. The single 'Lady Lynda' did score a top ten hit in the UK, reaching No.5 in Jan. '79

Original Release Date: US – 3/79, UK – 3/79
Serial No: US – Caribou JZ 35752
UK – Caribou S CRB 86081
Original Format: Vinyl
High Chart Pos/Weeks: US – #100(13), UK – #32(6)

The Beach Boys on CD: Single album CD's

THE BEACH BOYS
KEEPIN' THE SUMMER ALIVE

1	KEEPIN' THE SUMMER ALIVE	3:41
	(C. Wilson-R. Bachman) Murry Gage Music/Top Soil Music (admin. by Careers-BMG Music Publishing)	
2	OH DARLIN'	3:52
	(B. Wilson-M. Love) Beach Bum Music/Clairaudient Music Corp.	
3	SOME OF YOUR LOVE	2:34
	(B. Wilson-M. Love) Beach Bum Music/Clairaudient Music Corp.	
4	LIVIN' WITH A HEARTACHE	4:03
	(C. Wilson-R. Bachman) Murry Gage Music/Top Soil Music (admin. by Careers-BMG Music Publishing)	
5	SCHOOL DAY (RING! RING! GOES THE BELL)	2:50
	(C. Berry) Isalee Music Co.	
6	GOIN' ON	3:02
	(B. Wilson-M. Love) Beach Bum Music/Clairaudient Music Corp.	
7	SUNSHINE	2:50
	(B. Wilson-M. Love) Beach Bum Music/Clairaudient Music Corp.	
8	WHEN GIRLS GET TOGETHER	3:30
	(B. Wilson-M. Love) Beach Bum Music/Clairaudient Music Corp.	
9	SANTA ANA WINDS	3:12
	(B. Wilson-A. Jardine) Beach Bum Music/Al Jardine Music	
10	ENDLESS HARMONY	3:07
	(B. Johnston) Chappell & Co.	

Title: Keepin' The Summer Alive
Artist: The Beach Boys
Latest CD Release Date: Feb 26th, 1991
Record Label: Caribou
CD Ref. No: US: ZK 36283
 UK: 4683502
Country: US/UK/World
No. of Disks: 1
Format: Audio CD (re-mastered, 16 bit)
Audio: stereo

Album & Track Notes

This is the second album for CBS and performs just a badly as its predecessor.

Album History:

Released in March 1980, KTSA went to No.75 in the US, and stayed for six weeks. The album reached No.54 in the UK and spent three weeks on the chart. In May 1980, the 7" single, 'Livin' with a Heartache-Santa Ana winds' failed to chart – two great songs.

Original Release Date: US – 3/80, UK – 3/80
Serial No: US – Caribou FZ 37010,
 UK- Caribou S CRB 86109
Original Format: Vinyl
High Chart Pos/Weeks: US - #75(6), UK - #54(3)

1. Getcha Back (2:59)
2. It's Gettin' Late (3:26)
3. Crack At Your Love (3:36)
4. Maybe I Don't Know (3:53)
5. She Believes In Love Again (3:27)
6. California Calling (2:46)
7. Passing Friend (4:59)
8. I'm So Lonely (2:51)
9. Where I Belong (2:55)
10. I Do Love You (4:20)
11. It's Just A Matter Of Time (2:19)
12. Male Ego (3:32)

Title: The Beach Boys
Artist: The Beach Boys
CD Release Date: May, 1985
Record Label: Caribou
CD Ref. No: US: ZK 39946 (original release)
Europe: CRB 462530 2 (1935)
UK: EPC 4673632 (Oct, 1990)
Europe: CRB 46013 2
Country: US/UK/World
No. of Disks: 1
Format: Audio CD (re-mastered, 16 bit)
Audio: stereo

Album & Track Notes

The third album for CBS, 'The Beach Boys' was the first Beach Boys' album to be released on CD and was released after a five recording year gap. The CD was also released by **CBS (CRB 465013 2)** as part of the 'Memory Pop Shop' inexpensive CD series in 1989, it had an oddball cover (above)

Album History:

Released in April 1985, 'The Beach Boys' went to No.52 in the US, and lasted fourteen weeks on the chart. The album reached No.60 in the UK and spent two weeks on the chart. 'Getcha Back' reached No.26 in the US singles charts in May 1985.

Original Release Date: US – 5/85, UK – 6/85
Serial No: US – Caribou ZK 39946, UK- Caribou CRB 26378
Original Format: Vinyl
High Chart Pos/Weeks: US - #52(14), UK - #60(2)

Title: Still Cruisin'
Artist: The Beach Boys
Latest CD Release Date: August, 1989
Record Label: Capitol Records
CD Ref. No: US: 92639 (D 144379 – BMG)
 UK: CDP 7926392
ountry: US/UK/World
No. of Disks: 1
Format: Audio CD
Audio: stereo

CD Notes

The Beach Boys re-join Capitol for their penultimate CD and it does rather well. The album contains a number of re-releases and includes the Beach Boys' biggest selling record for years and their fourh US No.1 hit; 'Kokomo' is taken from the sound track of the film 'Coctail', the album performs quite well in the US. Brian Wilson has effectively left the Beach Boys at this point and is persuing a solo career and has already released his first album.

CD History:

Released in Aug. 1989, 'Still Cruisin' went to No.46 in the US, and lasted a respectable 22 weeks on the chart. The album failed to chart in the UK.

Original Release Date: US – 8/89, UK – 8/89
Serial No: US – Capitol CDP 92639
 UK - Caribou CDP 7926392
Original Format: Vinyl
High Chart Pos/Weeks: US - #46(22), UK – DNC

UK CD disk

Title: Summer In Paradise
Artist: The Beach Boys
Latest CD Release Date: August, 1998
Record Label: Brother Entertainment
CD Ref. No: CDP 724382 96322 6
Country: US/UK/World
No. of Disks: 1
Format: Audio CD
Audio: stereo

CD Notes & History:

Released in Aug. 1992 the album failed to make an impression on the US chart. The UK version, released in May '93 proved no more successful in the UK...a sad end indeed, good cover though!

Original Release Date: US – 8/92, UK – 5/93
Serial No: US – BBR 727-2
UK – EMI 0777 7 81036 2 2
Original Format: Vinyl
High Chart Pos/Weeks: US – DNC, UK – DNC

The Beach Boys on CD: Single album CD's

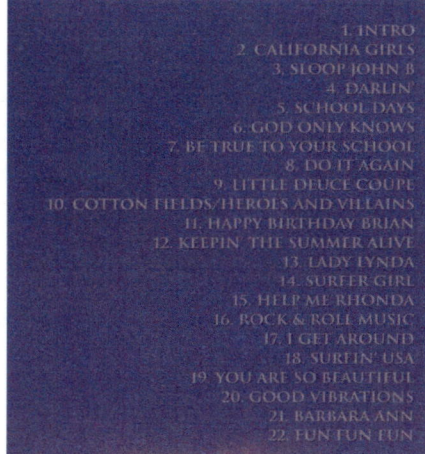

Title: Good Timin' (Live at Knebworth)
Artist: The Beach Boys
Latest CD Release Date: Oct. 2002
Record Label: Eagle Records
CD Ref. No: US: ER 20002 2
UK: Eagle (UK) 20002 2
Japan: VICP 62138
Country: US/UK/World
No. of Disks: 1
Format: Audio CD
Audio: stereo
Liner Notes: Mike Grant

CD Notes

The CD presents the Beach Boys playing live at Knebworth, England on June 21st 1980, the CD was produced by Mark Linett. This was apparently the last time all six original Beach Boys played together in the UK. The accompanying video portrays a very tired looking Brian Wilson and an equally exhausted looking Dennis Wilson. A great record all the same. The CD was released in the UK in Oct, 2002 – In Japan (Victor Entertainment) in Dec, 2002 and finally in the US in March, 2003

Original Release Date: US – 3/03, UK – 10/02
Serial No: US – ER 20002 2, UK – ER 20002 2
Original Format: CD
High Chart Pos/Weeks: US - DNC, UK - DNC

The Beach Boys on CD: Single album CD's

Title: The Originals
Artist: The Beach Boys
Latest CD Release Date: 1997
Record Label: Capitol/EMI Records
CD Ref. No: 7243 8 56069 2 2 (box)
7243 8 56070 2 8 (Summer Days)
7243 8 56071 2 7 (TODAY!)
7243 8 56072 2 6 (Smiley Smile)
Country: UK
No. of Disks: 3
Format: Audio CD
Audio: mono/stereo

CD Notes

Released to celebrate the 100-year anniversary of EMI records this 3 CD box set was part of 'The Originals' series released by EMI in the UK. To my knowledge, the three CD's are the only mini album CD's to be released outside of Japan. This box set is now quite rare, the sound quality on all CD's is OK.

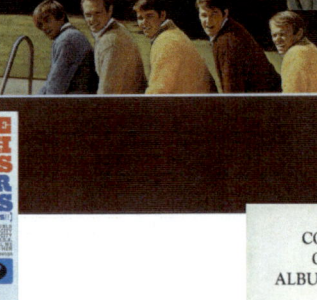

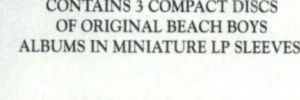

CONTAINS 3 COMPACT DISCS OF ORIGINAL BEACH BOYS ALBUMS IN MINIATURE LP SLEEVES.

7243 8 56069 2 2

SUMMER DAYS (AND SUMMER NIGHTS!!)	TODAY!	SMILEY SMILE
The Girl From New York City	Do You Wanna Dance?	Heroes And Villains
Amusement Parks U.S.A.	Good To My Baby	Vegetables
Then I Kissed Her	Don't Hurt My Little Sister	Fall Breaks And Back To Winter (W. Woodpecker Symphony)
Salt Lake City	When I Grow Up	
Girl Don't Tell Me	Help Me, Rhonda	She's Goin' Bald
Help Me, Rhonda	Dance, Dance, Dance	Little Pad
California Girls	Please Let Me Wonder	Good Vibrations
Let Him Run Wild	I'm So Young	With Me Tonight
You're So Good To Me	Kiss Me, Baby	Wind Chimes
Summer Means New Love	She Knows Me Too Well	Gettin' Hungry
I'm Bugged At My Ol'man	In The Back Of My Mind	Wonderful
And Your Dream Comes True	Bull Session With The "Big Daddy"	Whistle In

© 1997 THE COPYRIGHT IN THIS COMPILATION IS OWNED BY CAPITOL RECORDS INC. © 1997 EMI RECORDS LTD.

The Beach Boys on CD: Single album CD's

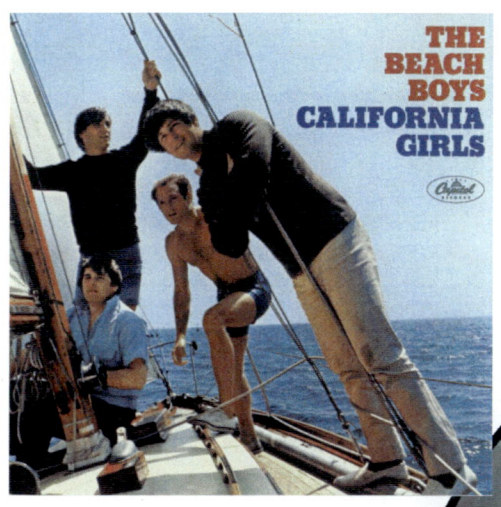

Title: California Girls
Artist: The Beach Boys
Latest CD Release Date: 1987
Record Label: Capitol Records
CD Ref. No: CDP 7 48046 2
Country: US
No. of Disks: 1
Format: Audio CD
Audio: mono/stereo

CD Notes

I have no idea why this CD was released

The Beach Boys on CD: Single album CD's

Title: Lost and Found (currently: Studio sessions '61'62)
Artist: The Beach Boys
Latest CD Release Date: 1991/95 & Nov, 21st 2000
Record Label: 1991: DCC
 2000: Burning Airlines
CD Ref. No: DZS 054
 038894 001266
Country: US
No. of Disks: 1
Format: Audio CD
Audio: mono/stereo
Liner Notes: Denis Diken/Paul Urbahns

CD Notes

This CD was originally released by DCC. The tracks on the CD are recordings made by the Beach Boys before signing to Capitol Records in 1962. From an historical viewpoint, these recording are important, aurally; these recordings are poor quality. The original re-engineering 1991, was carried out by Steve Hofmann. A Japanese long-box version of this CD exists

The Japanese Version

The current version

48

Title: Stars and Stripes Vol.1
Artist: Other Artists (The Beach Boys backing vocals)
Latest CD Release Date: 1996
Record Label: River North
CD Ref. No: 7 51416 1205 2 2
Country: US
No. of Disks: 1
Format: Audio CD
Audio: stereo
Liner Notes: Various

CD Notes

This compact disk was released (or did it escape?) in 1996. The executive producer was Mike Love with production by Brian Wilson & Joe Thomas. This is not a Beach Boys album, rather it is bunch of C&W singers covering well-known Beach Boys songs; the Beach Boys provide background vocals and some instrumentation. This is volume one, I cannot wait for volume 2. Highlights; Willie Nelson singing 'The Warmth of the Sun'...the lowlights; everything else (IMO)

The Beach Boys on CD: Single album CD's

Redferns

The Twofers

In 1990 Capitol records released CD versions of the studio albums in the form of 8 re-mastered twofer CD's, these were the first releases of the Beach Boys back catalogue to appear on CD. The twofers consisted of original album pairs on a single CD, along with CD liner notes. The idea of the twofer was not new; two Beach Boys albums in a single release dates back to the mid 60 s. Released in 1972, Carl and the Passion was coupled with a re-released Pet Sounds. In 1974, Capitol released gatefold vinyl pairs (Wild Honey/20-20 & Friends/Smiley Smile). Each of the original Capitol CD twofer contained bonus tracks consisting of: previously released singles, alternate mixes, studio outtakes and/or previously unreleased recordings. In 1990, Pet Sounds and the Beach Boys' Christmas Album were released on CD as single re-mastered CD s. The twofers were also released in the UK, Canada and Japan. The original eight twofers were:

    Surfin Safari/Surfin U.S.A.
    Surfer Girl/Shut Down Volume 2
    Little Deuce Coupe/All Summer Long
    Concert/Live in London (Beach Boys 69)
    Today!/Summer Days (and Summer Nights)
    Beach Boys Party!/Stack-o-Tracks
    Smiley Smile/Wild Honey
    Friends/20/20

In 1994 (date not known) Capitol in the US discontinued the twofers and released the individual Studio Albums in CD format for the first time. These CD s were released without the twofer liner notes and contained no bonus material. The twofers continued to be sold in the US as imports from the UK and Canada, the Canadian and especially the UK twofers had different CD case back covers than the original US versions, the Japanese versions had a fold over sleeve showing both albums on the front cover. In 2000, the Brother albums were released by Capitol on twofers (under license from Brother Records) and in March 2001 Capitol released new 24 bit HCDC versions of the original twofers containing essentially the same tracks as the 1990 twofer releases but with infinitely better sound quality. The Brother twofers are:

    Sunflower/Surf s Up
    Carl and the Passions So Tough /Holland
    15 Big Ones/Love You
    M.I.U. Album/L.A. (Light Album)
    Keepin' the Summer Alive/The Beach Boys (1985)

The Beach Boys **In Concert** remains as a single CD's along with **Still Cruisin'** and **Summer in Paradise** which have yet to appear in twofer format. In summary, the following twofer series exist; sets A-E are now out of print (OOP) but are still available at various outlets:

Series A:	BMG (record club) 1990 twofer series (same as D, different covers
Series B:	Canadian Capitol-EMI 1990 twofer series (same as D, different covers)
Series C:	UK EMI-Capitol 1990 twofer series (same as D, different covers)
Series D:	US Capitol 1990 twofer series
Series E:	Japanese Toshiba-EMI 1990 twofer series (same as D, just different cover sleeve)
Series F:	Brother 2000 twofers
Series G:	Re-mastered HDCD Capitol twofers (Capitol albums only)

All of the current twofers include booklets which provide liner notes, photographs, bonus track details and other technical information. The front cover of all the twofer booklets (and CD's) is the cover of the first named album, the booklets also include images of the original album back covers (unlike the 1990 Caribou single album CD releases), and some of the 'Brother' twofers contain liner notes/comments from well known music artists and/or writers. The detail of the various twofer sets is provided/illustrated on the following pages – they are presented in the following order; Series G, F, D, C, B, A (The Japanese twofer series is detailed in the chapter, 'Land of the Rising Song'. The main illustration on the following pages shows the reverse of the CD jewel case and track listings.

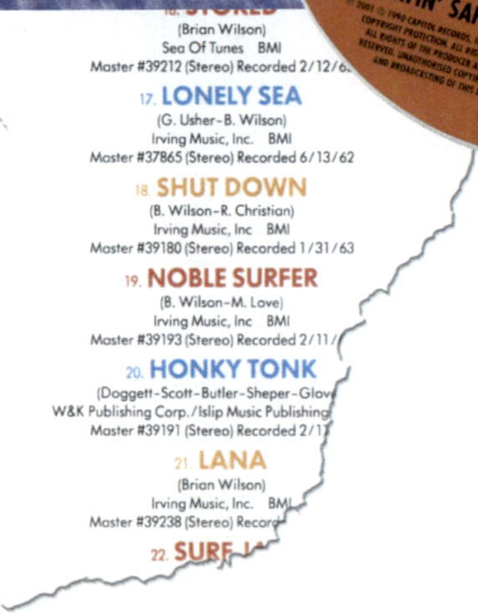

SURFIN' SAFARI

1. SURFIN' SAFARI
2. COUNTY FAIR
3. TEN LITTLE INDIANS
4. CHUG-A-LUG
5. LITTLE MISS AMERICA
6. 409
7. SURFIN'
8. HEADS YOU WIN - TAILS I LOSE
9. SUMMERTIME BLUES
10. CUCKOO CLOCK
11. MOON DAWG
12. THE SHIFT

SURFIN' U.S.A.

13. SURFIN' U.S.A.
14. FARMER'S DAUGHTER
15. MISIRLOU
16. STOKED
17. LONELY SEA
18. SHUT DOWN
19. NOBLE SURFER
20. HONKY TONK
21. LANA
22. SURF JAM
23. LET'S GO TRIPPIN'
24. FINDERS KEEPERS

BONUS TRACKS

25. CINDY, OH CINDY
26. THE BAKER MAN
27. LAND AHOY

Title: Surfin' Safari/Surfin' U.S.A.
Release Date: 13th Mar. 2001
Record Label: Capitol
CD Ref. No: 7243 5 31517 2 0
Country: US
No. of Disks: 1
Format: Audio CD
Audio: HDCD (24 bit)
Liner Notes: David Leaf

Album & Track Notes

Remastered to digital and transferred to CD via HDCD technology the Capitol twofer CD were re-released in early 2001, no remixing of the original tapes was carried out. These twofers contain the same booklet as the original 1990 releases and essentially comprise of a CD with a greatly improved sound quality; essentially the re-engineered sound is an attempt to get as close a copy (as is currently technically possible) to the original analog sound of the original tape and vinyl & needle. The bonus tracks include:-

Track 25: Cindy, Oh Cindy
Track 26: The Baker Man
Track 27:. Land Ahoy

SURFER GIRL
1. SURFER GIRL
2. CATCH A WAVE
3. THE SURFER MOON
4. SOUTH BAY SURFER
5. THE ROCKING SURFER
6. LITTLE DEUCE COUPE
7. IN MY ROOM
8. HAWAII
9. SURFERS RULE
10. OUR CAR CLUB
11. YOUR SUMMER DREAM
12. BOOGIE WOODIE

SHUT DOWN VOLUME 2
13. FUN, FUN, FUN
14. DON'T WORRY BABY
15. IN THE PARKIN' LOT
16. "CASSIUS" LOVE VS. "SONNY" WILSON
17. THE WARMTH OF THE SUN
18. THIS CAR OF MINE
19. WHY DO FOOLS FALL IN LOVE
20. POM POM PLAY GIRL
21. KEEP AN EYE ON SUMMER
22. SHUT DOWN, PART II
23. LOUIE LOUIE
24. DENNY'S DRUMS

BONUS TRACKS
25. FUN, FUN, FUN (SINGLE VERSION)
26. IN MY ROOM (GERMAN VERSION)
27. I DO

Title: Surfer Girl/Shut Down Volume 2
Release Date: 13th Mar. 2001
Record Label: Capitol
CD Ref. No: 7243 5 31515 2 2
Country: US
No. of Disks: 1
Format: Audio CD
Audio: HDCD (24 bit)
Liner Notes: David Leaf

Album & Track Notes

In booklet Brian Wilson provides some insight into the recordings on the CD and puts the music into an historical context; Brian gives us some background on the tunes 'In My Room', 'Fun, Fun, Fun' and other well known songs. The bonus tracks include:-

Track 25: Fun, Fun, Fun (single version)
Track 26: In My Room (German version)
Track 27: I Do

Title: Little Deuce Coupe/All Summer Long
Release Date: 13th Mar. 2001
Record Label: Capitol
CD Ref. No: 7243 5 31516 2 2
Country: US
No. of Disks: 1
Format: Audio CD
Audio: HDCD (24 bit)
Liner Notes: David Leaf

Album & Track Notes

Unusual colouring on the CD disk...the colour is switched on the swirl (now corrected). The bonus tracks include:-

Track 25:   Be True To Your School (single version)
Track 26:   All Dressed Up For School
Track 27:   Little Honda (alternate take)
Track 28:   Don't Back Down (alternate take)

Version with the swirl colours corrected

Title: Concert/Live In London
Release Date: 13th Mar. 2001
Record Label: Capitol
CD Ref. No: 7243 5 31861 2 8
Country: US
No. of Disks: 1
Format: Audio CD
Audio: HDCD (24 bit)
Liner Notes: David Leaf

Album & Track Notes

The 'live' twofer; the bonus tracks include:-

Track 26:   Don't Worry Baby
Track 27:   Heroes & Villains

TODAY!

1. DO YOU WANNA DANCE
2. GOOD TO MY BABY
3. DON'T HURT MY LITTLE SISTER
4. WHEN I GROW UP (TO BE A MAN)
5. HELP ME, RONDA (LP VERSION)
6. DANCE, DANCE, DANCE
7. PLEASE LET ME WONDER
8. I'M SO YOUNG
9. KISS ME BABY
10. SHE KNOWS ME TOO WELL
11. IN THE BACK OF MY MIND
12. BULL SESSIONS WITH "BIG DADDY"

SUMMER DAYS (AND SUMMER NIGHTS!!)

13. THE GIRL FROM NEW YORK CITY
14. AMUSEMENT PARKS U.S.A.
15. THEN I KISSED HER
16. SALT LAKE CITY
17. GIRL DON'T TELL ME
18. HELP ME, RHONDA (SINGLE RECORD VERSION)
19. CALIFORNIA GIRLS
20. LET HIM RUN WILD
21. YOU'RE SO GOOD TO ME
22. SUMMER MEANS NEW LOVE
23. I'M BUGGED AT MY OL' MAN
24. AND YOUR DREAMS COME TRUE

BONUS TRACKS

25. THE LITTLE GIRL I ONCE KNEW (SINGLE)
26. DANCE, DANCE, DANCE (ALTERNATE TAKE)
27. I'M SO YOUNG (ALTERNATE TAKE)
28. LET HIM RUN WILD (ALTERNATE TAKE)
29. GRADUATION DAY (STUDIO VERSION)

Title: TODAY!/All Summer Long
Release Date: 13th Mar. 2001
Record Label: Capitol
CD Ref. No: 7243 5 31639 2 1
Country: US
No. of Disks: 1
Format: Audio CD
Audio: HDCD (24 bit)
Liner Notes: David Leaf

Album & Track Notes

The bonus tracks include:-

Track 25: The Girl I Once Knew (single)
Track 26: Dance, Dance, Dance (alternate)
Track 27: I'm So Young (alternate)
Track 28: Let Him Run Wild (alternate)
Track 29: Graduation Day (studio version)

Title: Party!/Stack-O-Tracks
Release Date: 13th Mar. 2001
Record Label: Capitol
CD Ref. No: 7243 5 31641 2 6
Country: US
No. of Disks: 1
Format: Audio CD
Audio: HDCD (24 bit)
Liner Notes: David Leaf/Mark Linett

Album & Track Notes

The bonus tracks include:-

Track 28:   Help Me, Rhonda
Track 29:   California Girls
Track 30:   Our Car Club

The Beach Boys on CD: Twofers

Title: Smiley Smile/Wild Honey
Release Date: 13th Mar. 2001
Record Label: Capitol
CD Ref. No: 7243 5 31862 2 7
Country: US
No. of Disks: 1
Format: Audio CD
Audio: HDCD (24 bit)
Liner Notes: David Leaf

Album & Track Notes
The bonus tracks include:-

Track 23:   Heroes & Villains (alternate)
Track 24:   Good Vibrations (various sessions)
Track 25:   Good Vibrations (early take)
Track 26:   You're Welcome
Track 27:   Their Hearts Were Full of Spring
Track 28:   Can't Wait Too Long

58

The Beach Boys on CD: Twofers

Title: Friends/2020
Release Date: 13th Mar. 2001
Record Label: Capitol
CD Ref. No: 7243 5 31638 2 2
Country: US
No. of Disks: 1
Format: Audio CD
Audio: HDCD (24 bit)
Liner Notes: David Leaf

Album & Track Notes

In this booklet Brian Wilson provides some insight into the recordings on the CD and discusses the vocal contributions on both albums in some detail. 20/20 was the Beach Boys 20th album for Capitol and was the last studio album for Capitol as the original group

Track 25:   Break Away
Track 26:   Celebrate The News
Track 27:   We're Together Again
Track 28:   Walk On By
Track 29:   Old Folks At Home/Ol' Man River

Title: Sunflower/Surf's Up
Release Date: 18th July 2000
Record Label: Capitol (Brother)
CD Ref. No: 7243 5 25692 2 9
Country: US
No. of Disks: 1
Format: Audio CD
Audio: 24 bit remastered
Liner Notes: Timothy White

Album & Track Notes

The 'Brother' twofers were first released in 2000 by Capitol Records (under license from Brother). The liner notes and historical background notes for this twofer is written by Timothy White. Unlike the Capitol twofers, no bonus tracks are provided. The booklet contains images of the back covers of the original vinyl releases and many other images of the Beach Boys.

For Further Reading: The Nearest Faraway Place (Brian Wilson, the Beach Boys, and the southern California experience) by Timothy White - ISBN 0-8050-2266-X

The Beach Boys on CD: Twofers

Title: Carl & The Passions/Holland
Release Date: 15th August 2000
Record Label: Capitol (Brother)
CD Ref. No: 7243 5 25694 2 7
Country: US
No. of Disks: 1
Format: Audio CD
Audio: 24 bit re-mastered
Liner Notes: Scott McCaughey

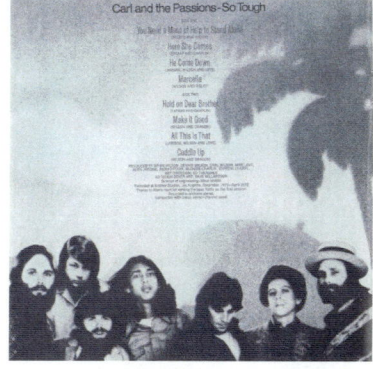

Album & Track Notes

Track comments are provided by Scott McCaughey, the booklet also contains album comments from Elton John (Carl & the Passions) and Tom Petty (Holland). The CD also contains the Mount Vernon and Fairway (A Fairy Tale) recording (original released as a separate EP with the Holland album)

The Beach Boys on CD: Twofers

Title: 15 Big Ones/Love You
Release Date: 15th August 2000
Record Label: Capitol (Brother)
CD Ref. No: 7243 5 27945 2 2
Country: US
No. of Disks: 1
Format: Audio CD
Audio: 24 bit re-mastered
Liner Notes: Denis Diken

Album & Track Notes

Track comments and background information is provided by Denis Diken (15 Big Ones). Peter Buck of R.E.M. provides the song notes and comments for 'Love You'. 15 Big Ones was touted as the 'Brian's back' album in 1976; Brian Wilson had been in the 'doldrums' for some time prior to the album.

The Beach Boys on CD
(an illustrated Guide)

The Beach Boys

Advance Reader

I hope you all enjoy the book. I would appreciate any constructive comments and if you spot any problems, can you draw them to my attention by noting the page number and provide a short description...Happy Christmas - Joe, Dec. 2003

Joe Thomas
No.7 Avoca Park
Blackrock
Co. Dublin
IRELAND
rathmich@gofree.indigo.ie

Title: M.I.U. Album/L.A. (Light Album)
Release Date: 15th August 2000
Record Label: Capitol (Brother)
CD Ref. No: 7243 5 27950 2 4
Country: US
No. of Disks: 1
Format: Audio CD
Audio: 24 bit re-mastered
Liner Notes: Jeff Tamarkin

Album & Track Notes

Track comments are provided by Jeff Tamarkin. These two album are often found in the 'worst Beach Boys' category...unfairly

Title: Keepin The Summer Alive/The Beach Boys
Release Date: 15th August 2000
Record Label: Capitol (Brother)
CD Ref. No: 7243 5 25694 2 7
Country: US
No. of Disks: 1
Format: Audio CD
Audio: 24 bit re-mastered
Liner Notes: Andrew G. Doe

Album & Track Notes

The booklet contains commentary from Randy Bachman (The Bachman Turner Overdrive – "You Ain't Seen Nothing Yet' fame); he who also co-wrote (with Carl) a couple of songs on 'Keepin' The Summer Alive'. The general booklet notes are provided by Andrew G. Doe.

For further Reading: The Complete Guide to the Music of The Beach Boys by Andrew Doe & John Tobler: ISBN 0-7119-5595-6 (out of print)

1990 US twofer series

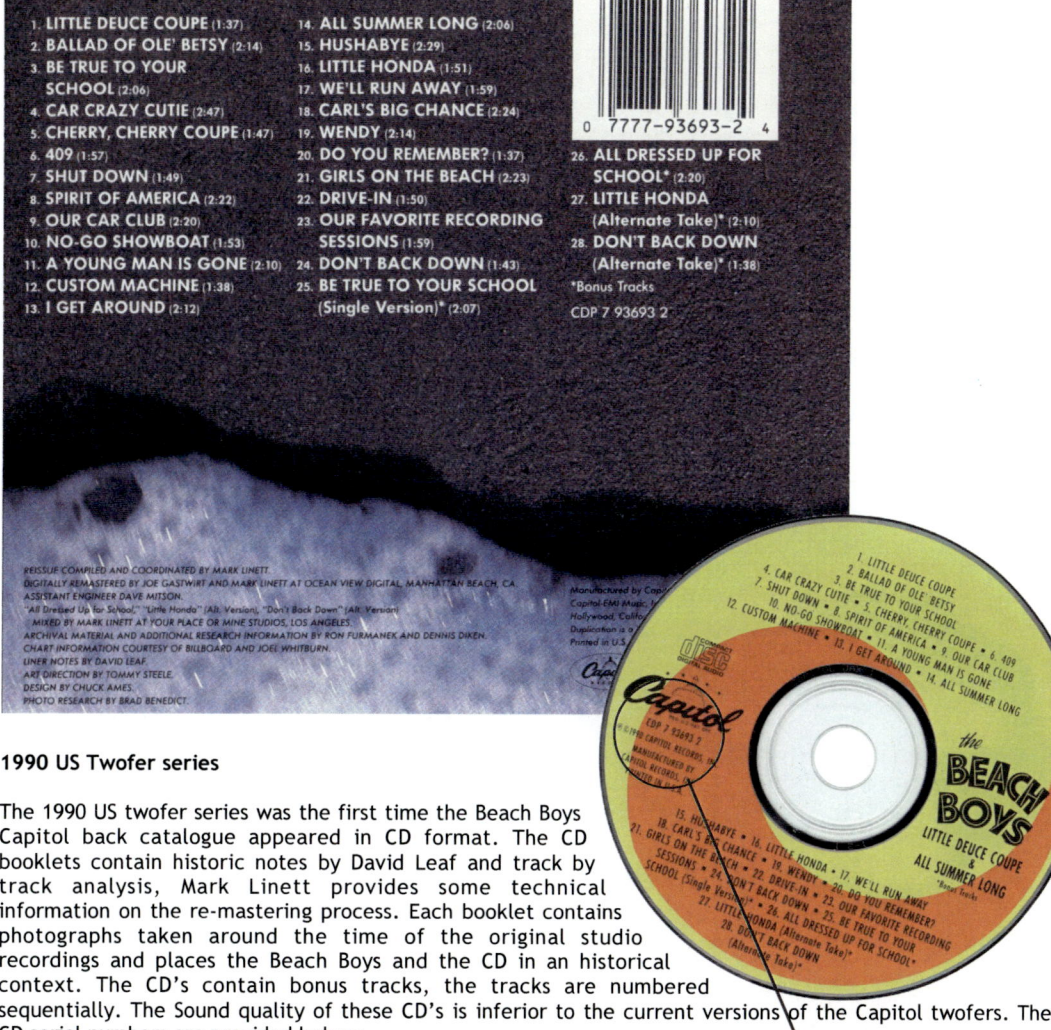

1990 US Twofer series

The 1990 US twofer series was the first time the Beach Boys Capitol back catalogue appeared in CD format. The CD booklets contain historic notes by David Leaf and track by track analysis, Mark Linett provides some technical information on the re-mastering process. Each booklet contains photographs taken around the time of the original studio recordings and places the Beach Boys and the CD in an historical context. The CD's contain bonus tracks, the tracks are numbered sequentially. The Sound quality of these CD's is inferior to the current versions of the Capitol twofers. The CD serial numbers are provided below:-

Surfin Safari/Surfin U.S.A.	CDP 7 93691 2
Surfer Girl/Shut Down Volume 2	CDP 7 93692 2
Little Deuce Coupe/All Summer Long	CDP 7 93693 2
Today!/Summer Days (and Summer Nights)	CDP 7 93694 2
Concert/Live in London (Beach Boys 69)	CDP 7 93695 2
Smiley Smile/Wild Honey	CDP 7 93696 2
Friends/20/20	CDP 7 93697 2
Beach Boys Party!/Stack-o-Tracks	CDP 7 93697 2

1990 UK twofer series

1990 UK Twofer series

The UK twofer series was released in 1990 and differs from its US 1990 counterpart in packaging only; the musical content on the disk is identical. The distinguishing features of the UK CDs are as follows:-

a) The back cover of the Jewel case is coloured and contains mini pictures of the album sleeves
b) The actual CD states that the disk was 'MADE IN UK'
c) The CD is given a UK number in the form CZ xxx and the booklet has the UK CD number stamped on the back cover
d) The front cover describes the bonus tracks and has a coloured band across the top

1990 Canadian twofer series

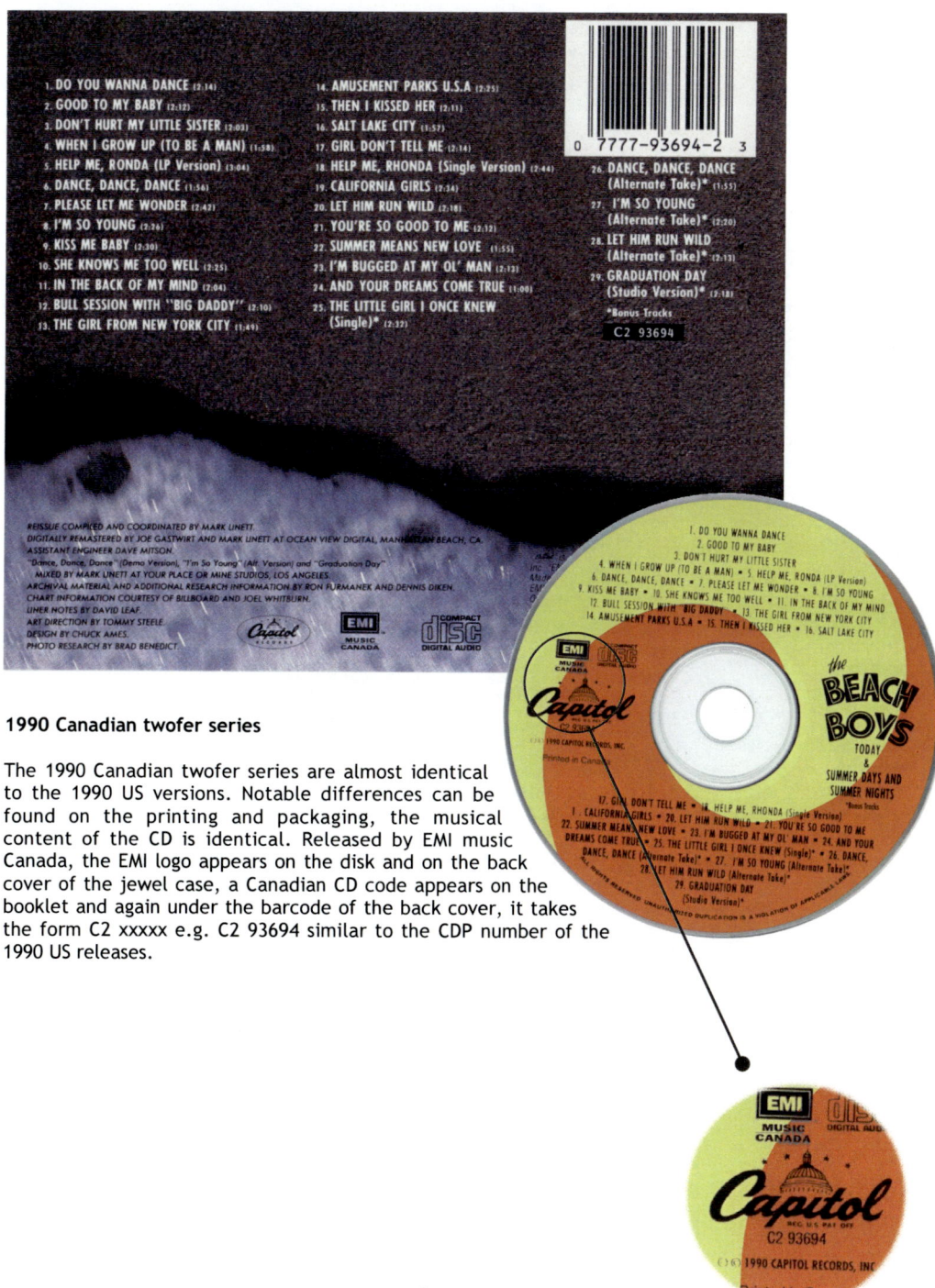

1990 Canadian twofer series

The 1990 Canadian twofer series are almost identical to the 1990 US versions. Notable differences can be found on the printing and packaging, the musical content of the CD is identical. Released by EMI music Canada, the EMI logo appears on the disk and on the back cover of the jewel case, a Canadian CD code appears on the booklet and again under the barcode of the back cover, it takes the form C2 xxxxx e.g. C2 93694 similar to the CDP number of the 1990 US releases.

1990 BMG twofer series

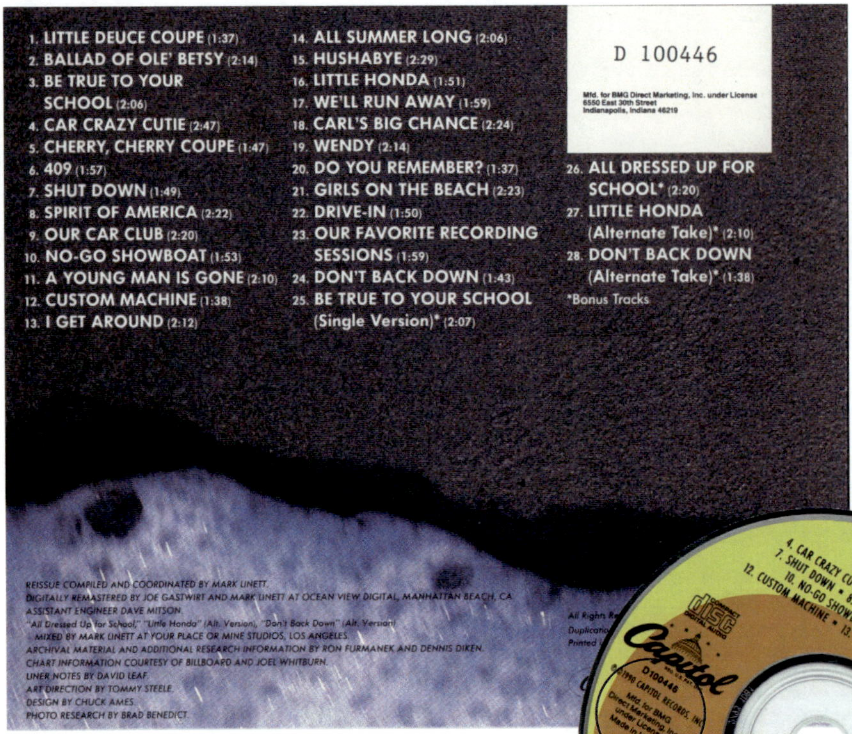
1. LITTLE DEUCE COUPE (1:37)
2. BALLAD OF OLE' BETSY (2:14)
3. BE TRUE TO YOUR SCHOOL (2:06)
4. CAR CRAZY CUTIE (2:47)
5. CHERRY, CHERRY COUPE (1:47)
6. 409 (1:57)
7. SHUT DOWN (1:49)
8. SPIRIT OF AMERICA (2:22)
9. OUR CAR CLUB (2:20)
10. NO-GO SHOWBOAT (1:53)
11. A YOUNG MAN IS GONE (2:10)
12. CUSTOM MACHINE (1:38)
13. I GET AROUND (2:12)
14. ALL SUMMER LONG (2:06)
15. HUSHABYE (2:29)
16. LITTLE HONDA (1:51)
17. WE'LL RUN AWAY (1:59)
18. CARL'S BIG CHANCE (2:24)
19. WENDY (2:14)
20. DO YOU REMEMBER? (1:37)
21. GIRLS ON THE BEACH (2:23)
22. DRIVE-IN (1:50)
23. OUR FAVORITE RECORDING SESSIONS (1:59)
24. DON'T BACK DOWN (1:43)
25. BE TRUE TO YOUR SCHOOL (Single Version)* (2:07)
26. ALL DRESSED UP FOR SCHOOL* (2:20)
27. LITTLE HONDA (Alternate Take)* (2:10)
28. DON'T BACK DOWN (Alternate Take)* (1:38)
*Bonus Tracks
D 100446
Mfd. for BMG Direct Marketing, Inc. under License
6550 East 30th Street
Indianapolis, Indiana 46219
REISSUE COMPILED AND COORDINATED BY MARK LINETT.
DIGITALLY REMASTERED BY JOE GASTWIRT AND MARK LINETT AT OCEAN VIEW DIGITAL, MANHATTAN BEACH, CA
ASSISTANT ENGINEER DAVE MITSON.
"All Dressed Up for School," "Little Honda" (Alt. Version), "Don't Back Down" (Alt. Version)
MIXED BY MARK LINETT AT YOUR PLACE OR MINE STUDIOS, LOS ANGELES.
ARCHIVAL MATERIAL AND ADDITIONAL RESEARCH INFORMATION BY RON FURMANEK AND DENNIS DIKEN.
CHART INFORMATION COURTESY OF BILLBOARD AND JOEL WHITBURN.
LINER NOTES BY DAVID LEAF.
ART DIRECTION BY TOMMY STEELE.
DESIGN BY CHUCK AMES.
PHOTO RESEARCH BY BRAD BENEDICT.

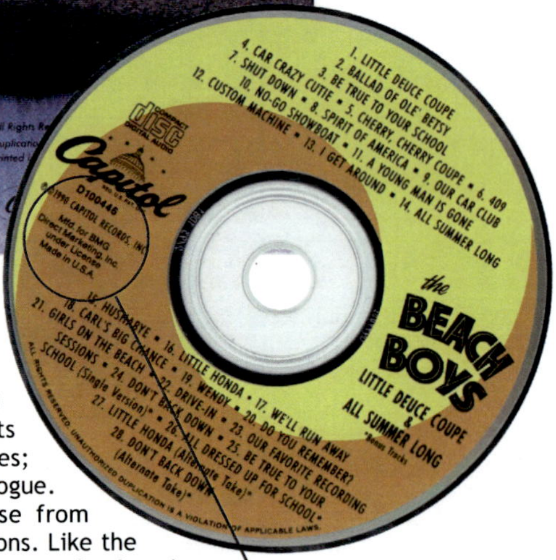
Capitol
D100446
the BEACH BOYS
LITTLE DEUCE COUPE
&
ALL SUMMER LONG

1990 BMG twofer series

BMG is the world largest record club and markets CD's (sells CD's: http://www.bmgmusic.com/index.jhtml) to its members under license from the major record companies; BMG currently has twenty two Beach Boys CD's in its catalogue. The 1990 BMG twofer series was released under license from Capitol and are again almost identical to the 1990 US versions. Like the Canadian versions, notable differences from the US versions can be found on the printing and packaging; the musical content of the CD is identical. A BMG CD code number appears at the back of the booklet and again on the back cover of the jewel case, it takes the form D 100xxx e.g. D 100446. The 1990 BMG catalogue numbers are listed below along with the current BMG catalogue numbers (in brackets)

Capitol
REG. U.S. PAT. OFF.
D100446
℗©1990 CAPITOL RECORDS, INC.
Mfd. for BMG
Direct Marketing, Inc.
under License

	1990	Current
Surfin Safari/Surfin U.S.A.	D 100448	(D 1387794)
Surfer Girl/Shut Down Volume 2	D 100447	(D 1387786)
Little Deuce Coupe/All Summer Long	D 100446	(D 1387802)
Today!/Summer Days (and Summer Nights)	D 100449	(D 1387778)
Concert/Live in London (Beach Boys 69)	D ??????	(D 1400670)
Smiley Smile/Wild Honey	D ??????	(D 1400654)
Friends/20/20	D ??????	(D 1400621)
Beach Boys Party!/Stack-o-Tracks	D 100450	(D 1400639)
Sunflower/Surf's Up		(D 1407196)

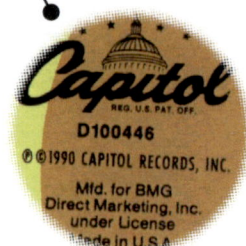

Title: Surfin U.S.A/Surfer Girl
Release Date: June 09, 1989
Record Label: Mobile Fidelity Sound Lab
CD Ref. No: UDCD 521
Country: US
No. of Disks: 1
Format: Audio CD
Audio: mono/stereo
Liner Notes: minimal

CD Notes: The first CD twofer. The sleeve Includes a warning about the sound quality (strange but true...for such an expensive product)

Redferns

The Pet Sounds Chronicle

Pet Sounds, The Beach Boys 12th Album (10th in the UK) was released in the US in May 1996 and was released in the UK the following month, June 1966. The album was essentially created in the first quarter of 1966 and marked the highpoint of Brian Wilson's creative output to date. Along with lyricist Tony Asher, a group of superb session musicians and technicians and mostly in the absence of the rest of the Beach Boys, Brian Wilson created what is now regarded by many as the finest work of popular music created in the last century. The prowess of Pet Sounds did not happen overnight; rather it has progressed to this state gradually over the last thirty-odd years or so. Pet Sounds was classified gold in 1997, and is now officially platinum. In 1966, the general reaction to the 'sound' of Pet Sounds in the US was underwhelming and a number of factors contributed to its relative poor showing on the American charts. Pet Sounds reached the No.10 position but its progress was hampered by Capitol's untimely release of the compilation, 'The Best of the Beach Boys' in early July 1966. The US singles releases from the album were greeted with mixed success: **Caroline No** (a Brian Wilson solo release, reached No.32, April), **Sloop John B** (No. 3, May) and the double A-side single, **Wouldn't It Be Nice** (No.8 Sept)/ B-Side **God Only Knows** (No.29, Sept). Pet Sounds met with greater success in the UK, the album hit the No.2 spot in late July - the UK singles **Sloop John B** (released before the album) went to No.2 in May and **God Only Knows** hit the No.2 spot in August. So why then does Pet Sounds now receive such high praise and honour? Perhaps like Brian Wilson once mused about himself; Pet Sounds just wasn't made for its time. Today many people salivate at the mere mention of Pet Sounds; I know individuals who talk sagely about its content and do not own a copy, but that's OK. Pet Sounds has stood the test of time and the plaudits it receives today and in recent years, although belated, are undoubtedly deserved - it is my favourite album.

In 1990, Pet Sounds was re-mastered from the original tapes and released on CD - it has been all up hill since then. We now have various versions on CD: The mono version; a CD version to the original album, the stereo version, the twofer mono/stereo version and the DCC gold version along with the Capitol Gold versions. In 1997 Capitol provided us with The Pet Sounds Sessions box set; a fitting tribute to the album and Brian Wilson. There are other versions; Pet Sounds Live, the FAME release in the UK, various Japanese versions ((no less than ten) and in 2003 the release of Pet Sounds on DVD Audio; a stunning re-engineering of the original studio tapes. All of these versions are presented in release date order and are described in the following pages. The first version of Pet Sounds to appear on CD was in Japan in late 1998, released as part of the Toshiba-EMI 'Greenline' series.

For further information on Pet Sounds the following references will be helpful:

The Beach Boys Pet Sounds: The Greatest Album of the Twentieth Century - Kingley Abbott: Helter Shelter Publishing ISBN 1-900924-30-7

I Just Wasn't Made For These Times: Brian Wilson and the Making of Pet Sounds (The Vinyl Frontier) - Charles L. Granata: MQ Publications Ltd; ISBN: 1-903318-57-2

Brian Wilson Presents Pet Sounds Live DVD Video - Pet Stories: Sanctuary SVE3046

The Beach Boys on CD: Pet Sounds Chronicle

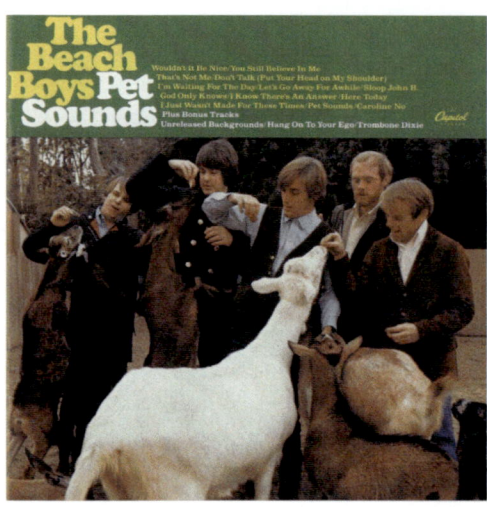

Track Listing...

1. Wouldn't It Be Nice
2. You Still Believe In Me
3. That's Not Me
4. Don't Talk (Put Your Head On My Shoulder)
5. I'm Waiting For The Day
6. Let's Go Away For Awhile
7. Sloop John B
8. God Only Knows
9. I Know There's An Answer
10. Here Today
11. I Just Wasn't Made For These Times
12. Pet Sounds
13. Caroline No

14. Unreleased Backgrounds
15. Hang Onto Your Ego
16. Trombone Dixie

Title: Pet Sounds
Release Date: 1990
Record Label: Capitol-EMI
CD Ref. No: CDP 548421 (D 100513...BMG version)
Country: US
No. of Disks: 1
Format: Audio CD
Audio: mono (Re-Mastered)
Liner Notes: David Leaf

Album & Track Notes

The first US release of Pet Sounds on CD, the original tapes were remastered to digital format in 1987 under the direction of the infamous Dr. Eugene Landy. The re-issue was coordinated by Mark Linett. The CD contains three bonus tracks and the CD booklet provides liner notes by David Leaf and extensive technical and historic song/track notes. The booklet also includes many pictures of the promo photo shoot at San Diego Zoo, including a picture of all six Beach Boys at the elephant pen. The booklet contains a foreword by Brian Wilson and an excellent little 'potted' history of the period by David Leaf. This version of Pet Sounds is still widely available. There is also a version of this CD marketed by BMG direct marketing, the CD number is D100513

Track Listing...

1. Wouldn't It Be Nice
2. You Still Believe In Me
3. That's Not Me
4. Don't Talk (Put Your Head On My Shoulder)
5. I'm Waiting For The Day
6. Let's Go Away For Awhile
7. Sloop John B
8. God Only Knows
9. I Know There's An Answer
10. Here Today
11. I Just Wasn't Made For These Times
12. Pet Sounds
13. Caroline No

14. Unreleased Backgrounds
15. Hang Onto Your Ego
16. Trombone Dixie

Title: Pet Sounds
Release Date: 1993 (disputed)
Record Label: Fame
CD Ref. No: CDP 7 48421 2
Country: UK
No. of Disks: 1
Format: Audio CD
Audio: mono
Liner Notes: David Leaf

Album & Track Notes

This version of Pet Sounds was released in the UK in 1993 and is identical to the 1990 Capitol release. The CD claims to be stereo, this cannot be the case and is not in fact (I've listened to the CD). I have been reliably informed by Mark Linett that a stereo version of Pet Sound was not even discussed until 1985 and was first presented on the Pet Sound Session box set.

Track Listing...

1. Wouldn't It Be Nice
2. You Still Believe In Me
3. That's Not Me
4. Don't Talk (Put Your Head On My Shoulder)
5. I'm Waiting For The Day
6. Let's Go Away For Awhile
7. Sloop John B
8. God Only Knows
9. I Know There's An Answer
10. Here Today
11. I Just Wasn't Made For These Times
12. Pet Sounds
13. Caroline No

14. Conclusion (Train & Dogs)
15. Hang Onto Your Ego

Title: Pet Sounds
Release Date: March 20th, 1993
Record Label: DCC
CD Ref. No: GZS 1035
Country: US
No. of Disks: 1
Format: Audio CD
Audio: mono
Liner Notes: David Leaf

Album & Track Notes

This version of Pet Sounds was released in 1993 by DCC (Direct Compact Classics). DCC released CD (usually 24 KT. Gold) versions of well known/famous album releases. This CD is now out of print. The accompanying booklet is an abbreviated version of the 1990 Capitol booklet. These CD were targeted at specific markets (usually people with more money than sense, myself included). The content of the CD was digitally remastered by Steve Moffat, the sound quality is not improved by virtue of the fact that the CD incorporates a gold film ☺ ; a nice collectors item

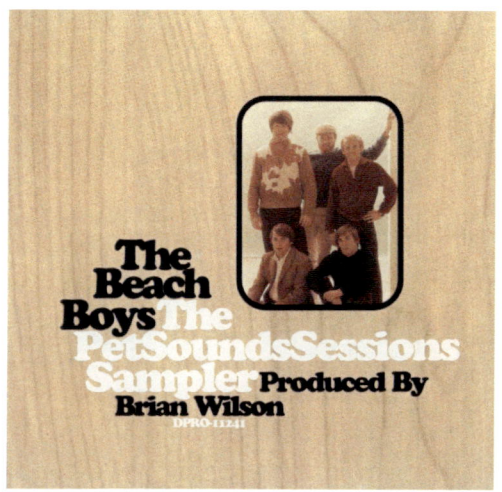

Track Listing...

1. Wouldn't It Be Nice Vocals only)
2. I Just Wasn't made For These Times (Vocal only)
3. Here Today (Track only)
4. Trombone Dixie (Track only)
5. Good Vibrations (Track Only)
6. Caroline, No (Track Only)
7. God Only Knows (Alternate version)
8. God Only Knows (Lounge mix, with sax solo)
9. I Know There's An Answer
10. Caroline, No (Promo Spot)
11. Caroline, No (Original speed, mono)

12-24 The Stereo mix (first time release)

Title: Pet Sounds Sessions Sampler
Release Date: 1996/67
Record Label: Capitol Records Inc.
CD Ref. No: DPRO-11241
Country: US
No. of Disks: 1
Format: Audio CD
Audio: mono/mono
Liner Notes: n/a

Album & Track Notes

This is the Pet Sounds sampler promo CD. The CD was released in advance of the released of the Pet Sounds Session box set. The promo provides a general selection of tunes from the recording sessions as well as the first stereo version of the full album (ironically the first 'official' stereo version appears on a promotional disk)

The Beach Boys on CD: Pet Sounds Chronicle

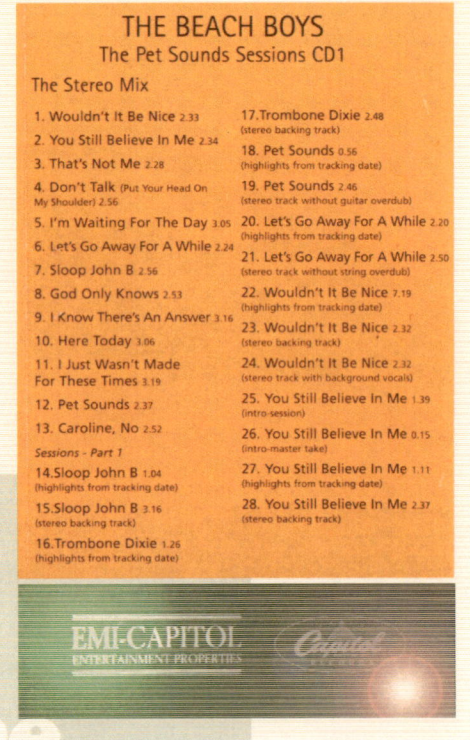

Title: Pet Sounds Session 'advance listening' Promo Set
Release Date: 1996
Record Label: Capitol-EMI Records Ltd.
CD Ref. No: disk #1 CDPP 025
disk #2 CDPP 026
disk #3 CDPP 027
disk #4 CDPP 028
Country: UK
No. of Disks: 4
Format: Audio CD
Audio: Mono & Stereo
Liner Notes: A4 type: David Leaf, Mark Linett

Album & Track Notes

A four disk Pet Sounds Sessions 'advance listening' promotional pack, this set was released in the UK and includes the complete box set recordings. The package also included some photographs of the Beach Boys and a typed A4 copy of the eventual contents of the main booklet. Very rare and very collectable.

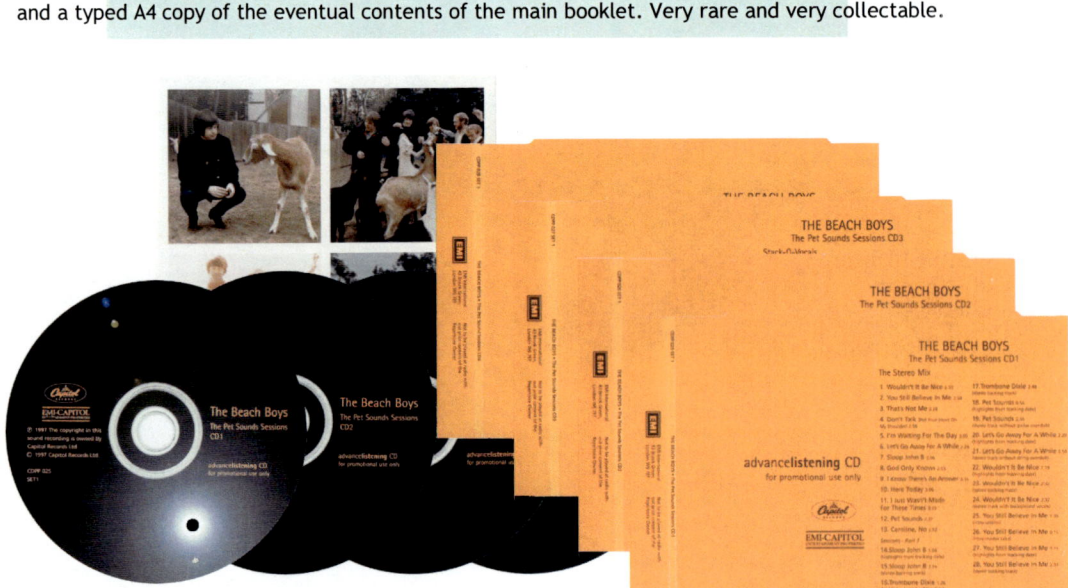

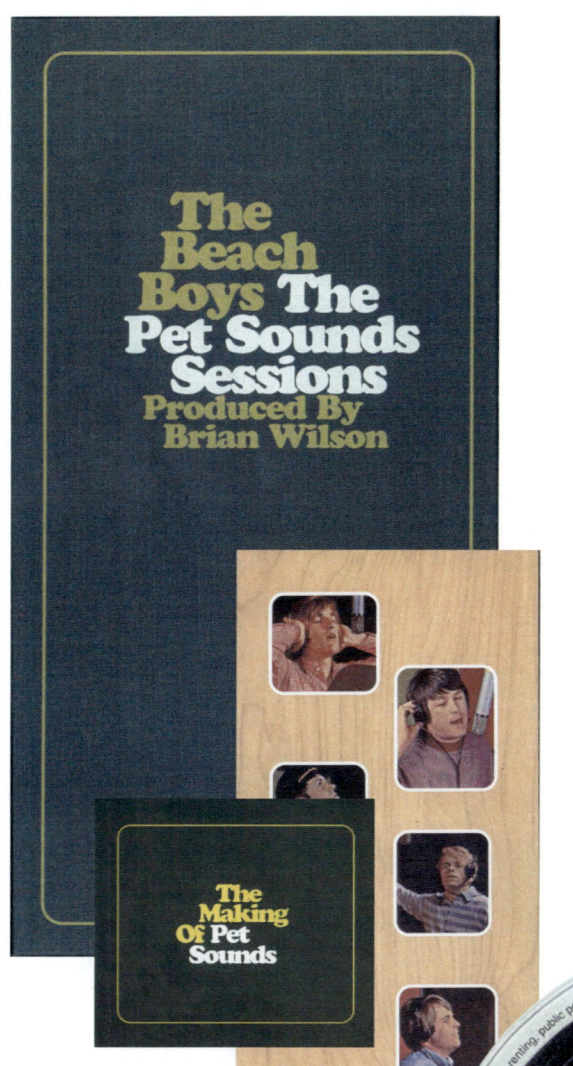

The Pet Sounds Session box set was released in November, 1997 to celebrate the 30th anniversary of the original release of the Pet Sounds Album. The box provides a fantastic array of material including; 4 disks of music, a historical booklet "The Making of Pet Sounds" and the main product booklet. The main booklet provides many photographs of the Beach Boys in 1966 and places the creation of Pet Sound in its historical context; it also provides details of track/song characteristics as well as the song lyrics and gives a history of how the album and the album single releases performed in the pop charts at that time.. The 'Making of Pet Sounds' booklet includes a foreword by Mike Love, transcript of an interview with Pet Sounds lyricist Tony Asher and short biographies of some of the main players; engineers and musicians. The booklet also provides commentary and recollections from all of the band members about the making of Pet Sounds. The box contains 4 disks; the first disk is the 'stereo' mix of Pet Sounds produced and released for the anniversary, the second and third disks contain mainly session material; backing tracks, solo vocals etc., and the fourth disk (the bonus disk) is the original mono version of Pet Sounds. Mark Linett contributes to the main booklet by providing an interesting insight into the 'sound engineering' of Pet Sounds, notes on the Brian Wilson original production techniques and the eventual re-engineering/production provide the reader with an insider view of the project.

Title: Pet Sounds Sessions
Release Date: Nov. 1997
Record Label: Capitol-EMI
CD Ref. No: CDP 7243 8 37662 2 2
  Disk #1 8 37663 2
  Disk #2 8 37664 2
  Disk #3 8 37665 2
  Disk #4 8 37666 2
Country: US
No. of Disks: 4
Format: Audio CD
Audio: mono/stereo
Liner Notes: Various

Disk 1 of 3

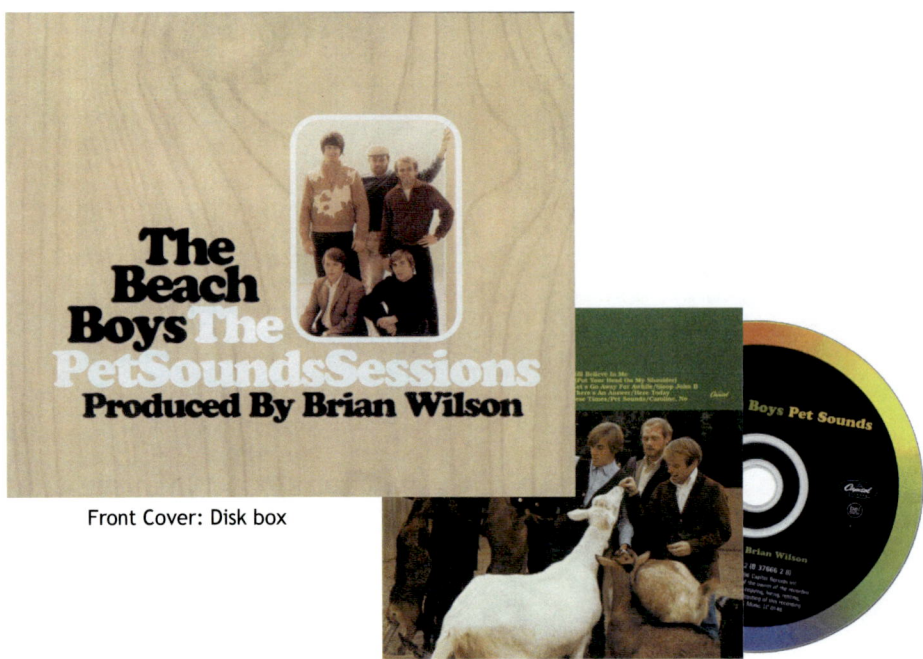

Front Cover: Disk box

Bonus Disk: Pet Sounds

Track Listing

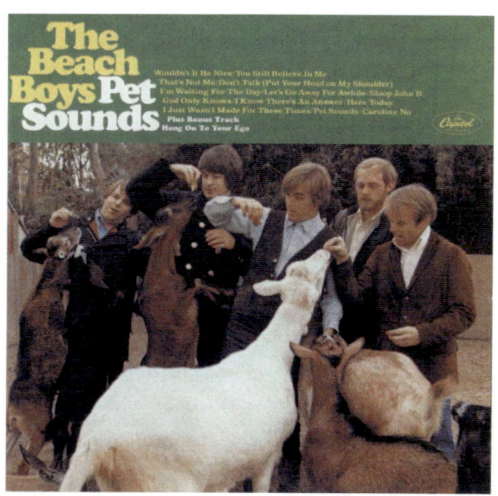

Track Listing...

1. Wouldn't It Be Nice
2. You Still Believe In Me
3. That's Not Me
4. Don't Talk (Put Your Head On My Shoulder)
5. I'm Waiting For The Day
6. Let's Go Away For Awhile
7. Sloop John B
8. God Only Knows
9. I Know There's An Answer
10. Here Today
11. I Just Wasn't Made For These Times
12. Pet Sounds
13. Caroline No
14. hang Onto Your Ego

15-27   The Stereo Version

Title: Pet Sounds (mono & stereo)
Release Date: 1999
Record Label: Capitol
CD Ref. No: CDP 521241
Country: US
No. of Disks: 1
Format: Audio CD
Audio: mono/stereo
Liner Notes: Brad Elliot

Album & Track Notes

This version of Pet Sounds was the first stereo & mono version and was released in late 1999. The liner notes were written by Brad Elliot, these notes were to be replaced in the 2001 version of this CD. This CD was digitally re-mastered by Ron McMaster. This CD can be distinguished from the later version; two short white lines of text appear on the front cover.

The Beach Boys on CD: Pet Sounds Chronicle

Track Listing...

1. Wouldn't It Be Nice
2. You Still Believe In Me
3. That's Not Me
4. Don't Talk (Put Your Head On My Shoulder)
5. I'm Waiting For The Day
6. Let's Go Away For Awhile
7. Sloop John B
8. God Only Knows
9. I Know There's An Answer
10. Here Today
11. I Just Wasn't Made For These Times
12. Pet Sounds
13. Caroline No

Title: Pet Sounds
Release Date: 4th Sept. 2000
Record Label: Capitol
CD Ref. No: CDP 7243 5 27319 2 3
Country: US
No. of Disks: 1
Format: Audio CD
Audio: mono HDCD (24 bit)
Liner Notes: Track notes & Mark Linett

Album & Track Notes

This version of Pet Sounds was released in 2000 and was a re-engineered version of the original Pet Sounds. No re mixing was performed but a denser sound was created by writing higher density digital information onto the CD (HDCD).

Track Listing...

1. Wouldn't It Be Nice
2. You Still Believe In Me
3. That's Not Me
4. Don't Talk (Put Your Head On My Shoulder)
5. I'm Waiting For The Day
6. Let's Go Away For Awhile
7. Sloop John B
8. God Only Knows
9. I Know There's An Answer
10. Here Today
11. I Just Wasn't Made For These Times
12. Pet Sounds
13. Caroline No
14. hang Onto Your Ego

15-27   The Stereo Version

Title: Pet Sounds (mono & Stereo)
Release Date: 2001
Record Label: Capitol
CD Ref. No: CDP 72435 26266 2 5
Country: US
No. of Disks: 1
Format: Audio CD
Audio: mono/stereo
Liner Notes: David Leaf & Mark Linett

Album & Track Notes

This version of Pet Sounds was released in 2001 and combines the stereo and mono versions onto one CD; the mono and stereo versions are presented on this CD along with a new updated booklet. The CD provides 24 bit HDCD quality sound.

Track Listing...

1. Show Inro
2. Wouldn't It Be Nice
3. You Still Believe In Me
4. That's Not Me
5. Don't Talk (Put Your Head On My Shoulder)
6. I'm Waiting For The Day
7. Let's Go Away For Awhile
8. Sloop John B
9. God Only Knows
10. I Know There's An Answer
11. Here Today
12. I Just Wasn't Made For These Times
13. Pet Sounds
14. Caroline No

Title: Brian Wilson Presents Pet Sounds
Release Date: 2002
Record Label: Sanctuary/ BriMel Records
CD Ref. No: SANCD118 *(TOCP-66088 in Japan)*
Country: US
No. of Disks: 1
Format: Audio CD
Audio: stereo
Liner Notes: David Leaf

Album & Track Notes

Brian Wilson and his band (Jeffrey Foskett & The Wondermints, Darian Sahanaja et al) peformed Pet Sounds live at the Royal Festival Hall, London in late January 2002. The concert was recorded and then mixed in the studio by Mark Linett; the result is this CD. The booklet (hard to read) has notes by David Leaf and provides the background and sets the scene for the live performances. A really great CD! On the Japanese version of this CD, there are two bonus tracks; 'Meant For You' & 'Friends' – released by Toshiba-EMI; TOCP-66088 - **strange but true!**

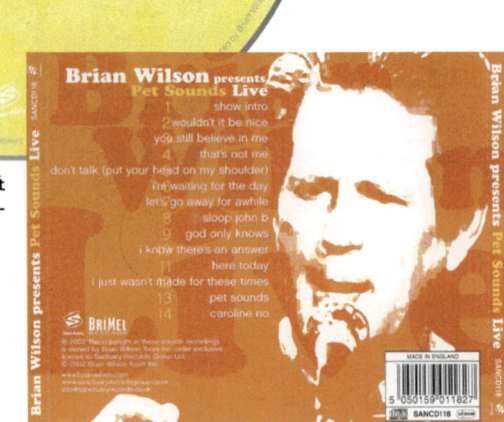

Track Listing...

1. Wouldn't It Be Nice
2. You Still Believe In Me
3. That's Not Me
4. Don't Talk (Put Your Head On My Shoulder)
5. I'm Waiting For The Day
6. Let's Go Away For Awhile
7. Sloop John B
8. God Only Knows
9. I Know There's An Answer
10. Here Today
11. I Just Wasn't Made For These Times
12. Pet Sounds
13. Caroline No

14. Unreleased Backgrounds
15. Wouldn't It Be Nice (session highlights)
16. Wouldn't It Be Nice (alternative mix, no vocal)
17. God Only Knows (session highlights)
18. God Only Knows (...a cappella tag)
19. I Just Wasn't Made For These Times (...a cappella tag)
20. Summer Means New Love

Title: Pet Sounds DVD 5.Audeo
Release Date: US: July, 22nd, 2003
UK: Sept. 8th, 2003
Record Label: Capitol
CD Ref. No: DVD 72434 77937 9 0
Country: US
No. of Disks: 1
Format: DVD Audio
Audio: stereo
Liner Notes: David Leaf
Technical Notes: Mark Linett

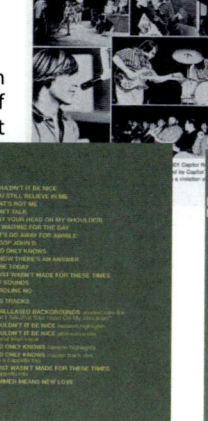

Album & Track Notes

This is a DVD and was released in 2003. The DVD contain all sorts of stuff; an enlarged version of Pet Sounds (7 bonus tracks) all in stunning surround sound 5.1 Other bonus material includes; The 1966 Pet Sounds promo film, a 1997 Pet Sounds Sessions documentary, the original Sloop John B promo film along with a Pet Sounds 'sessionography' and Beach Boys discography. The DVD also includes a hidden track; an instrumental version of 'Here Today' ", the Pet Sound booklet is once more updated...This is an outstanding product in terms of sound quality and additional material

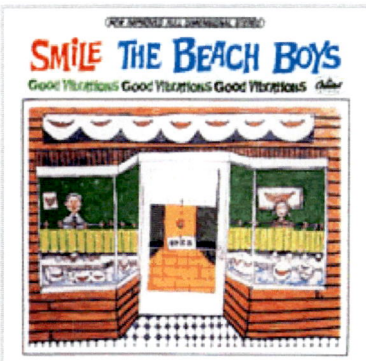

(Original LP cover artwork)

Smile (a tragedy in many part)

In late 1966/early 1967, the much-anticipated album SMILE (initially titled 'Dumb Angel') failed to be released. It seems to have taken almost forty years before a balanced and 'informed' reason for the 'no show' to develop. A lot of stuff has been written about SMILE and the Beach Boys in that period (very little of it contemporary) and the simplest conclusion (drawn out of historical hindsight) seems to be that there were numerous forces acting against SMILE in 1967 and that in the end, the negative elements prevailed, and Brian Wilson yielded under the pressure............

On the positive side and acting in favour of the Brian Wilson's new music:

* The success of Pet Sound (Sales abroad, artistic credibility in the US)
* The stunning worldwide success of 'Good Vibrations'
* The drive of Brian Wilson and his use of various drugs
* The collaboration of/with Van Dyke Parks
* The Beach Boys had become hugely popular abroad (UK in particular)

On the negative side and acting against the project:

* The use of various drugs by Brian Wilson
* The content of the music and lyrical content was radically different
* The Beach boys were suing Capitol Records for royalty underpayment
* The Beach Boys fan/street credibility was on the brink in the US in late 1966
* In the main, some Beach Boys seemingly were not too gone on the new music/lyrics
* Van Dyke Parks (Brian's co-lyricist) left the project allegedly after 'having words' with Mike Love
* The US government were attempting to draft Carl Wilson for the Vietnam War
* Capitol Records apparently/allegedly did not like the new material
* Deadlines came and went

No doubt, Brian Wilson was doing bizarre things back in those days; it is however, well documented that his focus on the music was sharp. It is hard not to conclude that Brian Wilson was just fed up with the negative forces and pressure. He became isolated, it seems/perhaps he lost confidence in SMiLE and abandoned the project for a simpler, self serving existing - you can just imaging hearing him say, '...I've worked myself to the bone on this stuff and for you guys for years, hang it, I'm off!...' What a tragedy! The Beach boys (and Brian Wilson in particular) imploded at their musical peak. Brain Wilson declined (from the very top) in the following years and although he continued to write/produce great music, he would never reach the heights of that golden period; the period from the TODAY! album, through Pet Sounds, Good Vibrations and just beyond the beautiful music of SMILE.

It is hard to keep a good thing down and SMILE has leaked out in various forms over the years. Many people have **released** 'personal' versions of SMILE. Some guide to the intended track listing does exist; the album sleeve was produced in 1966. Many of the intended SMILE tracks subsequently appear on the albums that followed the aborted SMILE project, tracks not listed on the album sleeve have been unearthed and are included in some bootleg 'variants' of SMILE. On the following pages the best known 'manifestations' of the SMILE album will be illustrated, I have also written a small piece on the artwork (© Frank Holmes) of the SMILE project.. SMILE has become a phenomenon, there are tons of webs sites, chats rooms and other vehicles, all discussing the SMILE project and music, I have listed some of the more interesting locations for your investigation, I have also provided a list of book reference at the end of this section. In early 2004, Brian Wilson will tour Europe with 'SMILE live'...might the tragedy have a happy ending?

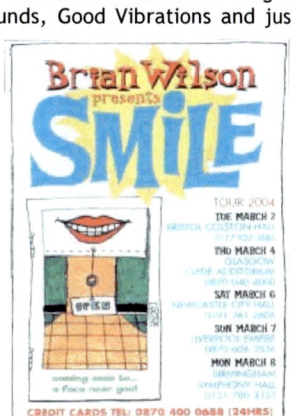

2004 SMiLE tour Flyer

The Beach Boys on CD: Smile

Title: Unsurpassed Master, Vol. 16, "SMiLE"
Release Date: 1999
Record Label: Sea of Tunes
CD Ref. No: C 9949
Country: World
No. of Disks: 1
Format: Audio CD
Audio: mono/stereo
Liner Notes: N/A

The Beach Boys on CD: Smile

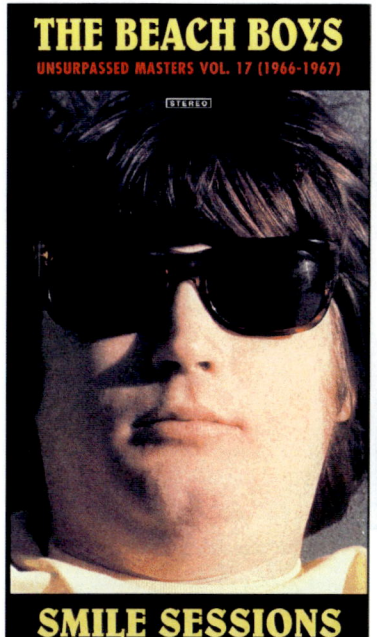

Title: Uns. Master, Vol. 17, "SMiLE Sessions"
Release Date: 1999
Record Label: Sea of Tunes
CD Ref. No: C 9950/51/52
Country: World
No. of Disks: 3
Format: Audio CD
Audio: mono/stereo
Liner Notes: N/A

The Beach Boys on CD: Smile

Record Label: VIGOTONE
Release Date: 1999
CD Ref. No: VIGO 110/111
Country: World
No. of Disks: 2
Format: Audio CD
Audio: mono/stereo
Liner Notes: N/A

Disc One
1. Heroes And Villains (B. Wilson/V.D. Parks)
2. Do You Like Worms (B. Wilson)
3. Medley: The Old Master Painter/You Are My Sunshine (H. Gillespie/B. Smith/J. Davis)
4. Wonderful (B. Wilson/V.D. Parks)
5. Child Is Father Of The Man (B. Wilson/V.D. Parks)
6. Prayer (B. Wilson)
7. Cabin-Essence (B. Wilson/V.D. Parks)
8. Good Vibrations (B. Wilson/M. Love)
9. Vege-Tables/I'm In Great Shape (B. Wilson/V.D. Parks)
10. Wind Chimes (B. Wilson)
11. Mrs. O'Leary's Cow (B. Wilson)
12. Cool Cool Water (B. Wilson/M. Love)
13. Surf's Up (B. Wilson/V.D. Parks)
14. Prayer (B. Wilson)
15. I Love To Say Dada (B. Wilson)
16. Untitled (She's Goin' Bald) (B. Wilson/M. Love/V.D. Parks)
17. Untitled (With Me Tonight) (B. Wilson)
18. Wonderful (B. Wilson/V.D. Parks)
19. Child Is Father Of The Man (B. Wilson/V.D. Parks)
20. You're Welcome (B. Wilson)
21. Heroes And Villains (B. Wilson/V.D. Parks)
thru
25. Do You Like Worms (B. Wilson)

Disc Two
1. Good Vibrations (B. Wilson/M. Love)
2. Cabin-Essence (B. Wilson/V.D. Parks)
3. Surf's Up (B. Wilson/V.D. Parks)
4-5. Tones/Tune X (B. Wilson)
6. Medley: The Old Master Painter/You Are My Sunshine (H. Gillespie/B. Smith/J. Davis)
7. George Fell Into His French Horn (B. Wilson)
8. Mrs. O'Leary's Cow (B. Wilson)
9. Barnyard (B. Wilson)
10. The Woodshop Song (B. Wilson)
11. Holidays (B. Wilson)
12. Prayer (B. Wilson)
13. Surf's Up (B. Wilson/V.D. Parks)
14. Smile Era Party

The Beach Boys on CD: Smile

Record Label: AB-outback
Release Date: 2003
CD Ref. No: AB-xxxx
Country: World
No. of Disks: 2
Format: Audio CD
Audio: mono/stereo
Liner Notes: Track Listing

This CD set appeared in 2003 and the content portrays a very personal view of SMiLE. Wonderfully presented is the music on these albums with an interesting array of non-SMiLE infusions making this the most unusual but interesting SMiLE offering to date. Try and get your hands on a copy of this CD set, you will not be disappointed.

The Beach Boys on CD: Smile

Title: Smile
Release Date: unknown
Record Label: Odeon
CD Ref. No: ST 9002
Country: Germany
No. of Disks: 1
Format: Audio CD
Audio: mono/stereo
Liner Notes: N/A

CD Notes: Just a great CD!

Smile Recordings

(which appear in later albums)

The definitive list of SMiLE tracks is not known; various people have assumed certain tracks to be SMiLE tracks (and indeed SMiLE era recordings) but have no hard evidence and so the intended and definitive SMiLE track listing or combination is not known. As mentioned earlier, a number of the ill-fated SMiLE tracks appeared on subsequent Beach Boys albums. On subsequent appearances, many of the SMiLE tracks were modified; overdubs were added, Carl Wilson sings/recorded a new lead vocal, a track was completely redone. The list below details the occurrence of Smile Tracks on vinyl or CD:

Good Vibrations	Single release & Smiley Smile
Wind Chimes	Smiley Smile (re-recorded) + as the unreleased SMiLE version on the 30 Year Box set
Wonderful	Smiley Smile (re-recorded) + as the unreleased SMiLE version on the 30 Year Box set
(Our) Prayer	20/20 (original Smile version + overdubs) + without overdubs on the 30 Year Box set
Cabinessence	20/20 (with the Carl Wilson Lead vocal)
Child Is the Father of the Man	(becomes a tag to Surf's Up on Surf's Up) + (Brian Solo on 30 Year Box Set)
Surf's Up	(Overdubs added + Carl Wilson lead vocal (poor cousin to the original Brian solo version on 30 Year Box Set)
Heroes & Villains	Smiley Smile (probably the intended version for SMiLE, same as the single version) + (5 versions/variants on the 30 Year Box Set)
Vega-Tables	Smiley Smile (re-recorded) + (original SMiLE material on the 30 Year Box set)
He Gives Speeches	Smiley Smile (morphed to She's going bald)
Love to say Dada	(morphed to Cool, Cool Water on Sunflower) + (original SMiLE on 30 Year Box set)
You're Welcome	Smiley Smile (twofer), for the first time
Do You Like Worms	appears on the 30 Years Box set for the first time

Smile artwork
©Frank Holmes

In 1966, Frank Holmes was commissioned to design and create the artwork for the SMiLE album cover and insert. The album cover was created but never made it onto the high street (apart from a mythical few – fact or fiction?). The insert included seven drawings which depicted imagery and scenes/themes from the lyrical content of the album compositions – The drawings are listed below -

- Surf's Up: "Two-step to lamps light""
- Surf's Up: "Diamond necklace play the pawn"
- Heroes and Villains: "The rain of bullets…"
- Vega-Tables
- Do You Like Worms: "Plymouth Rock roll over"
- Cabinessence: "Lost and Found"
- Cabinessence: "Uncover the corn fields"

Copies of the insert images and album cover can be obtained directly from Frank Holes at:-

http://www.frankholmes.com/purchase.htm

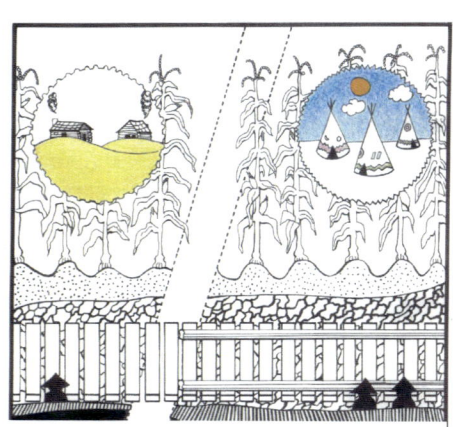

"Uncover the corn fields" © Frank Holmes

Smile - WEB references

http://www.thesmileshop.net/start.html - Still the best SMILE reference site

http://www.geocities.com/psychedelicate/hindsite.html - General

http://www.adriandenning.co.uk/smile.html - General

http://www.cabinessence.com/brian/ - The best Beach Boys reference site on the web

http://www.vvmo.com/ - get your special Beach Boys CD's here

http://smilealbum.tripod.com/links.html - SMILE links

Smile - book & article reference

http://cafecancun.com/bookarts/wilson.htm - Contemporary piece by Jules Siegel

Chapter 5: How Smile Got Lost – 'How Deep Is The Ocean' by Paul Williams (see App. VII)

Look, Listen, Vibrate, Smile -   **Domenic Priore** (Feb. 1997)
Publisher: Small Press Distribution
ISBN: 0867194170

Back To the Beach -   Edited by **Kingsley Abbott** (Jan. 2003)
Publisher: Helter Skelter
ISBN: 1-900924-46-3

Official Compilations

In 1966, just weeks after the release of Pet Sounds, Capitol records released the first Beach Boys compilation; it was titled 'The Best of the Beach Boys'. This was followed in 1967 with 'The Best of The Beach Boys Vol.2 and then with Vol. 3 in 1968. These three albums along with the other 17 studio albums constituted the complete Beach Boys Capitol catalogue up to and including the last studio album 20/20 in 1969. The content (quantity & content) of these three compilations was different on the UK releases and the second US volume is available in two versions. The US version of the first compilation was the only version to make it to CD format. The illustration of the opposite page provides the details of these first Capitol-EMI compilation releases. After these releases and throughout the 'vinyl era', Capitol continued to release/licence numerous compilations and in 1974 the giant 'Endless Summer' was released; this was followed in 1975 when Capitol released 'Spirit of America'. Both of these compilations made it onto CD and are still widely available. In 1976 EMI (UK) release '20 Golden Greats'; this too has made it to CD and is available. In 1981, Caribou (Brother) released 'Ten Years of Harmony' (now a double CD) and in 1986 'Made in USA' was released by Capitol records. Throughout the 1990's and into the new millennium numerous other CD compilations have been released the most notable being the box set '30 Years of the Beach Boys, Beach Boys Good Vibrations'. In 2003, Capitol-EMI released 'Sounds of the Summer'; it was a US top 20 hit. On the following pages all of the 'official' compilation releases are detailed in chronological order. The compilations 'Best of The Capitol Years' and the box set 'Thirty Years of the Beach Boys' are dealt with separately at the end of this section; the 'official releases' section is followed by the Capitol-EMI Special Market CD releases from 1990 to date.

BEST OF THE BEACH BOYS

UK

Best of The Beach Boys

Surfin' Safari
Surfin' U.S.A.
Little Deuce Coupe
Fun, Fun, Fun
I Get Around
All Summer Long
In My Room
Do You Wanna Dance
Help me, Rhonda
California Girls
Barbara Ann
You're So Good To Me
Sloop John B.
God Only Knows

Best of The Beach Boys Vol.2

Surfer Girl
Don't Worry Baby
Wendy
When I Grow Up To Be A Man
Good To My Baby
Dance, Dance, Dance
Then I Kissed Her
Girl From New York City
Girl Don't Tell Me
The Little Girl I Once Knew
Mountain of Love
Here Today
Wouldn't It Be Nice
Good Vibrations

Best of The Beach Boys Vol.3

Do It Again
The Warmth Of The Sun
409
Catch a Wave
Lonely Sea
Long Tall Texan
Wild Honey
Darlin'
Please Let Me Wonder
Let Him Run Wild
Country Air
I Know There's An Answer
Friends
Heroes and Villains

USA

Best of The Beach Boys Vol.1

Surfin U.S.A.
Catch a Wave
Surfer Girl
Little Deuce Coupe
In My Room
Little Honda
Fun, Fun, Fun
Warmth of the Sun
Louie, Louie
Kiss Me, Baby
You're So Good To Me
Wendy

Best of The Beach Boys Vol.2

Barbara Ann
When I Grow Up
Long Tall Texan
Please Let Me Wonder
409
Let Him Run Wild
Don't Worry Baby
Surfin' Safari
Little Saint Nick
California Girls
Help Me, Rhonda
I Get Around

Best of The Beach Boys Vol.3

God Only Knows
Dance, Dance, Dance
409
The Little Girl I Once Knew
Frosty the Snowman
Girl Don't Tell Me
Surfin'
Heroes & Villains
She Knows Me Too Well
Darlin'
Good Vibrations

Title: Best Of The Beach Boys
Release Date: Nov. 23rd, 1988
Record Label: Capitol Records
CD Ref. No: CDP 7 91318 2
BMG 123946
Country: US
No. of Disks: 1
Format: Audio CD
Audio: mono/stereo
Liner Notes: N/A

Album History

The CD version of the 1966 'Best of the Beach Boys' album, this CD was the only original 'Best of...' series to make it to CD. The original Album was a huge chart success; In the US, the album was released in July 1966 and spent 78 weeks in the charts reaching a high position of No. 8. In the UK, the album entered the charts in Nov. 1966 and spent 142 week on the charts reaching a high position of No. 2. The album/CD would eventualy be a double platinum seller

The Beach Boys on CD: Official Compilations

Title: Endless Summer
Release Date: 1988
Record Label: Capitol
CD Ref. No: CDP 077774-64672-7
Country: US
No. of Disks: 1
Format: Audio CD
Audio: stereo
Liner Notes: N/A

Album Notes

The original double album vinyl version of 'Endless Summer' was released in June 1974 and became a huge chart success and went gold. Reaching the No.1 position in the US in July that year, the album spent an amasing 156 weeks on the US charts and sparked renewed interest in the music of the Beach Boys. Although it was released in the UK, it made no impact on the UK charts. The CD version was released in 1987and was augmented by the addition of 'Good Vibrations'. Various versions (different packaging, same CD content) of 'Endless Summer' turn up in Europe; the original UK CD (2 version) and the EMI Gold CD, pressed in Holland and sold in the German/European Market. The DCC 24 Karet Gold version (GZS-1076) was released in 1995 and corrected/incorporated the original mono mixes of many of the tracks. The DCC version was re-engineered by Mark Linett and Larry Walshe and re-mastered by Steve Hofmann. The original album artwork was by Keith McConnell and was only re-produced fully on the DCC CD version. 'Endless Summer' and the follow-up 'Spirit of America' both reached gold status and filled the gap between the release of 'Holland' '73 & '15 Big Ones' '76; both compilations relied almost exclusively on the Beach Boys early/mid 60's recordings

Track list & times:-

#	Title	Time
1.	Surfin' Safari	02:06
2.	Surfer Girl	02:27
3.	Catch a Wave	02:08
4.	The Warmth Of The Sun	02:52
5.	Surfin' U.S.A	02:27
6.	Be True To Your School	02:06
7.	Little Deuce Coupe	01:39
8.	In My Room	02:13
9.	Shut Down	01:50
10.	Fun, Fun, Fun	02:02
11.	I Get Around	02:13
12.	Girls On The Beach	02:25
13.	Wendy	02:16
14.	Let Him Run Wild	02:22
15.	Don't Worry Baby	02:47
16.	California Girls	02:40
17.	Girl Don't Tell Me	02:18
18.	Help Me, Rhonda	03:09
19.	You're So Good To Me	02:12
20.	All Summer Long	02.07
21.	Good Vibrations	03.34

The Beach Boys on CD: Official Compilations

EMI UK (original release)

EMI UK (Music for pleasure series)

EMI European version

The Beach Boys on CD: Official Compilations

Arranged and produced by BRIAN WILSON
except **Surfin' Safari** produced by Murry Wilson and
Shut Down produced by Nick Venet.

Recorded at Western Studios, Hollywood, CA
Recording and mixing engineer: Chuck Britz
Surfin' U.S.A. and **Shut Down** recorded at Capitol Studios, Hollywood, CA
Good Vibrations recorded by Chuck Britz at Western
(with Larry Levine at Gold Star and Bruce Botnick at Sunset Sound).

Surfin' Safari taken from Capitol LP 1808 "Surfin' Safari"
Surfin' U.S.A., Shut Down taken from Capitol LP 1890 "Surfin' U.S.A."
Surfer Girl, Catch A Wave, Little Deuce Coupe and **In My Room**
taken from Capitol LP 1981 "Surfer Girl"
Fun, Fun, Fun, The Warmth Of The Sun and **Don't Worry Baby**
taken from Capitol LP 2027 "Shut Down, Volume 2"
I Get Around, All Summer Long, Wendy and **Girls On The Beach**
taken from Capitol LP 2110 "All Summer Long"
**Girl Don't Tell Me, Help Me, Rhonda, California Girls, You're So Good
To Me** and **Let Him Run Wild** taken from Capitol LP 2354 "Summer Days
(And Summer Nights!!)"
Be True To Your School taken from the Capitol single 5069
Good Vibrations taken from Brother LP 9001 "Smiley Smile"

*Surfin' Safari, Be True To Your School, I Get Around, Let Him Run Wild,
California Girls, Girl Don't Tell Me, Help Me, Rhonda, You're So Good To Me,
All Summer Long* and *Good Vibrations* appear on this compact disc in their
original mono mixes. No stereo mixes were made at the time these selections
were recorded.

1. **SURFIN' U.S.A.** *(Stereo)* Lead vocal: Mike Love
   (Chuck Berry-Brian Wilson) Recorded 1/63
2. **SURFER GIRL** *(Stereo)* Lead vocal: Brian Wilson
   (Brian Wilson) Recorded 6/63
3. **CATCH A WAVE** *(Stereo)* Lead vocal: Mike Love
   (Brian Wilson) Recorded 7/63
4. **THE WARMTH OF THE SUN** *(Stereo)*
   Lead vocal: Brian Wilson
   (Brian Wilson-Mike Love) Recorded 1/64
5. **SURFIN' SAFARI** *(Mono)* Lead vocal: Mike Love
   (Brian Wilson-Mike Love) Recorded 6/62
6. **BE TRUE TO YOUR SCHOOL** *(Mono)* (Hit single version)
   Lead vocal: Mike Love
   (Brian Wilson) Recorded 9/63 Featuring THE HONEYS
7. **LITTLE DEUCE COUPE** *(Stereo)* Lead vocal: Mike Love
   (Brian Wilson-Roger Christian) Recorded 6/63
8. **IN MY ROOM** *(Stereo)* Lead vocal: Brian Wilson
   (Brian Wilson-Gary Usher) Recorded 7/63
9. **SHUT DOWN** *(Stereo)* Lead vocal: Mike Love
   (Brian Wilson-Roger Christian) Recorded 1/63
10. **FUN, FUN, FUN** *(Stereo)* Lead vocal: Mike Love
    (Brian Wilson-Mike Love) Recorded 1/64
11. **I GET AROUND** *(Mono)*
    Lead vocals: Mike Love and Brian Wilson
    (Brian Wilson) Recorded 4/64
12. **GIRLS ON THE BEACH** *(Stereo)* Vocal: Group
    (Brian Wilson) Recorded 5/64 From the Motion Picture "The Girls On The Beach"
13. **WENDY** *(Stereo)* Lead vocals: Mike Love and Brian Wilson
    (Brian Wilson) Recorded 4/64
14. **LET HIM RUN WILD** *(Mono)* Lead vocal: Brian Wilson
    (Brian Wilson) Recorded 3/65
15. **DON'T WORRY BABY** *(Stereo)* Lead vocal: Brian Wilson
    (Brian Wilson-Roger Christian) Recorded 2/64
16. **CALIFORNIA GIRLS** *(Mono)* Lead vocal: Mike Love
    (Brian Wilson-Mike Love) Recorded 4/65
17. **GIRL DON'T TELL ME** *(Stereo)* Lead vocal: Carl Wilson
    (Brian Wilson) Recorded 4/65
18. **HELP ME, RHONDA** *(Mono)* (Hit single version)
    Lead vocal: Al Jardine
    (Brian Wilson) Recorded 2/65
19. **YOU'RE SO GOOD TO ME** *(Mono)* Lead vocal: Brian Wilson
    (Brian Wilson) Recorded 5/65
20. **ALL SUMMER LONG** *(Mono)* Lead vocal: Mike Love
    (Brian Wilson) Recorded 5/64
21. **GOOD VIBRATIONS** *(Mono)* Lead vocal: Carl (with Mike)
    (Brian Wilson-Mike Love) Recorded 2-6/66

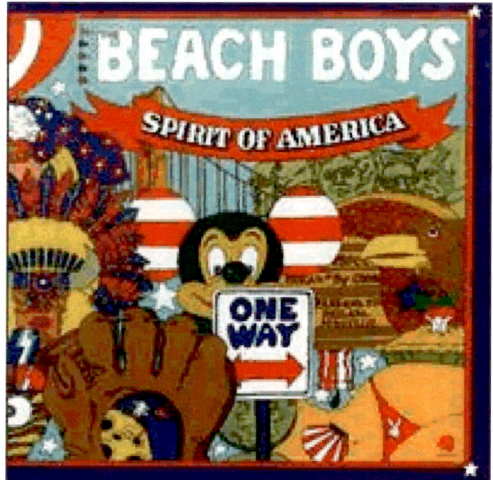

Track list & times:-

1. Dance, Dance, Dance
2. Break Away
3. Young Man Is Gone, A
4. 409
5. Little Girl I Once Knew, The
6. Spirit Of America
7. Little Honda
8. Hushabye
9. Hawaii
10. Drive-In
11. Good To My Baby
12. Tell Me Why
13. Do You Remember?
14. This Car Of Mine
15. Please Let Me Wonder
16. Why Do Fools Fall In Love
17. Custom Machine
18. Barbara Ann
19. Salt Lake City
20. Don't Back Down
21. When I Grow Up (To Be A Man)
22. Do You Wanna Dance
23. Graduation Day

Title: Spirit of America
Artist: The Beach Boys
Release Date: 1988
Record Label: Capitol Records
CD Ref. No: 077774-66182-9
Country: US
No. of Disks: 1
Format: Audio CD
Audio: mono/stereo
Liner Notes: N/A

Album Notes

Originally released in April 1975, 'Spirit of America' (Capitol SVBB 11384) entered the US charts in May '75, reached a top spot of No.8, spent 43 weeks on the chart and reached gold status. Capitol records (and the Beach Boys) were doing well; the last two releases would spend a total of almost 200 weeks on the US charts (almost exclusively on the back of the early 60's recordings). Like 'Endless Summer', 'Spirit of America' made no impact in the UK charts. Released in 1996 there is a DCC gold version of this album, GZS-1089

The Beach Boys on CD: Official Compilations

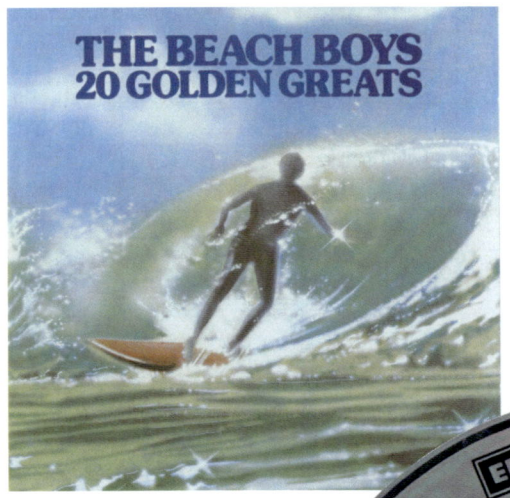

Title: 20 Golden Greats
Artist: The Beach Boys
Release Date: 1987
Record Label: EMI/Capitol
CD Ref. No: CDP 7 46738 2
Country: UK
No. of Disks: 1
Format: Audio CD
Audio: mono/stereo
Liner Notes: N/A

Album Notes

The EMI equivalent of the 'Endless Summer' album and timed perfectly for the Summer of 1976 the original album (EMI EMTV1) reached No.1, the Beach Boys first UK No.1 album; it stayed on the charts for a huge 86 weeks up to 1981. Interesting to note that 15 Big Ones was released just two weeks after this compilation and completelty bombed in the UK. The CD is still widely available.

Track listing:
1. SURFIN' U.S.A.
2. FUN, FUN, FUN*
3. I GET AROUND
4. DON'T WORRY BABY*
5. LITTLE DEUCE COUPE*
6. WHEN I GROW UP (To Be A Man)
7. HELP ME RHONDA
8. CALIFORNIA GIRLS
9. BARBARA-ANN
10. SLOOP JOHN B
11. YOU'RE SO GOOD TO ME*
12. GOD ONLY KNOWS
13. WOULDN'T IT BE NICE
14. GOOD VIBRATIONS
15. THEN I KISSED HER
16. HEROES AND VILLAINS
17. DARLIN'
18. DO IT AGAIN
19. I CAN HEAR MUSIC*
20. BREAK AWAY

Disc 1	Disc 2
1. ADD SOME MUSIC TO YOUR DAY	1. DARLIN'
2. ROLLER SKATING CHILD	2. LADY LYNDA
3. DISNEY GIRLS	3. SEA CRUISE
4. IT'S A BEAUTIFUL DAY	4. THE TRADER
5. CALIFORNIA SAGA/CALIFORNIA	5. THIS WHOLE WORLD
6. WONTCHA COME OUT TONIGHT	6. DON'T GO NEAR THE WATER
7. MARCELLA	7. SURF'S UP
8. ROCK AND ROLL MUSIC	8. COME GO WITH ME
9. GOIN' ON	9. DEIRDRE
10. IT'S OK	10. SHE'S GOT RHYTHM
11. COOL, COOL WATER	11. RIVER SONG
12. SAN MIGUEL	12. LONG PROMISED RAD
13. SCHOOL DAY (RING! RING! GOES THE BELL)	13. FEEL FLOWS
14. GOOD TIMIN'	14. 'TIL I DIE
15. SAIL ON SAILOR	

Title: Ten Years of Harmony
Artist: The Beach Boys
Release Date: 1987
Record Label: Caribou
CD Ref. No: 465670 2
Country: UK/US
No. of Disks: 1
Format: Audio CD
Audio: stereo
Liner Notes: Lyrics

Album & Track Notes

This compilation was released by Caribou in 1981 and consisted of 29 songs from the Beach Boys Warner/Caribou period, this was the only Beach Boys compilation released by Caribou. The CD was released in both the UK and the US (different versions (mixes on some tracks) US ref: 2ZK 37445); a 'digitaly re-mastered' version was released by SONY Music in 1991 (SONY Music had bought CBS in 1988). The CD is dominated by tracks from Surf's Up/Holland and M.I.U./L.A. and (light) on tracks from Sunflower and Love You. The compilation includes three previously unreleased tracks including 'San Miguel'. This is a really great compilation, get the 1991 version if you can, it's quite rare.

The Beach Boys on CD: Official Compilations

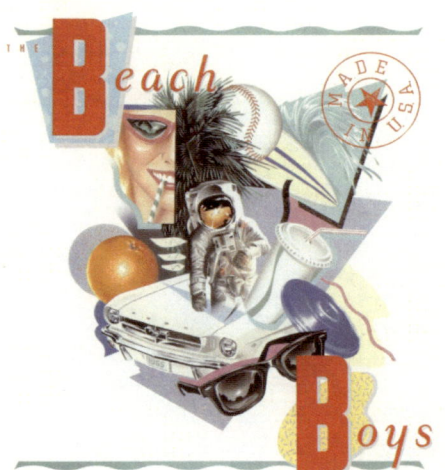

Title: Made in U.S.A
Artist: The Beach Boys
Release Date: July, 1986
Record Label: Capitol Records
CD Ref. No: CDP 7 46324 2
Country: US
No. of Disks: 1
Format: Audio CD
Audio: mono/stereo
Liner Notes: David Leaf

Album & Track Notes

This compilation was released by Capitol in 1986 to celebrate 25 years of the Beach Boys and included a selection of hit/miss singles. The CD was released the same year and was also available from BMG (D 264143). The liner notes are provided by David Leaf, the record peaked at No.96 in the US and spent only 12 weeks on the chart. The record was dedicated to the memory of Dennis Wilson who had died in Dec. 1983.

102

1.	I Get Around	15.	You're So Good To Me
2.	Surfin' U.S.A.	16.	God Only Knows
3.	Fun Fun Fun	17.	Then I Kissed Her
4.	Little Deuce Coupe	18.	Wouldn't It Be Nice
5.	Surfin' Safari	19.	Heroes And Villains
6.	Help Me Rhonda	20.	Wild Honey
7.	California Girls	21.	Do It Again
8.	Don't Worry Baby	22.	Friends
9.	When I Grow up (To Be A Man)	23.	Darlin'
10.	Dance Dance Dance	24.	Bluebirds Over The Mountain
11.	The Little Girl I Once Knew	25.	I Can Hear Music
12.	Barbara Ann	26.	Break Away
13.	Good Vibrations	27.	Cotton Fields
14.	Sloop John B.	28.	California Dreamin'

Title: Summer Dreams
Artist: The Beach Boys
Release Date: June, 1990
Record Label: EMI-Capitol
CD Ref. No: CDP 79 4620 2
Country: UK/US
No. of Disks: 1
Format: Audio CD
Audio: mono/stereo
Liner Notes: Peter Doggett

Album & Track Notes

This compilation was released by EMI in 1990 and contained 28 'classic' tracks. The liner are notes are written by Peter Doggett the editor of 'Record Collector'. The CD claims 'stereo' but this is not the case, the sound quality is inconsistant. The CD is still widely available. The compilation reached No.2 in the UK and spent a total of 17 weeks on the chart.

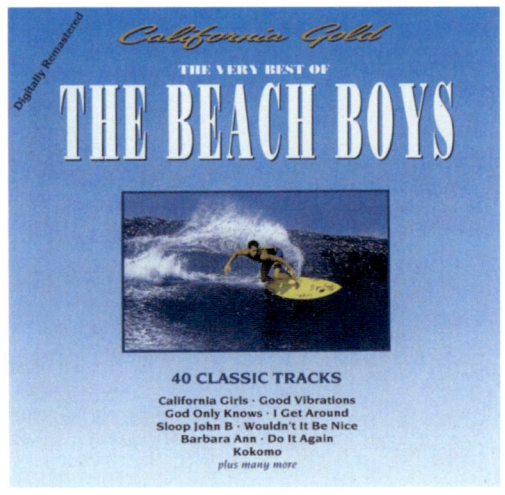

Title: California Gold (The Very Best of The Beach Boys)
Artist: The Beach Boys
Release Date: 1990
Record Label: Capitol
CD Ref. No: 7 965492
Country: Unknown
No. of Disks: 2
Format: Audio CD
Audio: mono/stereo
Liner Notes: Rob Burt

Album & Track Notes

This compilation was released by Capitol in 1990 and contains a giant 40 tracks. Liner notes are provided by Rob Burt? This is an oddity in that the tracks span the full length of the Beach Boys Capital years; 1963 right up to Still Cruisin', a first claimed by some more recent compilations. The CD is still available on the internet. The sound quality is OK.

The Beach Boys on CD: Official Compilations

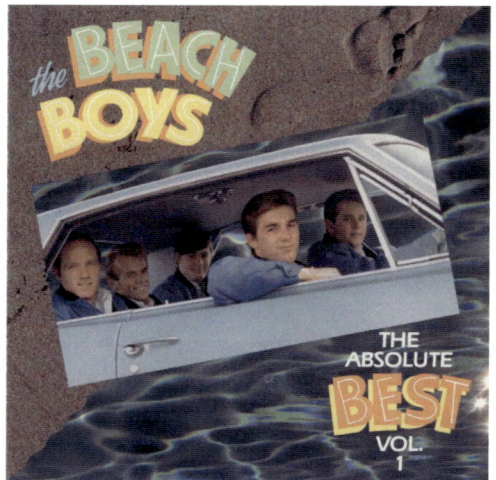 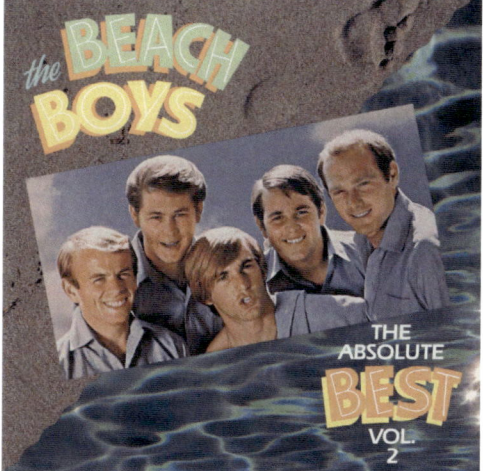

Title: Absolute Best Vols. 1 & 2
Artist: The Beach Boys
Release Date: 1991
Record Label: Capitol-EMI
CD Ref: CDP 7 96795 2/96796 2
Country: US
No. of Disks: 1
Format: Audio CD
Audio: mono/stereo
Liner Notes: Lyrics

Album & Track Notes

These two compilations were released the year after the 1990 release of the Capitol twofers and essentially constitute the best of the twofers; the best of the Capitol years. Two great compilations and although 16 bit technolgy was still quite poor, these tunes are presented with the best digital quality available at that time. The inclusion of 'California Dreaming' on the second disk is a little odd. These CD's are still widely available

The most of
THE BEACH BOYS
20 ORIGINAL TRACKS
featuring
Do It Again
California Girls
Surfin' Safari
Good Vibrations
Fun Fun Fun
plus many more

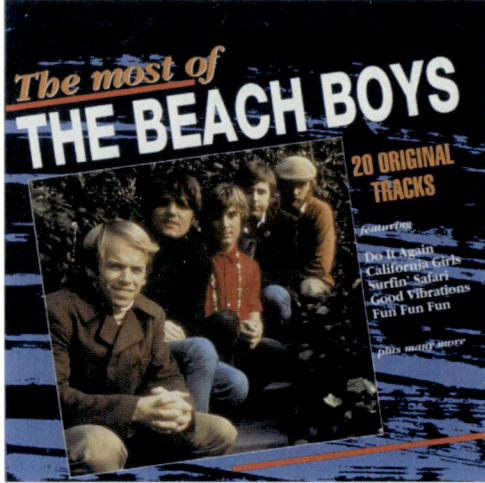

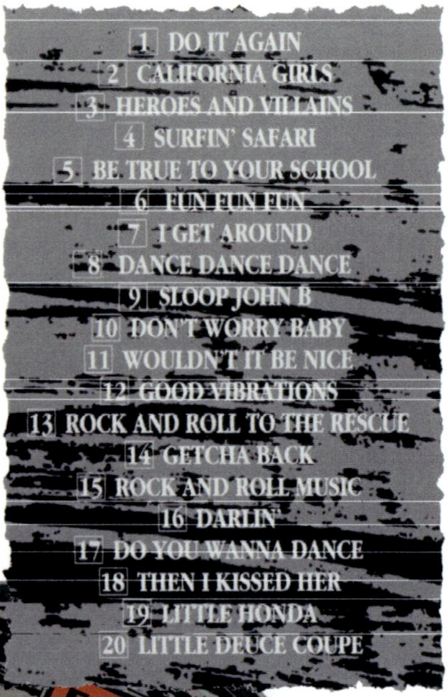

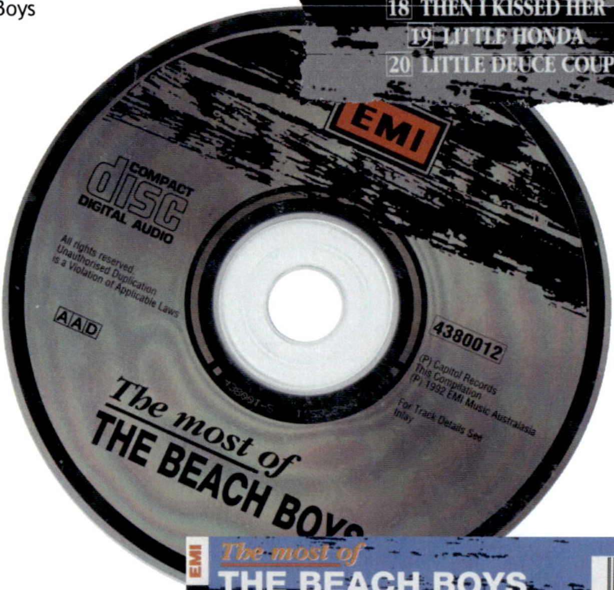

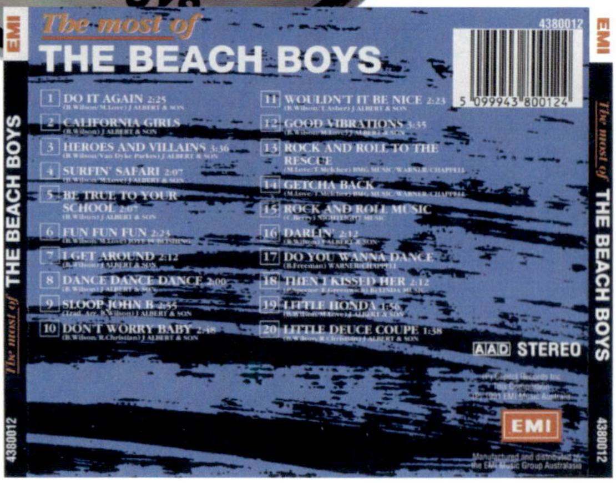

1 DO IT AGAIN
2 CALIFORNIA GIRLS
3 HEROES AND VILLAINS
4 SURFIN' SAFARI
5 BE TRUE TO YOUR SCHOOL
6 FUN FUN FUN
7 I GET AROUND
8 DANCE DANCE DANCE
9 SLOOP JOHN B
10 DON'T WORRY BABY
11 WOULDN'T IT BE NICE
12 GOOD VIBRATIONS
13 ROCK AND ROLL TO THE RESCUE
14 GETCHA BACK
15 ROCK AND ROLL MUSIC
16 DARLIN'
17 DO YOU WANNA DANCE
18 THEN I KISSED HER
19 LITTLE HONDA
20 LITTLE DEUCE COUPE

Title: The Most of The Beach Boys
Artist: The Beach Boys
Release Date: 1992
Record Label: EMI Australasia
CD Ref: 4380012
Country: Australia
No. of Disks: 1
Format: Audio CD
Audio: mono/stereo
Liner Notes: Lyrics

Album & Track Notes

20 Hits...Next!

EMI
COMPACT disc DIGITAL AUDIO
All rights reserved
Unauthorised Duplication
is a Violation of Applicable Laws
AAD
4380012
(P) Capitol Records
This Compilation
(P) 1992 EMI Music Australasia
For Track Details See Inlay
The most of
THE BEACH BOYS

EMI
The most of
THE BEACH BOYS
4380012
1 DO IT AGAIN 2:25
2 CALIFORNIA GIRLS
3 HEROES AND VILLAINS 3:36
4 SURFIN' SAFARI 2:07
5 BE TRUE TO YOUR SCHOOL 2:07
6 FUN FUN FUN 2:24
7 I GET AROUND 2:12
8 DANCE DANCE DANCE 2:00
9 SLOOP JOHN B
10 DON'T WORRY BABY 2:48
11 WOULDN'T IT BE NICE 2:23
12 GOOD VIBRATIONS 3:35
13 ROCK AND ROLL TO THE RESCUE
14 GETCHA BACK
15 ROCK AND ROLL MUSIC
16 DARLIN' 2:12
17 DO YOU WANNA DANCE
18 THEN I KISSED HER 2:12
19 LITTLE HONDA 1:56
20 LITTLE DEUCE COUPE 1:38
AAD STEREO
The most of THE BEACH BOYS
4380012

The Beach Boys on CD: Official Compilations

Title: I Love You
Artist: The Beach Boys
Release Date: 1993 (re: May, 1999)
Record Label: EMI
CD Ref. No: 0777 7 89576 2
Country: UK
No. of Disks: 1
Format: Audio CD
Audio: stereo
Liner Notes: Gerald Mahlowe

Album & Track Notes

Orinaly released in 1993, this compilation was re released by EMI in 1999 within the 'Music for Pleasure' series. The CD contains some tracks not normally found on Beach Boys compilations; 'Good To My Baby', 'Devoted to You' and others. Brief notes are provided by Gerald Mahlowe. Available for 'washers' on the internet and other outlets.

The Beach Boys on CD: Official Compilations

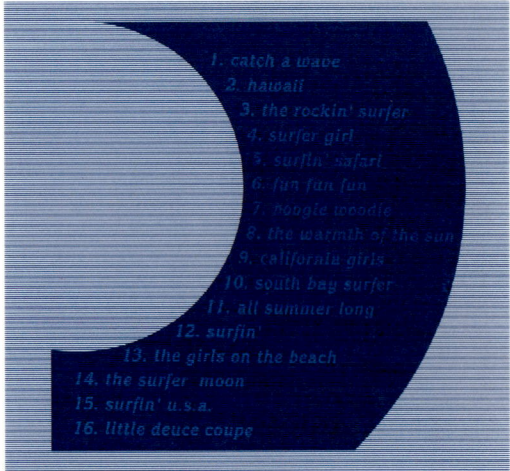

Artist: Let's go Surfin'
Release Date: 1994
Record Label: EMI-Australia
CD Ref. No: 8144372
Country: Australia
No. of Disks: 1
Format: Audio CD
Audio: mono/stereo
Liner Notes: Unknown

Album & Track Notes

Heavy on the Surfing theme, this CD was released by EMI Australia in 1995. Puny liner notes and average sound quality, buy it for a euro, you know it makes sense.

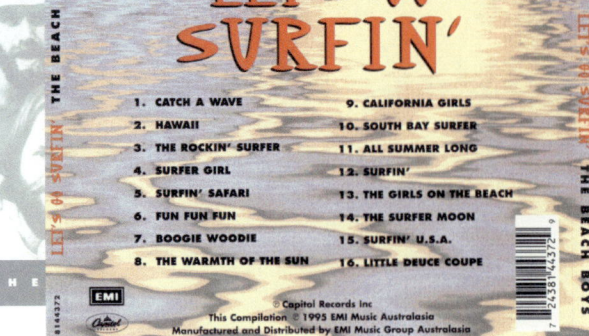

The Beach Boys on CD: Official Compilations

Title: Best of Vol. 3
Artist: The Beach Boys
Release Date: 1995
Record Label: EMI
CD Ref. No: 8329112 (Vol.1)/8329102(Vol.2)
Country: Australia
No. of Disks: 1
Format: Audio CD
Audio: mono/stereo
Liner Notes: Unknown

Album & Track Notes

This compilation was released by EMI Australia and is Vol. 3 of a re-released three set 'Best of...' series. The covers of Vol 1. & Vol.2 are shown above. If the track listing is anything to go by, zero attention to chronology was observed. These CD's are as rare as hens teeth, I got these copies from an Australian.

109

The Beach Boys on CD: Official Compilations

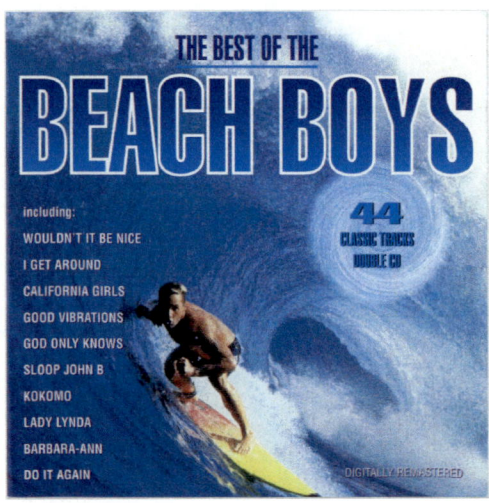

Title: The Best of The Beach Boys
Artist: The Beach Boys
Latest CD Release Date: 1995
Record Label: EMI Records Ltd.
CD Ref. No: 724 8 34472 2 0
Country: UK
No. of Disks: 2
Format: Audio CD
Audio: Mono & Stereo (Re-Mastered)
Liner Notes: Patrick Humphreys

Track Listing, Disk 1 (Titles & Time)...

1.	California Girls (mono)	2:38
2.	Surfin' U.S.A.	2:27
3.	Little Deuce Coupe	1:39
4.	Fun Fun Fun (mono)	2:20
5.	Surfer Girl	2:28
6.	I Get Around (mono)	2:13
7.	Girls On The Beach	2:22
8.	Don't Worry Baby	2:47
9.	When I Grow Up (To Be A Man) (mono)	2:01
10.	All Summer Long (mono)	2:05
11.	Wendy	2:14
12.	Do You Wanna Dance	2:11
13.	Dance Dance Dance (mono)	1:59
14.	In My Room	2:14
15.	Help Me Rhonda (mono)	2:47
16.	Then I Kissed Her (mono)	2:14
17.	Little Girl I Once Knew, The (mono)	2:31
18.	Barbara-Ann (mono)	2:06
19.	Sloop John B. (mono)	2:57
20.	You're So Good To Me (mono)	2:16
21.	Caroline No (mono)	2:52
22.	God Only Knows (mono)	2:50
23.	Wouldn't It Be Nice (mono)	2:22
24.	Heroes And Villains (mono)	2:35

Total Playing time: 58:22

Track Listing, Disk 2 (Titles & Time)...

1.	Good Vibrations (mono)	3:37
2.	Darlin' (mono)	2:12
3.	Wild Honey (mono)	2:37
4.	Friends	2:31
5.	Do It Again	2:25
6.	Bluebirds Over The Mountain	2:52
7.	I Can Hear Music	2:38
8.	Break Away	2:54
9.	Cottonfields (The Cotton Song) (mono)	3:01
10.	Forever	2:38
11.	Tears In The Morning	4:06
12.	Disney Girls	4:08
13.	Surf's Up	4:11
14.	Sail On Sailor	3:20
15.	Rock And Roll Music	2:29
16.	Here Comes The Night	4:34
17.	Lady Lynda	4:01
18.	Sumahama	4:11
19.	California Dreamin'	3:11
20.	Kokomo	3:35

Total Playing time: 1:05:21

Album & Track Notes

This double CD was released by EMI in 1995 and contains a whopping 44 'digitally remastered' tracks. The liner notes (by Patrick Humphries) provide a concise history of the Beach Boys 30+ years of recording and each track is annotated with composer, date and publisher information. The track selection is excellent and is presented in chronological order. About half of the tracks are mono. The CD's are housed in a single CD jewel case. Relatively rare, this CD provides great value for money. The compilation got to No.25 in the UK charts (July, 1995). This is the only compilation to include the '45' single version (Mar. 1979) of the upbeat re-make 'Here Come the Night'

The Beach Boys on CD: Official Compilations

Title: 20 Good Vibrations
Artist: The Beach Boys
Release Date: Apr. 1995
Record Label: Capitol
CD Ref. No: 7243 829418 2 8
Country: US
No. of Disks: 1
Format: Audio CD
Audio: mono/stereo
Liner Notes: N/A

Album & Track Notes

This compilation was released by Capitol in 1995. In 1994 Capitol had released the skelital single album CD's and had already discontinued the 1990 twofer releases. This looks like an attempt to revitalise the surf/car theme of the early Beach Boys years. Since it was not issued as Vol. 1 (the 1999 re-issue was) the mind boggles at what was being attempted here. Versions of this CD were also marketed by BMG (CD No. D108298) and manufactured by Columbia House (CD No. 529418).

1. SURFIN' SAFARI
   (B. Wilson / M. Love)
2. SURFIN' U.S.A.
   (C. Berry / B. Wilson)
3. SURFER GIRL
   (Brian Wilson)
4. LITTLE DEUCE COUPE
   (B. Wilson/R. Christian)
5. BE TRUE TO YOUR SCHOOL
   (Brian Wilson)
6. FUN, FUN, FUN
   (B. Wilson/M. Love)
7. I GET AROUND
   (Brian Wilson)
8. SHUT DOWN
   (B. Wilson/R. Christian)
9. DANCE, DANCE, DANCE
   (B. Wilson/C. Wilson)
10. DO YOU WANNA DANCE
    (Bobby Freeman)
11. HELP ME, RHONDA
    (Brian Wilson)
12. CALIFORNIA GIRLS
    (Brian Wilson)
13. BARBARA ANN
    (Barbara Ann)
14. SLOOP JOHN B
    (arr. Brian Wilson)
15. WOULDN'T IT BE NICE
    (B. Wilson/T. Asher)
16. GOOD VIBRATIONS
    (B. Wilson/M. Love)
17. 409
    (B. Wilson/G. Usher)
18. GOD ONLY KNOWS
    (B. Wilson/T. Asher)
19. CATCH A WAVE
    (Brian Wilson)
20. KOKOMO
    (Phillips/Love/Melcher/McKenzie)
    Courtesy Walt Disney Music Company

The Beach Boys on CD: Official Compilations

Title: The Best of The Beach Boys
Artist: The Beach Boys
Release Date: 1996
Record Label: EMI - Australia
CD Ref. No: 1572092
Country: Australia
No. of Disks: 1
Format: Audio CD
Audio: mono/stereo
Liner Notes: N/A

Album & Track Notes

EMI Australia, 14 tracks – Ho Hum!

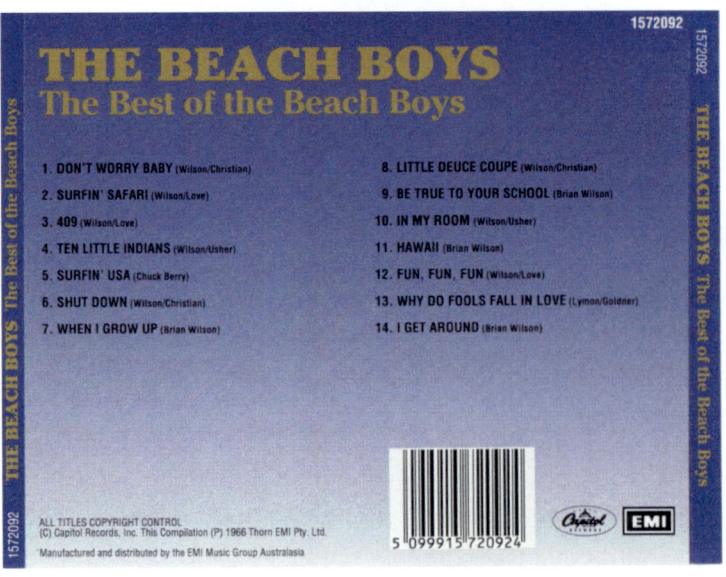

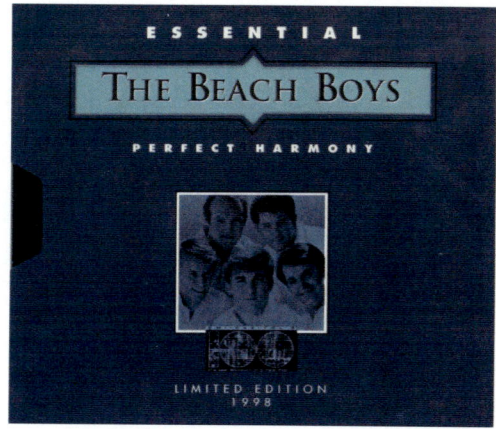

Title: Perfect Harmony
Artist: The Beach Boys
Release Date: 1997
Record Label: EMI
CD Ref. No: 72438 21277 2 7
Country: UK/US
No. of Disks: 1
Format: Audio CD
Audio: mono/stereo
Liner Notes: Dennis Diken

Album & Track Notes

This compilation was released by EMI to celebrate it's 100th year aniversary. The idea seems to be to portray it's most popular artists and their principle characteristics; in the case of the Beach Boys, 'harmony'...It 'misses the net' on a few songs but generally speaking it's a nice collection. A promo version of this CD is also available, but quite rare. Although a 'limited editon' the CD is readily available. The product is nicely packaged, the inner disk & notes are covered by the dark blue outer sleeve; the notes by Dennis Diken draw on writings by David Leaf and others sources.

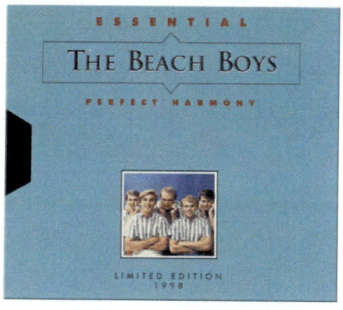

The Beach Boys on CD: Official Compilations

Title: Greatest Hits
Artist: The Beach Boys
Release Date: June 29th, 1998
Record Label: EMI/Capitol
CD Ref. No: 72434 95696 2
Country: UK
No. of Disks: 1
Format: Audio CD
Audio: mono/stereo
Liner Notes: N/A

Album & Track Notes

This compilation was released by EMI/Capitol in 1998. Good selection of tracks (29), good value, readily available. This CD is often refered to as an Australian compilation. It reached No.28 in the UK chart (July, '98)

114

Track listing:-

1. Soulful old man sunshine (1)
2. Soulful old man sunshine (2)
3. Radio concert promo
4. Medley
5. Surfer Girl
6. Help Me Ronda
7. Kiss Me Baby
8. California Girls
9. Good Vibrations
10. Heroes & Villains (1)
11. Heroes & Villains (2)
12. God Only Knows
13. Radio Concert Promo (2)
14. Wonderful/Don't Worry Bill
15. Do It Again
16. Loop De Loop
17. Barbara
18. Till I Die
19. Long Promised Road
20. All Alone
21. Brian's Back
22. Endless Harmony

Title: Endless Harmony
Artist: The Beach Boys
Release Date: Aug/Sept 1998
Record Label: Capitol/EMI
CD Ref. No: 72434 96391 2 6
Country: US/UK
No. of Disks: 1
Format: Audio CD
Audio: mono/stereo
Liner Notes: Brad Elliot

Album & Track Notes

This compilation was released by Capital/EMI and is the soundtrack of the VH-1 TV documentary; 'Endless Harmony, The Story of The Beach Boys'. All 21 tracks (excluding the radio promo's) were unreleased versions up to the release of this CD. The CD includes some 'Smile' tracks/versions and various other versions of well known songs, the Dennis songs are just great. The CD is widely available

Title: The Dutch Singles Collection
Artist: The Beach Boys
Release Date: Sept 1998
Record Label: EMI Music Holland
CD Ref. No: 7243 4 96507 2 5
Country: Holland/UK
No. of Disks: 1
Format: Audio CD
Audio: mono/stereo
Liner Notes: N/A

Album & Track Notes

This compilation was released by EMI Music Holland BV in 1998 and included the singles releases in Holland (Netherlands). Quite rare now, and difficult to obtain. The only compilation (that I know of) with the 'Fat Boys' single inlcuded; an eclectic and honest mix of Beach Boys recordings…I love it.

The Beach Boys on CD: Official Compilations

Title: Greatest Hits
Artist: The Beach Boys
Release Date: 1999
Record Label: Capitol/EMI
CD Ref. No: 7243 5 21648 2 0
Country: UK
No. of Disks: 1
Format: Audio CD
Audio: mono/stereo
Liner Notes: Peter Doggett

Album & Track Notes

This seems to be a re-release of the 1998 CD (above) of the same name. This compilation was released by EMI/Capitol in 1999 and provides the same 29 tracks. The product is repackaged and liner notes are provided by Peter Doggett. This CD should not be confused with the French CD "Le Meilleur des Beach Boys" which sports the same front cover. Again, good value and readily available.

The Beach Boys on CD: Official Compilations

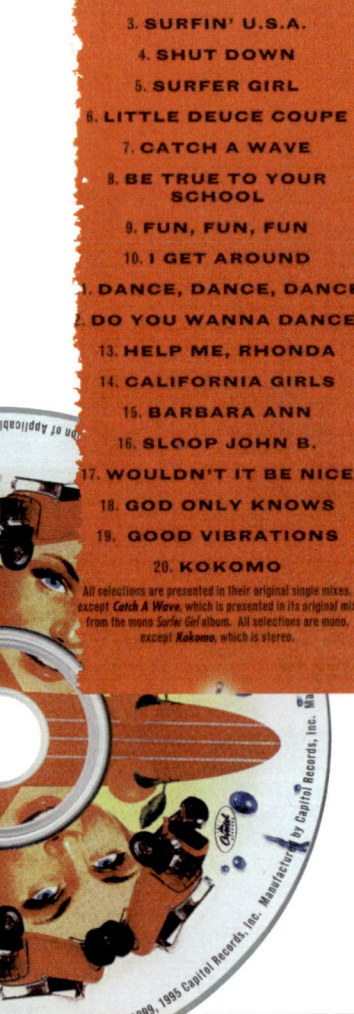

Title: 20 Good Vibrations
Artist: The Beach Boys
Release Date: 1999
Record Label: Capitol
CD Ref. No: 7243 5 21860 2 0
Country: UK/US
No. of Disks: 1
Format: Audio CD (24 bit)
Audio: stereo
Liner Notes: Lyrics

Album & Track Notes

This compilation was released by Capitol in Sept. 1999 and is a 24 bit remastered version similar (different track order) to that of the 1995 release, this time named Vol. 1. as it is the first of a three CD series providing the Beach Boys single chart hits in order of success & date. The CD contains liner notes by Brad Elliot who provides some historic background to the recordings. The CD is widely available, a version was also released by Columbia House (CDP 521860)

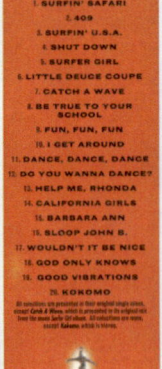

Title: The Greatest Hits Vol. 2
Artist: The Beach Boys
Release Date: 1999
Record Label: Capitol/EMI
CD Ref. No: 7243 5 20238 2 0
Country: US/UK
No. of Disks: 1
Format: Audio CD (24 bit)
Audio: mono/stereo
Liner Notes: Brad Elliot

Album & Track Notes

This compilation was released by Capitol in Sept. 1999; It is superior to the Vol. 1 collection although the majority of the 'hits' were minor hits. The CD contains historical background notes by Brad Elliot & detailed notes on the chart success of each track. A great '24 bit HDCD density' compilation.

The Beach Boys on CD: Official Compilations

Artist: Le Meilleur Des Beach Boys
Release Date: 1999
Record Label: EMI-France
CD Ref. No: 521 429 2
Country: France
No. of Disks: 1
Format: Audio CD
Audio: mono/stereo
Liner Notes: Martial Martinay

Album & Track Notes

This compilation was released by EMI-France in Sept. 1999. A collection of French? Beach Boys singles. Nicely packaged, sound quality good

The Beach Boys on CD: Official Compilations

1. Add Some Music To Your Day
2. Susie Cincinnati*
3. This Whole World
4. Tears In The Morning
5. Long Promised Road
6. 'Til I Die
7. Surf's Up
8. Marcella
9. Sail On, Sailor
10. The Trader
11. California Saga
    (On My Way to Sunny Californ-(-a)*
12. Rock And Roll Music*
13. It's O.K.*
14. Honkin' Down The Highway
15. Peggy Sue
16. Here Comes The Night
17. Good Timin'
18. Sumahama
19. Goin' On
20. Come Go With Me
21. Getcha Back
22. California Dreamin'

*Original Single Versions
All tracks are 24-Bit Digitally Remastered.

Title: The Best of The Beach Boys 1970 – 1986 The Brother Years
Artist: The Beach Boys
Release Date: Feb(US)/June (UK), 2000
Record Label: Capitol/Brother/EMI
CD Ref. No: 7243 5 24514 2 8 (US)
7243 5 25000 2 4 (UK)
Country: UK/US
No. of Disks: 1
Format: Audio CD
Audio: stereo (24 bit)
Liner Notes: Brad Elliot

US CD cover

Album & Track Notes

This compilation is the third volume in the hits series and covers the Brother years 1970 – 1986. The US and UK versions are different; the UK version contains two extra tracks: 'Tears in The Morning' & 'Disney Girls', the Bruce Johnston songs. The CD contains liner notes by Brad Elliot and details on the chart success of each song. This CD is still in print. The magnificence of the post surf'n'cars Beach Boys is well presented on this CD but they are definitely not the best songs the Beach Boys produced during the Brother years…still, we might get a best songs CD some day, here's hoping!

121

The Beach Boys on CD: Official Compilations

Title: Endless Harmony
Artist: The Beach Boys
Release Date: 28th Mar, 2000
Record Label: Capitol/EMI
CD Ref. No: 7243 5 24002 2 5
Country: US
No. of Disks: 1
Format: Audio CD
Audio: mono/stereo
Liner Notes: Brad Elliot

Album & Track Notes

This compilation was re-released by Capitol/EMI in 2000 and partnered the release of the DVD version of the documentary; Endless Harmony "The Story of The Beach Boys". The packaging is upgraded and Mark Linett re-mixes some of the titles for the new CD, a great product made better. Two Japanese versions exist:-

Endless Harmony, 1998 Toshiba-EMI TOCP-50720
Endless Harmony, June 29th, 2002 Toshiba-EMI TOCP-66032

The Beach Boys on CD: Official Compilations

Title: The Very Best Of
Artist: The Beach Boys
Release Date: July 2001
Record Label: EMI-Capital
CD Ref. No: 7243 5 32615 2 8
Country: UK/US
No. of Disks: 1
Format: Audio CD
Audio: mono/stereo
Liner Notes: Lyrics

Album & Track Notes

This compilation was released by EMI in July 2001 and spans the total recording period from 1963 to the present date. The track listing is good but is extremely light on the Brother year recording; all tracks are digitally remastered. The tracks appear in a seamingly random order but it doesn't matter, it's a an extensive selection of great Beach Boys classics. The CD is still in print and widely available. The compilation reached No.31 in July 2001 in the UK.

Title: Hawthorn CA 'Birthplace of a Musical Legacy'
Artist: The Beach Boys
Release Date: July 2001
Record Label: Capitol/EMI/Brother
CD Ref. No: 7243 5 31583 2 3
Country: US
No. of Disks: 2
Format: Audio CD
Audio: mono/stereo
Liner Notes: Alan Boyd

Album & Track Notes

This compilation was released by Capitol/EMI/Brother in 2001. It's a 'hotch potch' of early stuff, rarities and odd versions including many acappella mixes and rare stereo versions all wrapped up in a nostalga bag. The vast majority of the tracks are previously unreleased. Alan Boyd provides track and historical notes, Mark Linett chips in with some technical sound information.

Title: Hits of The Beach Boys
Artist: The Beach Boys
Release Date: 2002
Record Label: EMI Records
CD Ref. No: 7243 5 40072 2 4
Country: UK
No. of Disks: 1
Format: Audio CD
Audio: mono/stereo
Liner Notes: N/A

Album & Track Notes

This compilation was released by EMI in 2002, as part of the EMI Gold series...why? Similar to the 1990 CEMA CD release in the 'Ten Best' series

The Beach Boys
Classics
selected by Brian Wilson

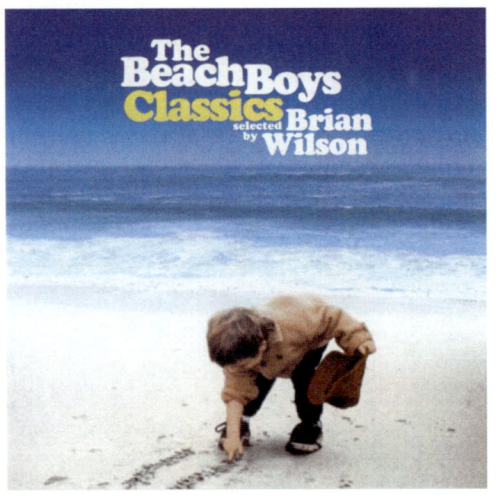

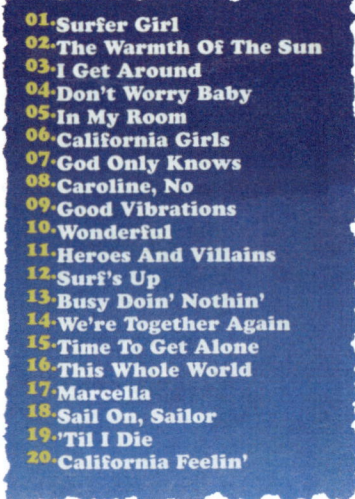

01·Surfer Girl
02·The Warmth Of The Sun
03·I Get Around
04·Don't Worry Baby
05·In My Room
06·California Girls
07·God Only Knows
08·Caroline, No
09·Good Vibrations
10·Wonderful
11·Heroes And Villains
12·Surf's Up
13·Busy Doin' Nothin'
14·We're Together Again
15·Time To Get Alone
16·This Whole World
17·Marcella
18·Sail On, Sailor
19·'Til I Die
20·California Feelin'

Title: Classics (selected by Brian Wilson)
Artist: The Beach Boys
Release Date: July, 2002
Record Label: Capitol-EMI
CD Ref. No: 7243 5 40087 2 6
Country: Japan/US
No. of Disks: 1
Format: Audio CD
Audio: mono/stereo
Liner Notes: Alan Boyd

The Beach Boys
Classics
selected by Brian Wilson

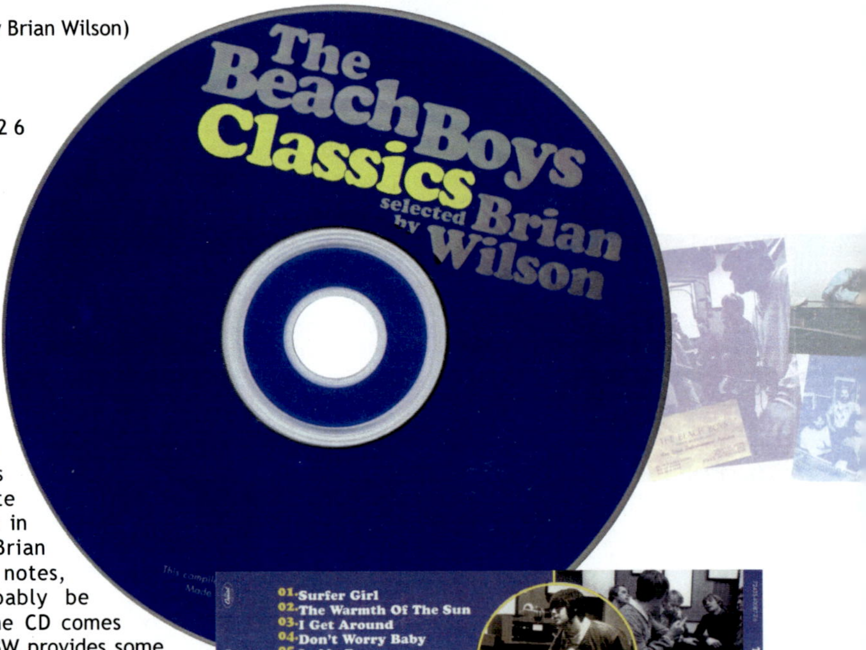

Album & Track Notes

This compilation was released by Capitol/EMI 2002. The list was compiled by Toshiba-EMI and ostensibly represents Brain Wilsons favourite recordings at that point in time; to paraphrase Brian Wilson from the liner notes, '...the list would probably be different tomorrow...' The CD comes with a booklet in which BW provides some notes on each song and some release notes are also provided. The CD is produced in HDCD format and the engineering is another Mark Linett/Joe Gastwirt affair and sounds spectacular on a 6 speaker surround sound system. The track listing is great (edging towards the moody in general) and includes the previously un-released Brian Wilson song 'California Feelin''. This CD is released in Japan as 'California Feelin'....'(TOCP-66030)

The Beach Boys Classics selected by Brian Wilson
01·Surfer Girl
02·The Warmth Of The Sun
03·I Get Around
04·Don't Worry Baby
05·In My Room
06·California Girls
07·God Only Knows
08·Caroline, No
09·Good Vibrations
10·Wonderful
11·Heroes And Villains
12·Surf's Up
13·Busy Doin' Nothin'
14·We're Together Again
15·Time To Get Alone
16·This Whole World
17·Marcella
18·Sail On, Sailor
19·'Til I Die
20·California Feelin'
See Hollywood and Vine
The Beach Boys Classics selected by Brian Wilson

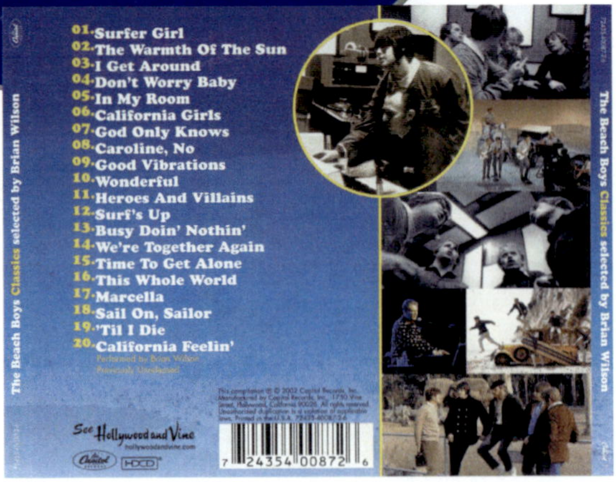

1. California Girls
2. I Get Around
3. Surfin' Safari
4. Surfin' U.S.A.
5. Fun, Fun, Fun
6. Surfer Girl
7. Don't Worry Baby (single version)
8. Little Deuce Coupe
9. Shut Down
10. Help Me, Rhonda (single version)
11. Be True To Your School (single version)
12. When I Grow Up (To Be A Man)
13. In My Room
14. God Only Knows
15. Sloop John B
16. Wouldn't It Be Nice
17. Getcha Back
18. Come Go With Me
19. Rock And Roll Music
20. Dance, Dance, Dance
21. Barbara Ann (single version)
22. Do You Wanna Dance?
23. Heroes And Villains
24. Good Timin'
25. Kokomo
26. Do It Again
27. Wild Honey
28. Darlin'
29. I Can Hear Music
30. Good Vibrations

Title: Sounds of Summer
Artist: The Beach Boys
Release Date: June 2003
Record Label: Capitol Records
CD Ref. No: 7243 5 82710 2 7
Country: US
No. of Disks: 1
Format: Audio CD
Audio: mono/stereo
Liner Notes: Alan Boyd

Album & Track Notes

This compilation was released by Capitol in the Summer of 2003 and was an instant hit, reaching No. 16 on the Billboard charts. The release coincided with the airing on TV (June 14, 2003) of the mini series 'The Beach Boys: An American Family'. Similar to the EMI 2001 release this CD includes 30 tracks and spans the years 1963 to 'Kokomo' but concentrates on the early 'summery' type hits. The liner notes are provided by Antony DeCurtis, notes are provided on chart history and once again the partnership of Mark Linett & Joe Gastwirt guarantees the sound & production quality. It's interesting to note that Blondie Chaplin and Ricky Fataar are not credited as members of the Beach Boys in the booklet credits (the tracks were recorded when BC/RF were not part of the Beach Boys)

The Beach Boys on CD: Official Compilations

Title: Long Promised Road
Artist: Carl Wilson
Release Date: 1998
Record Label: Capitol/EMI
CD Ref. No: DPRO12138
Country: US
No. of Disks: 1
Format: Audio CD
Audio: stereo
Liner Notes: Brad Elliot

Track Listing

Long Promised Road – The Beach Boys
    From the 1971 album Surf's Up.
Feel Flows – The Beach Boys
    From the 1971 album Surf's Up.
The Trader – The Beach Boys
    From the 1973 album Holland.
Full Sail – The Beach Boys
    From the 1979 album L.A. (Light Album).
Goin' South – The Beach Boys
    From the 1979 album L.A. (Light Album).
Keepin' the Summer Alive – The Beach Boys
    From the 1980 album KTSA.
Livin' with a Heartache – The Beach Boys
    From the 1980 album KTSA.
Hold Me – Carl Wilson
    From the 1981 album Carl Wilson.
Hurry Love – Carl Wilson
    From the 1981 album Carl Wilson.
Heaven – Carl Wilson
    From the 1981 album Carl Wilson.
What More Can I Say? – Carl Wilson
    From the 1983 album Youngblood.
Giving You Up – Carl Wilson
    From the 1983 album Youngblood.
One More Night Alone – Carl Wilson
    From the 1983 album Youngblood.
Rockin' All Over The World – Carl Wilson
    From the 1983 album Youngblood.
What You Do To Me – Carl Wilson
    From the 1983 album Youngblood.
Of the Times – Carl Wilson
    From the 1983 album Youngblood.
It's Gettin' Late – The Beach Boys
    From the 1985 album The Beach Boys.
Maybe I Don't Know – The Beach Boys
    From the 1985 album The Beach Boys.
Where I Belong – The Beach Boys
    From the 1985 album The Beach Boys.

CD Notes:

'Long Promised Road' is a limited edition CD and was released by Capitol/EMI, DPRO12138. The CD is a compilation consisting of the highlights of Carl Wilson's recordings over the years - with the Beach Boys and as a solo performer in the early 1980's. Track selection and liner notes are provided by Brad Elliott. Attendees at the **Carl Wilson Benefit Concert**, (Oct. 18th, 1998 - The Roxy in Los Angeles) received a copy as a memento.

The Beach Boys on CD: Official Compilations

The 'Good Vibrations' box set (**CDP 0777 7 81294 2 4**) was released in **June, 1993**, Title '30 Years of the Beach Boys' the original set contained six disks (five in the US) of music covering the recording history of the Beach Boys since 1962 to the present day. The current box set contains just five disks; the 6th disk is now a collector's item. The total number of tracks is 142 (147 if you have the 6th disk) and includes a varied array of unreleased tracks, different versions, radio spots and the entire un-released 'Smile' album (well, a version of it). The booklet notes are written by David Leaf and provide historical background in chronological order, the booklet also contains many pictures and historical records. The four main disks present the music in a chronological sequence. Disk one covers the surfing and cars era, disk two concentrates on the 'Pet Sounds' and 'Smile era. Disk four presents music from the final Capitol years and early Warner years while disk four concentrates on the Caribou output and the later years. The booklet also provides track notes yielding details of chart positions of the track itself or the album from which it came. The 'bonus disk is provided for the benefit of 'hard core Beach Boys fans' and provides an interesting selection of recordings and radio spots.

Overall, the box set is a great product and represents good value for money, it tends towards the period from 'Pet Sounds' onwards, an area sorely neglected in past compilations and therein lies it's strength. The set is still in print, the four disk are often sold separately now and the sixth bonus disk is almost impossible to find. The following page provides the complete track listings and pictures of the front covers of the individual CD's. The Japanese version (Toshiba-EMI) also includes the sixth disk. TOCP-8021~26

Bonus disk: No. 0777 7 89937 2 8 (UK/JP Versions only)

The Beach Boys on CD: Official Compilations

1
SURFIN' U.S.A. (DEMO VERSION) [PREVIOUSLY UNRELEASED] • LITTLE SURFER GIRL [PREVIOUSLY UNRELEASED]
SURFIN' (REHEARSAL) [PREVIOUSLY UNRELEASED] • SURFIN'
THEIR HEARTS WERE FULL OF SPRING (DEMO) [PREVIOUSLY UNRELEASED] • SURFIN' SAFARI • 409
PUNCHLINE (INSTRUMENTAL) [PREVIOUSLY UNRELEASED] • SURFIN' U.S.A. • SHUT DOWN • SURFER GIRL
LITTLE DEUCE COUPE • IN MY ROOM • CATCH A WAVE • THE SURFER MOON
BE TRUE TO YOUR SCHOOL • SPIRIT OF AMERICA • LITTLE SAINT NICK (45 RPM)
THINGS WE DID LAST SUMMER [PREVIOUSLY UNRELEASED] • FUN, FUN, FUN • DON'T WORRY BABY
WHY DO FOOLS FALL IN LOVE • THE WARMTH OF THE SUN
I GET AROUND • ALL SUMMER LONG • LITTLE HONDA • WENDY • DON'T BACK DOWN
DO YOU WANNA DANCE • WHEN I GROW UP (TO BE A MAN) • DANCE, DANCE, DANCE
PLEASE LET ME WONDER • SHE KNOWS ME TOO WELL
RADIO STATION JINGLES [PREVIOUSLY UNRELEASED]
CONCERT PROMO/HUSHABYE (LIVE) [PREVIOUSLY UNRELEASED]

2
CALIFORNIA GIRLS • HELP ME, RHONDA • THEN I KISSED HER • AND YOUR DREAMS COME TRUE
THE LITTLE GIRL I ONCE KNEW (45 VERSION) • BARBARA ANN (45 VERSION)
RUBY BABY (OUTTAKE) [PREVIOUSLY UNRELEASED] • KOMA (RADIO PROMO SPOT) [PREVIOUSLY UNRELEASED] • SLOOP JOHN B
WOULDN'T IT BE NICE • YOU STILL BELIEVE IN ME • GOD ONLY KNOWS
HANG ON TO YOUR EGO (ALTERNATE VERSION) [PREVIOUSLY UNRELEASED] • I JUST WASN'T MADE FOR THESE TIMES
PET SOUNDS • CAROLINE, NO • GOOD VIBRATIONS (45 VERSION) • OUR PRAYER [PREVIOUSLY UNRELEASED]
HEROES AND VILLAINS • HEROES AND VILLAINS (SECTIONS) [PREVIOUSLY UNRELEASED]
WONDERFUL [PREVIOUSLY UNRELEASED] • CABINESSENCE • WIND CHIMES
HEROES AND VILLAINS (INTRO) [PREVIOUSLY UNRELEASED] • DO YOU LIKE WORMS [PREVIOUSLY UNRELEASED]
VEGETABLES [PREVIOUSLY UNRELEASED] • I LOVE TO SAY DA DA [PREVIOUSLY UNRELEASED]
SURF'S UP [PREVIOUSLY UNRELEASED] • WITH ME TONIGHT

3
HEROES AND VILLAINS (45 VERSION) • DARLIN' • WILD HONEY • LET THE WIND BLOW
CAN'T WAIT TOO LONG (ALTERNATE VERSION) • COOL COOL WATER [PREVIOUSLY UNRELEASED] • MEANT FOR YOU
FRIENDS • LITTLE BIRD • BUSY DOIN' NOTHIN' • DO IT AGAIN • I CAN HEAR MUSIC
I WENT TO SLEEP • TIME TO GET ALONE • BREAKAWAY
COTTON FIELDS (THE COTTON SONG) (45 VERSION) • SAN MIGUEL
GAMES TWO CAN PLAY [PREVIOUSLY UNRELEASED] • I JUST GOT MY PAY [PREVIOUSLY UNRELEASED] • THIS WHOLE WORLD
ADD SOME MUSIC • FOREVER • OUR SWEET LOVE • H.E.L.P. IS ON THE WAY • 4TH OF JULY
LONG PROMISED ROAD • DISNEY GIRLS • SURF'S UP • 'TIL I DIE

4
SAIL ON SAILOR • CALIFORNIA • TRADER • FUNKY PRETTY • FAIRY TALE MUSIC
YOU NEED A MESS OF HELP TO STAND ALONE • MARCELLA • ALL THIS IS THAT
ROCK AND ROLL MUSIC • IT'S OK • HAD TO PHONE YA • THAT SAME SONG
IT'S OVER NOW [PREVIOUSLY UNRELEASED] • STILL I DREAM OF IT [PREVIOUSLY UNRELEASED] • LET US GO ON THIS WAY
THE NIGHT WAS SO YOUNG • I'LL BET HE'S NICE • AIRPLANE • COME GO WITH ME
OUR TEAM [PREVIOUSLY UNRELEASED] • BABY BLUE • GOOD TIMIN' • GOIN' ON • GETCHA BACK • KOKOMO

5
BONUS DISC • ALL TRACKS PREVIOUSLY UNRELEASED*
IN MY ROOM (DEMO) • RADIO SPOT • I GET AROUND (TRACK ONLY) • RADIO SPOT
DANCE, DANCE, DANCE (TRACKING SESSION) • HANG ON TO YOUR EGO (SESSIONS)
GOD ONLY KNOWS (TRACKING SESSION) • GOOD VIBRATIONS (SESSIONS) • HEROES AND VILLAINS (TRACK ONLY)
CABINESSENCE (TRACK ONLY) • SURF'S UP (TRACK ONLY) • RADIO SPOT • ALL SUMMER LONG (VOCALS)
WENDY (VOCALS) • HUSHABYE (VOCALS) • WHEN I GROW UP (TO BE A MAN) (VOCALS)
WOULDN'T IT BE NICE (VOCALS) • CALIFORNIA GIRLS (VOCALS) • RADIO SPOT
CONCERT INTRO/SURFIN' U.S.A. - LIVE 1964 • SURFER GIRL - LIVE 1964
BE TRUE TO YOUR SCHOOL - LIVE 1964 • GOOD VIBRATIONS - LIVE 1966
SURFER GIRL - LIVE IN HAWAII REHEARSALS - 1967

CDP 0777 7 81295 2 3

CDP 0777 7 81296 2 2

CDP 0777 7 81297 2 1

CDP 0777 81299 2 9

CDP 0777 7 81298 2 0

The Beach Boys on CD: Official Compilations

In 1980 under the guidance and leadership of Roy Gudge (Beach Boys Stomp, UK) and at the request of World records, the most extensive collection of Beach Boys recording was compiled and presented in a seven disk box set titled **'The Capitol Years'**. The tracks were selected by a group of 'Superfans' and the result is arguably the finest Beach Boys music compilation to date. In addition to the Beach Boys recordings, the seventh disk contained seventeen songs; produced (and mostly written) by Brian Wilson for other artists in the 1960's. The Beach Boys recording were presented on the first 6 disks and were grouped under the following headings: Summertime U.S.A (disk 1), California Dream (disk 2), Sunshine Music (disk 3), Changes (disk 4), Timeless (disk 5) & Break Away (disk 6). A number of tracks were 'reprocessed' to stereo and the result was a collection that would be hard to match today. The CD version of the first six vinyl disks (four CD's) is available and was released in 1999; a rarer Japanese box set of all seven disks turns up now and then on auction sites and other on-line retail outlets.

The Beach Boys on CD: Official Compilations

Title: The Capitol Years
Release Date: 2000
Record Label: Capitol-EMI
CD Ref. No: CDAX 971029/030/031/032
           Japan   TOCD-6151/52/53/54/56/57
Country: Australia
No. of Disks: 4
Format: Audio CD
Audio: mono/stereo
Liner Notes: Peter Ruem

Album & Track Notes

The CD version of the 1980 'Capitol Years set, minus the Brian Wilson Productions This is a 106 track compilation, every Beach Boys fan should own one of these sets. A seven CD Japanese version which mimics the original seven disk album release also exists.

The Booklet: not as extensive as the 1980 Album notes

Japanese seven disk Set

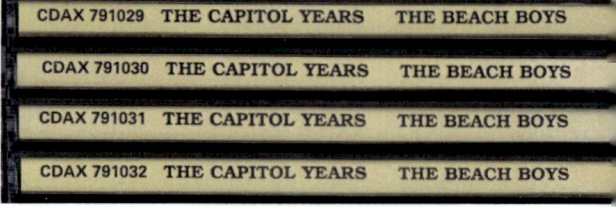

Four CD set with slip over case

The Beach Boys on CD: Special Markets

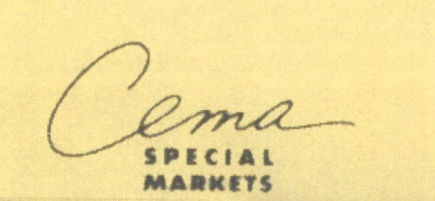

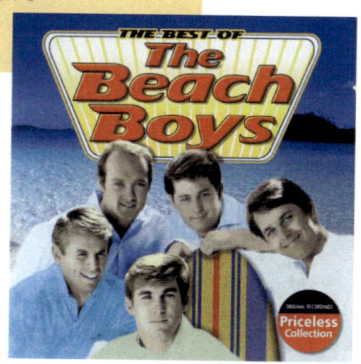

Capitol and EMI have released various Beach Boys compilations into 'Special Markets' and via a subsidiary, CEMA. Quite often a re-packaged release will appear ten years later and will be given a different name. The current name of this subsidiary is EMI-Capitol Music, Special Markets and their latest release is illustrated (right); this is a re-packaged version of older 1990 & 1997 collections. A number of independent companies also release compilations and special releases in association (under license) with EMI-Capitol Special markets. I have listed all of the currently available collections (I am sure there are others) in chronological order, CD notes are not provided except in special cases. The later part of this section includes the releases of the Dutch DISKY Company.

Title: The Beach Boys' Golden Stars
Artist: The Beach Boys
Latest CD Release Date: late 1990's
Record Label: Capitol Records (record club)
CD Ref. No: 65 424 4
Country: Germany
No. of Disks: 1
Format: Audio CD
Audio: mono/stereo

The Beach Boys on CD: Special Markets

Title: The Little Deuce Coupe
Artist: The Beach Boys
Latest CD Release Date: 1989
Record Label: Capitol-EMI SM (Canada)
CD Ref. No: CDL 57241
Country: US
No. of Disks: 1
Format: Audio CD
Audio: mono/stereo

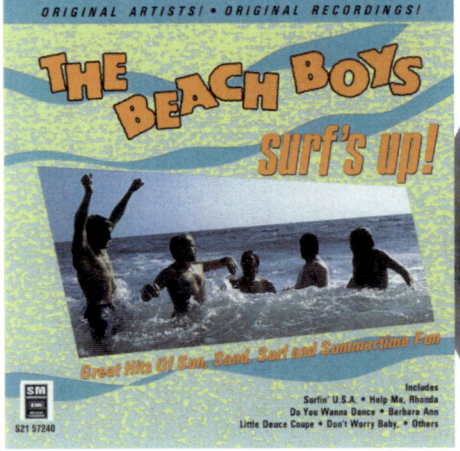

Title: The Beach Boys' Surf's Up
Artist: The Beach Boys
Latest CD Release Date: 1989
Record Label: EMI Music Canada
CD Ref. No: S21 57240
Country: US
No. of Disks: 1
Format: Audio CD
Audio: mono/stereo

Title: All Time Greatest Hits
Artist: The Beach Boys
Latest CD Release Date: 1990
Record Label: CEMA Special Markets
CD Ref. No: CDL 57355
Country: US
No. of Disks: 1
Format: Audio CD
Audio: mono/stereo

Title: All Summer Long
Artist: The Beach Boys
Latest CD Release Date: 1992
Record Label: Capitol-EMI SM (CEMA)
CD Ref. No: S21 57639
Country: Canada
No. of Disks: 1
Format: Audio CD
Audio: mono/stereo

Title: Greatest Car Songs
Artist: The Beach Boys
Latest CD Release Date: 1990
Record Label: CEMA Special Markets
CD Ref. No: S21 57241
Country: US
No. of Disks: 1
Format: Audio CD
Audio: mono/stereo

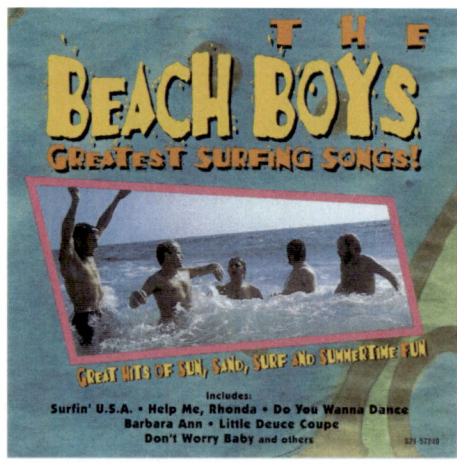

Title: Greatest Surfing Songs
Artist: The Beach Boys
Latest CD Release Date: Sept 8th, 1992
Record Label: CEMA Special Markets
CD Ref. No: S21 57240
Country: US
No. of Disks: 1
Format: Audio CD
Audio: mono/stereo

The Beach Boys on CD: Special Markets

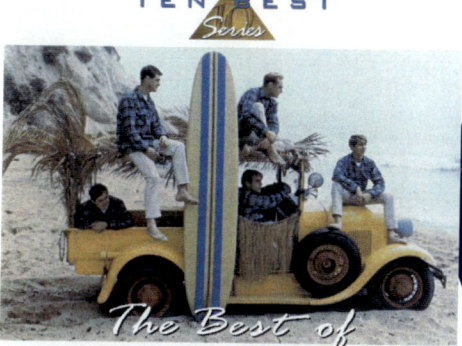
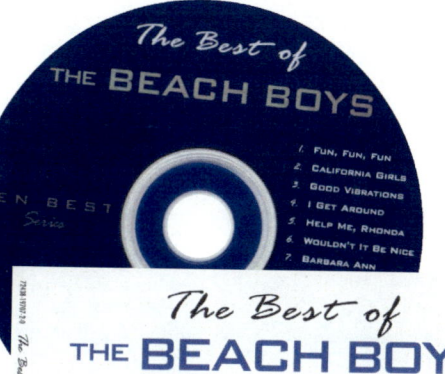

Title: The Best of The Beach Boys
Artist: The Beach Boys
Latest CD Release Date: 1997
Record Label: EMI-Capitol Special Markets
CD Ref. No: CDP 7243 8 19702 2 0
Country: US
No. of Disks: 1
Format: Audio CD
Audio: mono/stereo

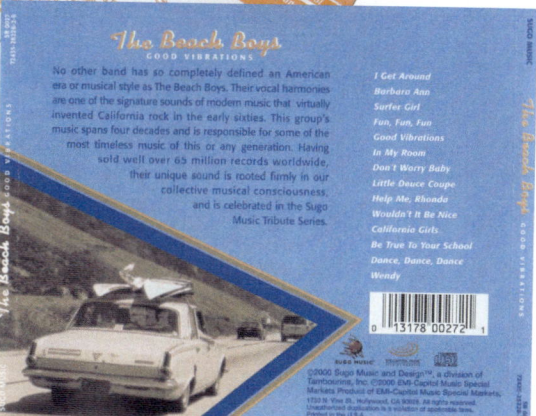

Title: Good Vibrations
Artist: The Beach Boys
Latest CD Release Date: 2000
Record Label: EMI-Capitol Special Market/SUGO Music
CD Ref. No: CDP 7243 5 28228 2 9
Country: US
No. of Disks: 1
Format: Audio CD
Audio: mono/stereo
Liner Notes: Yes

Title: 36 All Time Greatest Hits/Classics
Artist: The Beach Boys
Latest CD Release Date: 2000
Record Label: EMI-Capitol Special Markets
CD Ref. No: S23 18607
Country: US
No. of Disks: 3
Format: Audio CD
Audio: mono/stereo

Notes: Sold via TV only

Alternative Cover

Title: Summer Crush
Artist: The Beach Boys
Latest CD Release Date: 2001
Record Label: EMI-Capitol Special Markets/Hear Music
CD Ref. No: CDP 7243 5 33311 2 2
Country: US
No. of Disks: 1
Format: Audio CD
Audio: mono/stereo
Liner Notes: Ben Barnes & David R. Legry

CD Notes

Sold in Starbucks, this is a great compilation. You can get one for just a few dollars on eBay.

The Beach Boys on CD: Special Markets

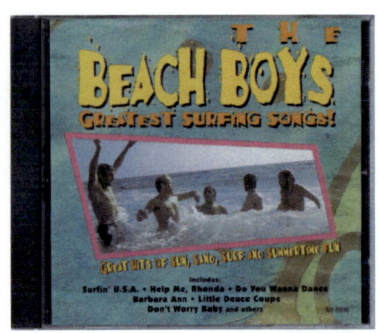

Title: Catch a Wave (Box Set)
Artist: The Beach Boys
Latest CD Release Date: 2001
Record Label: EMI-Capitol Special Markets
CD Ref. No: CDP 7243 5 36171 2 7
Country: US
No. of Disks: 1
Format: Audio CD
Audio: mono/stereo

CD Notes

A box which contains 3 CD's, good value at < 10$. The set is quite hard to find. The 3 CD are also sold as separate items. Same as earlier released (2000) long box below

The Beach Boys on CD: Special Markets

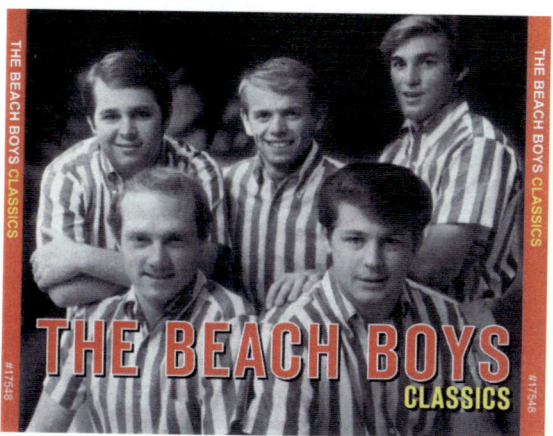

Title: 36 All-Time Greatest Hits, Classic Hits (long Box)
Artist: The Beach Boys
Latest CD Release Date: 2000
Record Label: EMI-Capitol Music Special Markets
CD Ref. No: S23 18607
Country: US
No. of Disks: 3
Format: Audio CD
Audio: mono/stereo

THE BEACH BOYS CLASSICS

Disc ONE
1. Surfin' U.S.A.
2. Surfer Girl
3. 409
4. Surfin' Safari
5. Little Deuce Coupe
6. Catch A Wave
7. In My Room
8. Fun, Fun, Fun
9. Shut Down
10. Your Summer Dream
11. Be True To Your School
12. Spirit Of America

Disc TWO
1. I Get Around
2. The Warmth Of The Sun
3. Dance, Dance, Dance
4. Don't Back Down
5. Wendy
6. Do You Wanna Dance
7. Hushabye
8. Help Me, Rhonda
9. All Summer Long
10. Little Honda
11. California Girls
12. Girls On The Beach

Disc THREE
1. Don't Worry Baby
2. Sloop John B
3. Wouldn't It Be Nice
4. Barbara Ann
5. God Only Knows
6. Then I Kissed Her
7. Good Vibrations
8. Wild Honey
9. The Little Girl I Once Knew
10. Do It Again
11. Girl Don't Tell Me
12. I Can Hear Music

www.timelessmusic.com
Hundreds of Rare & Hard to Find Titles

#17548
S23-18607

This compilation ©1995 EMI-Capitol Music Special Markets. ©2003 EDI • Product of EMI-Capitol Music Special Markets, 1750 N. Vine St. Hollywood, CA 90028. All rights reserved. Unauthorized duplication is a violation of all applicable laws. Distributed by EDI, P.O. Box 22738, Eugene, OR 97402 • Package Design by: EDI/Don Haugen

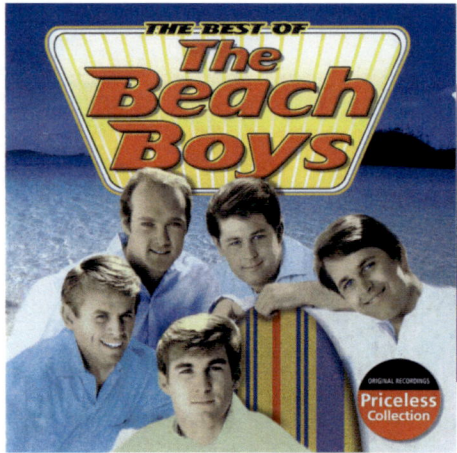

Title: The Best of The Beach Boys
Artist: The Beach Boys
Latest CD Release Date: 2003
Record Label: EMI-Capitol Music Special Markets
CD Ref. No: CDP 7243 8 19707 2 0
Country: US
No. of Disks: 1
Format: Audio CD
Audio: mono/stereo

The Beach Boys on CD: Special Markets

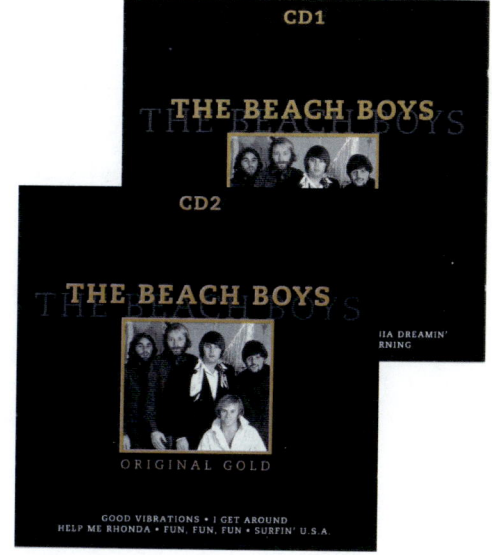

Title: Original Gold
Artist: The Beach Boys
Latest CD Release Date: 1999
Record Label: Disky
CD Ref. No: 72438 578921 (bar code)
　　　　　　　72438 579027 (bar code)
　　　　　　　HR 857712
　　　　　　　CD1 BX 857892
　　　　　　　CD2 BX 857902
Country: Holland
No. of Disks: 2
Format: Audio CD
Audio: mono/stereo

cd 1
1 Barbara Ann 2,04 • 2 Sloop John B. 2,55 • 3 Cotton fields 3,00
4 10 Little Indians 1,28 • 5 Getcha back 3,03 • 6 California 3,21
7 Rock and roll music 2,28 • 8 It's ok 2,11 • 9 Breakaway 2,54
10 Tears in the morning 4,05 • 11 Friends 2,32 • 12 Little Honda 1,52
13 Dance, dance, dance 2,00 • 14 The little girl I once knew (45 version) 2,37
15 Add some music (to your day) 3,34 • 16 Things we did last summer 2,28
17 Do you wanna dance 2,17 • 18 Spirit of America 2,21
19 California dreamin' 3,11 • 20 The surfer moon 2,17

cd 2
1 Good vibrations 3,37 • 2 Help me Rhonda 2,47 • 3 Surfin' U.S.A. 2,27
4 California girls 2,34 • 5 I get around 2,14 • 6 Surfin' safari 1,56
7 Surfer girl 2,06 • 8 Catch a wave 2,08 • 9 The warmth of the sun 2,52
10 Be true to your school 2,06 • 11 Little deuce coupe 1,39
12 In my room 2,12 • 13 Shut down 1,50 • 14 Fun, fun, fun 2,02
15 Girls on the beach 2,25 • 16 Wendy 2,15
17 Let him run wild 2,22 • 18 Don't worry baby 2,47
19 Girl don't tell me 2,18 • 20 You're so good to me 2,14
21 All summer long 2,07

The Beach Boys on CD: Special Markets

Title: California Dreamin'
Artist: The Beach Boys
Latest CD Release Date: 1998
Record Label: Disky
CD Ref. No: 7243 8 53422 4 (bar code)
SI 853422
Country: Holland
No. of Disks: 1
Format: Audio CD
Audio: mono/stereo

Title: All Summer Long
Artist: The Beach Boys
Latest CD Release Date: 1997
Record Label: Disky
CD Ref. No: 7243 8 78682 1
DC 878682
Country: Holland
No. of Disks: 1
Format: Audio CD
Audio: mono/stereo

Title: 20 Great Love Songs
Artist: The Beach Boys
Latest CD Release Date: 1996
Record Label: Disky
CD Ref. No: 7243 8 63072 8
 LS 863072
Country: US
No. of Disks: 1
Format: Audio CD
Audio: mono/stereo

The Beach Boys on CD: Special Markets

Title: The Beach Boys: 1962-1967
Artist: The Beach Boys
Latest CD Release Date: 1991
Record Label: Time Life Music
CD Ref. No: unknown
Country: US
No. of Disks: 2
Format: Audio CD
Audio: mono/stereo
Liner Notes: Geoffrey Himes

Album & CD Notes

The images shown are of the 2 vinyl album box set released by Time Life Music as part of the 'Rock'N'Roll Era' series in 1986. Released at around the same time, the CD version has escaped my grasp a number of times.

SIDE ONE
1. Fun, Fun, Fun (1964)
2. 409 (1962)
3. Surfer Girl (1963)
4. Be True to Your School (1963)
5. In My Room (1963)

SIDE TWO
1. I Get Around (1964)
2. Shut Down (1963)
3. When I Grow Up (To Be a Man) (1964)
4. Little Deuce Coupe (1963)
5. Wendy (1964)
6. Don't Worry Baby (1964)

SIDE THREE
1. California Girls (1965)
2. Dance, Dance, Dance (1964)
3. Barbara Ann (1966)
4. The Little Girl I Once Knew (1965)
5. Do You Wanna Dance? (1965)
6. Help Me, Rhonda (1965)

SIDE FOUR
1. Good Vibrations (1966)
2. Sloop John B. (1966)
3. Wouldn't It Be Nice? (1966)
4. God Only Knows (1966)
5. Heroes and Villains (1967)

Brian and his former wife Marilyn in the mid-'60s.

The Beach Boys on CD: Special Markets

Title: Their Greatest Hits & Finest Performances
Artist: The Beach Boys
Latest CD Release Date: 1991
Record Label: Readers Digest
CD Ref. No: #3932
Country: US
No. of Disks: 1
Format: Audio CD
Audio: mono/stereo

DISC 1: 1 • SURFIN' U.S.A. (2:27)   2 • SURFER GIRL (2:26)   3 • BE TRUE TO YOUR SCHOOL (2:06)   4 • CALIFORNIA GIRLS (2:45)   5 • WHEN I GROW UP (TO BE A MAN) (2:01)   6 • BARBARA ANN (2:04)   7 • GOOD VIBRATIONS (3:45)   8 • IN MY ROOM (2:13)   9 • HEROES AND VILLAINS (3:36)   10 • WOULDN'T IT BE NICE (2:22)   11 • SLOOP JOHN B. (2:55)   12 • HELP ME, RHONDA (2:45)   13 • DO YOU REMEMBER? (1:38)   14 • WHY DO FOOLS FALL IN LOVE? (1:59)   15 • HUSHABYE (2:40)   16 • DO YOU WANNA DANCE? (2:17)   17 • COTTON FIELDS (3:01)   18 • LOUIE, LOUIE (2:23)   19 • DANCE, DANCE, DANCE (1:59)   20 • LITTLE SAINT NICK (1:59)   21 • PAPA-OOM-MOW-MOW (2:27)   22 • HULLY GULLY (2:19)   23 • LONG, TALL TEXAN (2:29)   24 • FUN, FUN, FUN (2:17)   25 • LITTLE HONDA (1:39)   26 • SHUT DOWN (1:50)   27 • I GET AROUND (2:13)   28 • 409 (1:58)   29 • LITTLE DEUCE COUPE (1:39)   30 • DRIVE-IN (1:47)

The Beach Boys on CD: Licences Compilations

Compilations (other)

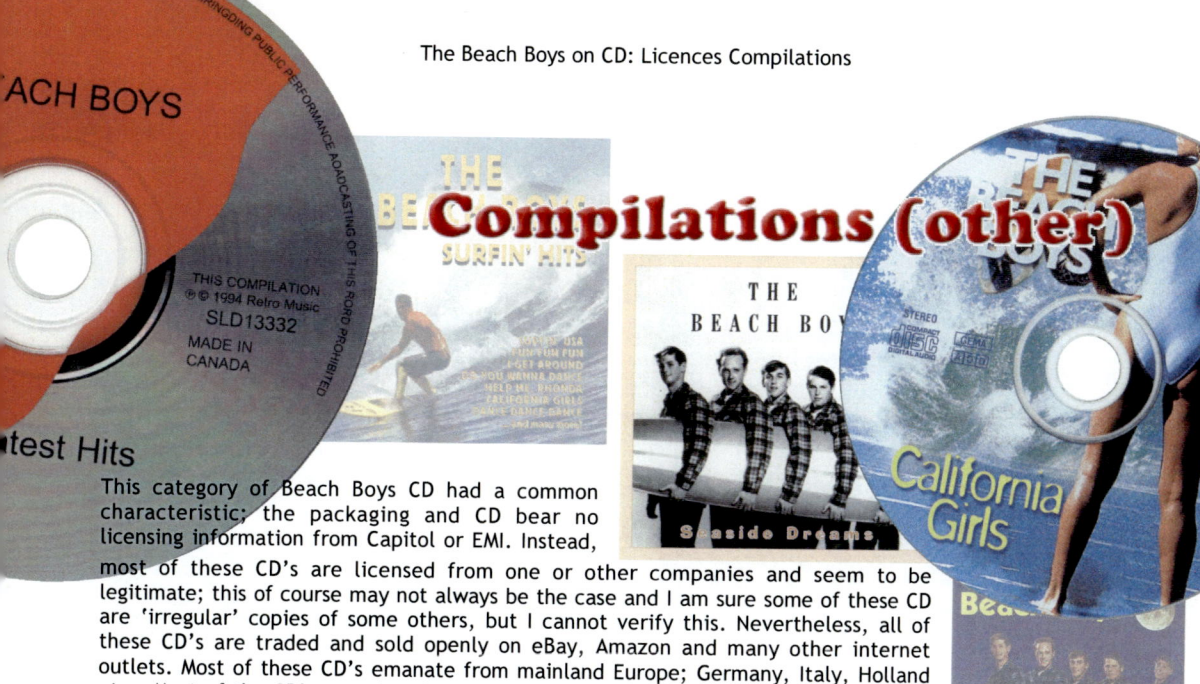

This category of Beach Boys CD had a common characteristic; the packaging and CD bear no licensing information from Capitol or EMI. Instead, most of these CD's are licensed from one or other companies and seem to be legitimate; this of course may not always be the case and I am sure some of these CD are 'irregular' copies of some others, but I cannot verify this. Nevertheless, all of these CD's are traded and sold openly on eBay, Amazon and many other internet outlets. Most of these CD's emanate from mainland Europe; Germany, Italy, Holland etc. Most of the CD's contain a limited set of Beach Boys recording and most songs are from early to mid 60's. Since many if these CDs do contain date information, they are not presented in date order. Those CD's which I think represent good value for money, or which have a superior track listing, are marked with a red spot.

Title: The Magic Collection
Artist: The Beach Boys
Latest CD Release Date: unknown
Record Label: Telstar
CD Ref. No: MEC 949018
Country: Holland
No. of Disks: 1
Format: Audio CD
Audio: mono/stereo

#	Track	Time	Credits
1.	BALBOA BLUES	3'46	(Murphy/Sarencino) Smooth Music Ltd.
2.	BARBIE	2'10	(Morgan) Guild Music Co.
3.	KARATE	2'25	(Wilson) Guild Music Co.
4.	LUAU	3'04	(Morgan) Guild Music Co.
5.	SURFER GIRL	2'18	(Wilson) EMI Music Pub Ltd.
6.	SURFER'S STOMP	3'20	(Daughty/Sarenceno) EMI Music Pub Ltd.
7.	SURFIN'	3.19	(Love/Wilson) Guild Music Co.
8.	SURFIN' SAFARI	2'58	(Wilson/Love) Guild Music Co.
9.	WHAT IS A YOUNG GIRL MADE OF	2'47	(Morgan) Prestige Music Ltd.
10.	WIPE OUT	3.09	(Berry Hill/Connolly/Fuller/Wilson) Dispute Nork.

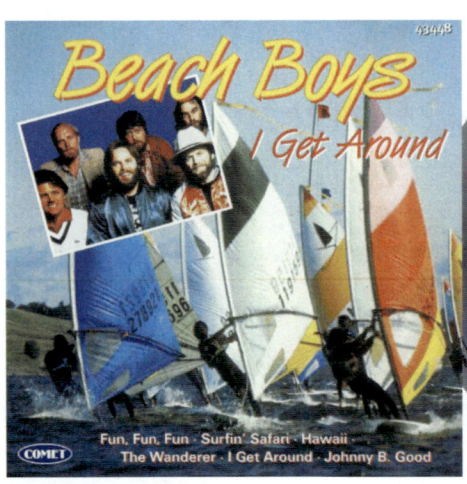

Title: I Get Around
Artist: The Beach Boys
Latest CD Release Date: unknown
Record Label: Comet
CD Ref. No: 43448
Country: UK/Germany
No. of Disks: 1
Format: Audio CD
Audio: mono/stereo

Title: Greatest Hits
Artist: The Beach Boys
Latest CD Release Date: 1987
Record Label: Hollywood
CD Ref. No: HCD-109
Country: US
No. of Disks: 1
Format: Audio CD
Audio: mono/stereo

The Beach Boys on CD: Licences Compilations

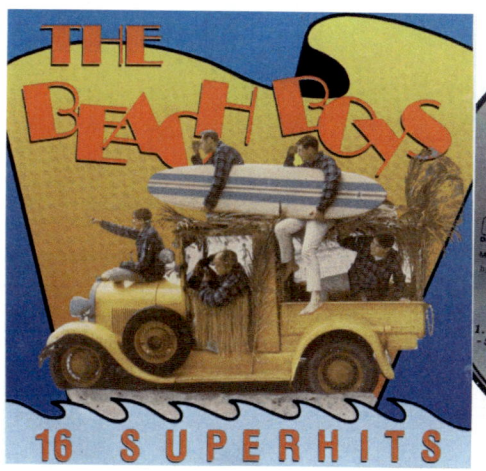

Title: 16 Superhits
Artist: The Beach Boys
Latest CD Release Date: 1988
Record Label: Duchesse
CD Ref. No: CD 352020
Country: Germany
No. of Disks: 1
Format: Audio CD
Audio: mono/stereo

Title: Fun, Fun, Fun (live)
Artist: The Beach Boys
Latest CD Release Date: 1989
Record Label: Lazer Light
CD Ref. No: 15164
Country: Germany
No. of Disks: 1
Format: Audio CD
Audio: stereo

The Beach Boys on CD: Licences Compilations

Title: Spirit of the 60's
Artist: The Beach Boys
Latest CD Release Date: 1991
Record Label: Time Life
CD Ref. No: TL 531/11
Country: US/Holland/UK
No. of Disks: 1
Format: Audio CD
Audio: mono/stereo

Title: California Dreamin'
Artist: The Beach Boys
Latest CD Release Date: 1992
Record Label: BR Music
CD Ref. No:
Country: Holland
No. of Disks: 1
Format: Audio CD
Audio: mono/stereo

Title: The Beach Boys
Artist: The Beach Boys
Latest CD Release Date: 1992
Record Label: Dynamic
CD Ref. No: ST 52083
Country: Germany
No. of Disks: 1
Format: Audio CD
Audio: mono/stereo

Tiitle: Surfin' Hits
Artist: The Beach Boys
Latest CD Release Date: 1993
Record Label: Aloha
CD Ref. No: AL 10-004
Country: Germany
No. of Disks: 1
Format: Audio CD
Audio: mono/stereo

Title: Greatest Hits (Prime Cuts)
Artist: The Beach Boys
Latest CD Release Date: 1994
Record Label: Retro Music
CD Ref. No: SLD 13332
Country: Canada
No. of Disks: 1
Format: Audio CD
Audio: mono/stereo

Title: Heroes & Villains (live)
Artist: The Beach Boys
Latest CD Release Date: 1995
Record Label: Smart Art
CD Ref. No: WZ 98003
Country: Germany
No. of Disks: 1
Format: Audio CD
Audio: mono/stereo

The Beach Boys on CD: Licences Compilations

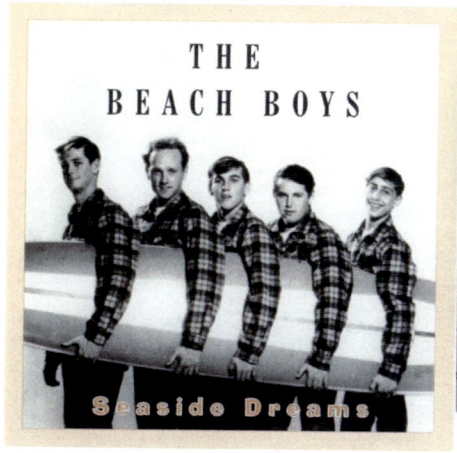

Title: Seaside Dreams
Artist: The Beach Boys
Latest CD Release Date: 1995
Record Label: A PRIORI Records
CD Ref. No: CD 791314
Country: Italy
No. of Disks: 1
Format: Audio CD
Audio: mono/stereo

Title: Surfer's Moon
Artist: The Beach Boys
Latest CD Release Date: 1995
Record Label: Back Biter
CD Ref. No: BB 61070
Country: Germany
No. of Disks: 1
Format: Audio CD
Audio: mono/stereo

The Beach Boys on CD: Licences Compilations

Title: Surf Dance Fun
Artist: The Beach Boys
Latest CD Release Date: 1995
Record Label: Back Biter
CD Ref. No: BB 61052
Country: Germany
No. of Disks: 1
Format: Audio CD
Audio: mono/stereo

Title: Original Surfin' Hits
Artist: The Beach Boys
Latest CD Release Date: 1995
Record Label: Curb Records
CD Ref. No: D2 77747
Country: US
No. of Disks: 1
Format: Audio CD
Audio: mono/stereo

The Beach Boys on CD: Licences Compilations

Title: 32 Great Songs
Artist: The Beach Boys
Latest CD Release Date: unknown (late 90's)
Record Label: StarLife
CD Ref. No: CD 91011
Country: Germany
No. of Disks: 2
Format: Audio CD
Audio: mono/stereo

Title: Fun, Fun, Fun
Artist: The Beach Boys
Latest CD Release Date: unknown
Record Label: Rainbow
CD Ref. No: RCD 5703
Country: Australia
No. of Disks: 1
Format: Audio CD
Audio: mono/stereo

The Beach Boys on CD: Licences Compilations

Title: Super Hits
Artist: The Beach Boys
Latest CD Release Date: unknown
Record Label: Evergreen
CD Ref. No: 2690842
Country: Korea
No. of Disks: 1
Format: Audio CD
Audio: mono/stereo

Title: Surfin'
Artist: The Beach Boys
Latest CD Release Date: 1988
Record Label: Telstar
CD Ref. No: TRCD 1001
Country: US
No. of Disks: 1
Format: Audio CD
Audio: mono/stereo

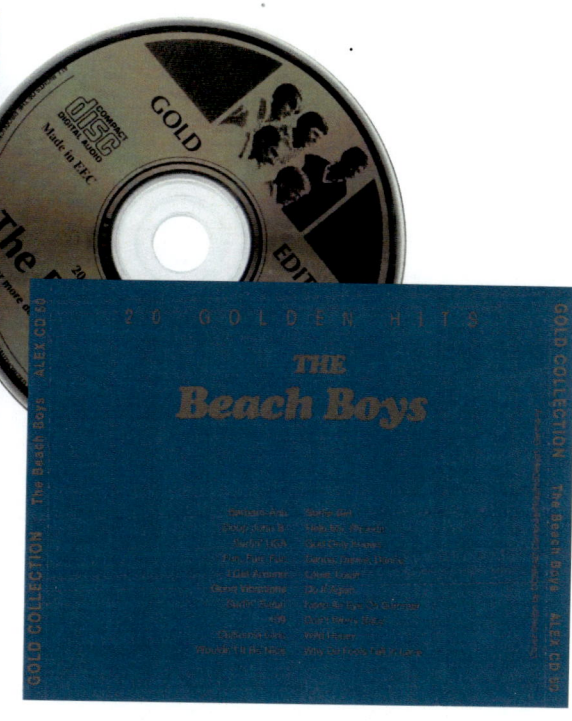

Title: Gold Collection
Artist: The Beach Boys
Latest CD Release Date: 1991
Record Label: ALEX
CD Ref. No: CD 050
Country: Germany
No. of Disks: 1
Format: Audio CD
Audio: mono/stereo

Title: The Wonderful World of The Beach Boys
Artist: The Beach Boys
Latest CD Release Date: 1993
Record Label: Remember
CD Ref. No: RMB 75634
Country: Portugal?
No. of Disks: 1
Format: Audio CD
Audio: mono/stereo

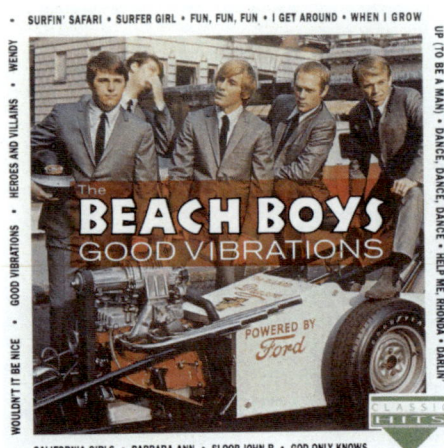

Title: Good Vibrations
Artist: The Beach Boys
Latest CD Release Date: 1994
Record Label: Cedar (Charly)
CD Ref. No: CRB 505
Country: Germany
No. of Disks: 1
Format: Audio CD
Audio: mono/stereo

Title: Sunny Times
Artist: The Beach Boys
Latest CD Release Date: 1995
Record Label: A PRIORI
CD Ref. No: CD 791304
Country: Italy
No. of Disks: 1
Format: Audio CD
Audio: mono/stereo

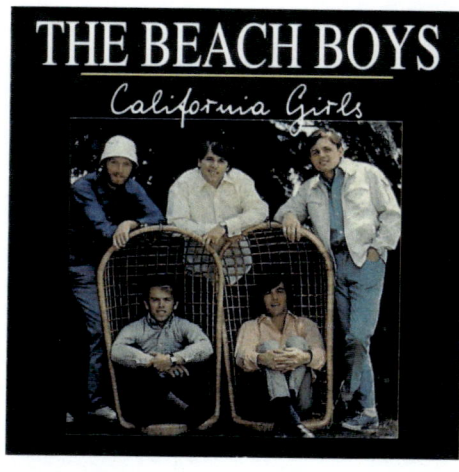

Title: California Girls
Artist: The Beach Boys
Latest CD Release Date: late 1997
Record Label: Eurosound/Gloabal Arts
CD Ref. No: 3309
Country: Germany
No. of Disks: 1
Format: Audio CD
Audio: mono/stereo

Title: Forever Surfin'
Artist: The Beach Boys
Latest CD Release Date: 1997
Record Label: A PRIORI
CD Ref. No: 791303
Country: Italy
No. of Disks: 1
Format: Audio CD
Audio: mono/stereo

The Beach Boys on CD: Licences Compilations

Title: The Great Beach Boys
Artist: The Beach Boys
Latest CD Release Date: 1993
Record Label: Goldies
CD Ref. No: GLD 63138
Country: Portugal?
No. of Disks: 1
Format: Audio CD
Audio: mono/stereo

Title: Surfin'
Artist: The Beach Boys
Latest CD Release Date: 2000
Record Label: Varese Sarabande
CD Ref. No: 302 066 085 2
Country: US
No. of Disks: 1
Format: Audio CD
Audio: mono/stereo

The Beach Boys on CD: Licences Compilations

Title: California Girls
Artist: The Beach Boys
Latest CD Release Date: 2001
Record Label: Universe (FNM)
CD Ref. No: 3309
Country: Germany (re-release)
No. of Disks: 1
Format: Audio CD
Audio: mono/stereo

Title: Fun, Fun, Fun (Beach Boys Best)
Artist: The Beach Boys
Latest CD Release Date: 1990
Record Label: VMV (EMI-Electrola)
CD Ref. No: 27200163 (CDF 670 573)
Country: Germany
No. of Disks: 1
Format: Audio CD
Audio: mono/stereo

Title: Good Vibrations Vol. 2
Artist: The Beach Boys
Latest CD Release Date: 2001
Record Label: Music Collection
CD Ref. No: Golden Pop History 73002
Country: Germany
No. of Disks: 1
Format: Audio CD
Audio: mono/stereo

Title: The Beach Boys Best
Artist: The Beach Boys
Latest CD Release Date: 1985 ?
Record Label: Jasrac
CD Ref. No: R 950101
Country: Japan
No. of Disks: 1
Format: Audio CD
Audio: mono/stereo

The Beach Boys on CD: Licences Compilations

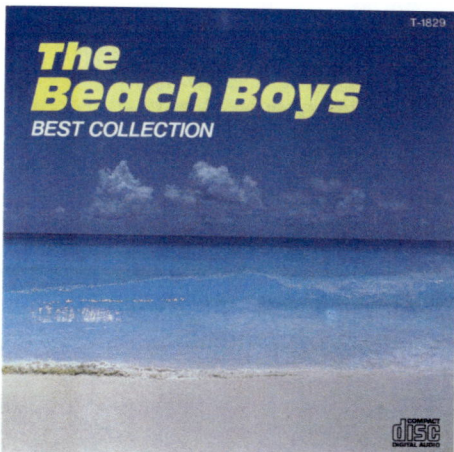

Title: The Beach Boys Best Collection
Artist: The Beach Boys
Latest CD Release Date: unknown
Record Label: Jasrac
CD Ref. No: R 250065
Country: Japan
No. of Disks: 1
Format: Audio CD
Audio: mono/stereo

Title: Good Vibrations (Beach Boys live)
Artist: The Beach Boys
Latest CD Release Date: 1983
Record Label: Fabbri Editori
CD Ref. No: MRL 060
Country: Italy
No. of Disks: 1
Format: Audio CD
Audio: stereo

Title: The Early Years
Artist: The Beach Boys
Latest CD Release Date: 1994
Record Label: Mastertone Multimedia
CD Ref. No: 10027
Country: UK
No. of Disks: 1
Format: Audio CD
Audio: mono/stereo

Title: Surf in the USA
Artist: The Beach Boys
Latest CD Release Date: 1994
Record Label: Music Reflection
CD Ref. No: 1402.2043-2
Country: Austria-Switzerland
No. of Disks: 1
Format: Audio CD
Audio: mono/stereo

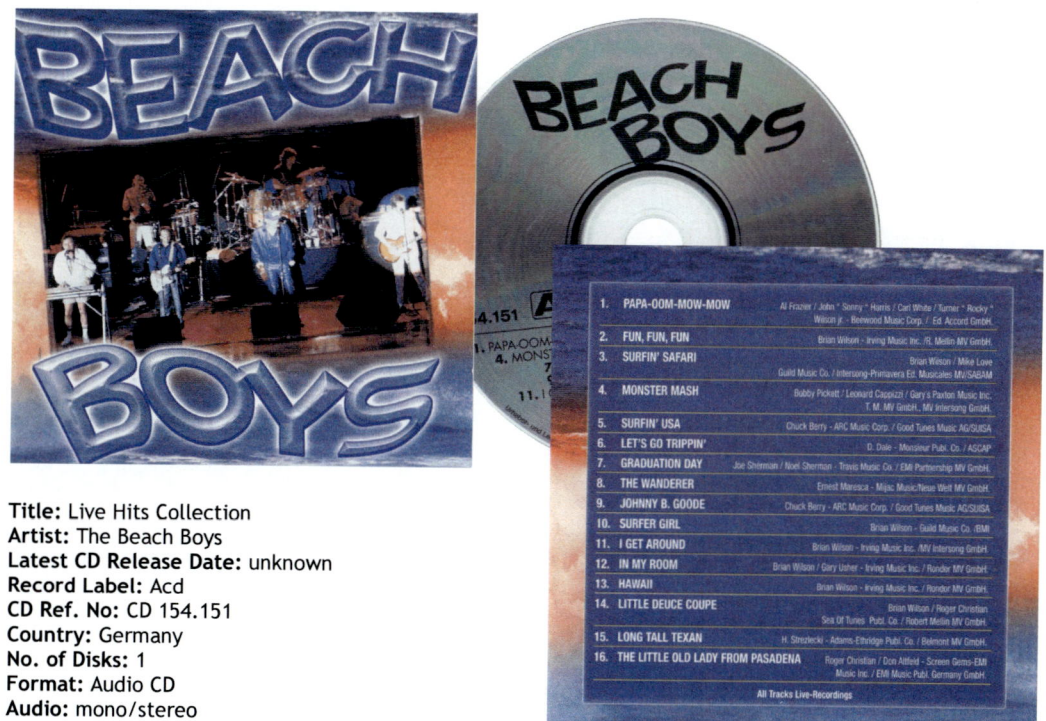

Title: Live Hits Collection
Artist: The Beach Boys
Latest CD Release Date: unknown
Record Label: Acd
CD Ref. No: CD 154.151
Country: Germany
No. of Disks: 1
Format: Audio CD
Audio: mono/stereo

Title: Beach Party (live in Montego Bay – 26/6/1982)
Artist: The Beach Boys
Latest CD Release Date: 1993
Record Label: International Broadcast Recordings
CD Ref. No: IRB 2025
Country: unknown
No. of Disks: 1
Format: Audio CD
Audio: stereo

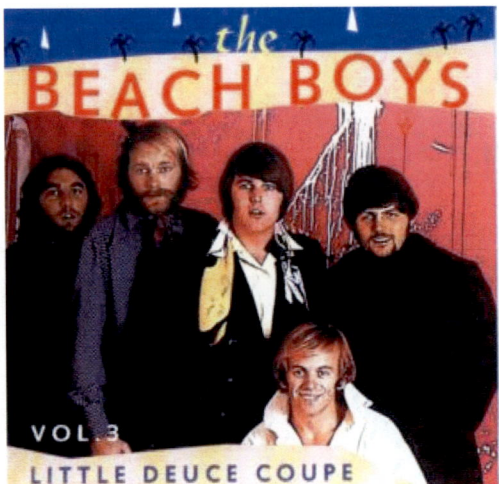

Title: Little Deuce Coupe Vol. 3
Artist: The Beach Boys
Latest CD Release Date: 1993
Record Label: Duchesse
CD Ref. No: CD 352143
Country: unknown
No. of Disks: 1
Format: Audio CD
Audio: mono/stereo

The Beach Boys have released two Christmas albums, 'The Beach Boys Christmas Album' (1664) and 'Ultimate Christmas (1998); the detail is provided on the following pages.

Although never released, tracks for a third album were recorded in 1977 at MIU. Some of these recordings now appear on the 'Ultimate Christmas album and were released in full on the Frontline bootleg.

Between the release of these two albums, a number of CD's have sprung up (mostly from CEMA; Emi-Capitol Special Markets)

and a few 'foreign' offerings have bubbled to the surface. Brief details of the variants are illustrated below. The Sea of Tunes bootleg, 'The Christmas Box', is illustrated in the 'Bootleg Sounds' chapter

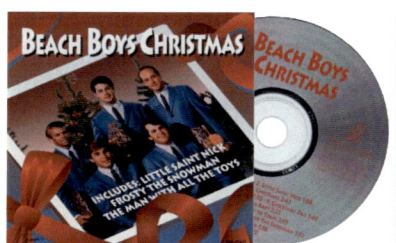

CEMA S21-17417

CEMA CDL 9012 (1991)

Frontline bootleg FLCD 14
(Recorded 1977 MIU)

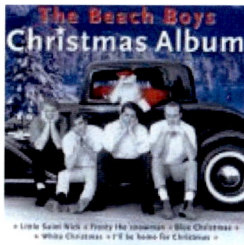

DISKY CH884092

CEMA 7243 5 27702 2 9
(LaserLight 21 718)

Dynamic 352094 (1992)

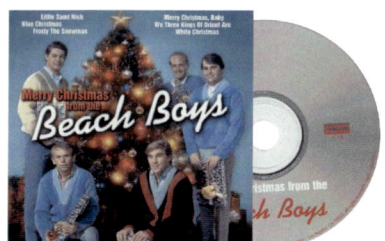

CEMA 07777 56620 2 3

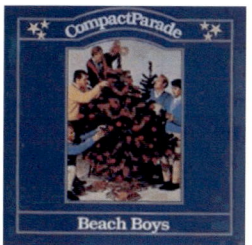

No Xmas songs ??

German: Universe UN 3 160

THE
BEACH BOYS'
CHRISTMAS ALBUM

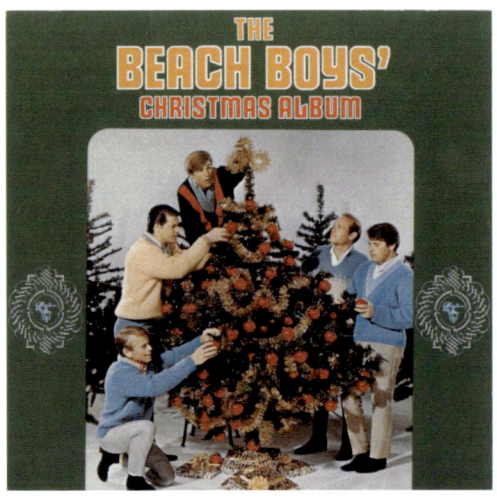

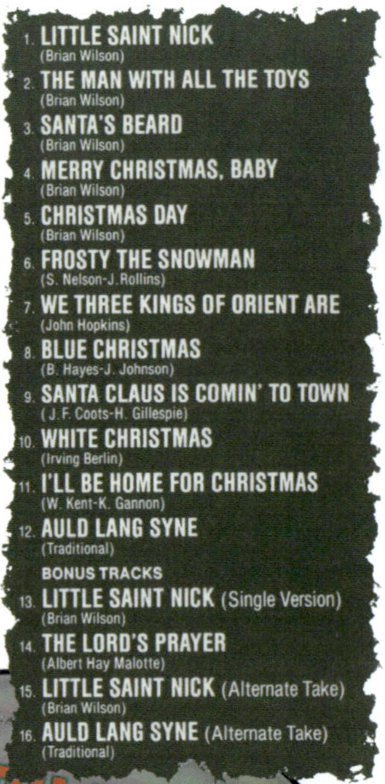
1. LITTLE SAINT NICK
(Brian Wilson)
2. THE MAN WITH ALL THE TOYS
(Brian Wilson)
3. SANTA'S BEARD
(Brian Wilson)
4. MERRY CHRISTMAS, BABY
(Brian Wilson)
5. CHRISTMAS DAY
(Brian Wilson)
6. FROSTY THE SNOWMAN
(S. Nelson-J. Rollins)
7. WE THREE KINGS OF ORIENT ARE
(John Hopkins)
8. BLUE CHRISTMAS
(B. Hayes-J. Johnson)
9. SANTA CLAUS IS COMIN' TO TOWN
(J. F. Coots-H. Gillespie)
10. WHITE CHRISTMAS
(Irving Berlin)
11. I'LL BE HOME FOR CHRISTMAS
(W. Kent-K. Gannon)
12. AULD LANG SYNE
(Traditional)
BONUS TRACKS
13. LITTLE SAINT NICK (Single Version)
(Brian Wilson)
14. THE LORD'S PRAYER
(Albert Hay Malotte)
15. LITTLE SAINT NICK (Alternate Take)
(Brian Wilson)
16. AULD LANG SYNE (Alternate Take)
(Traditional)

Title: The Beach Boys' Christmas Album
Artist: The Beach Boys
Latest CD Release Date: 1994
Record Label: Capitol/EMI Records
CD Ref. No: CDP 07777 910082 - 1988
CDP 07777 950842 - 1992
7243 8 30729 2 7 - 1994
D 133854 (BMG)
Country: US
No. of Disks: 1
Format: Audio CD
Audio: mono/stereo

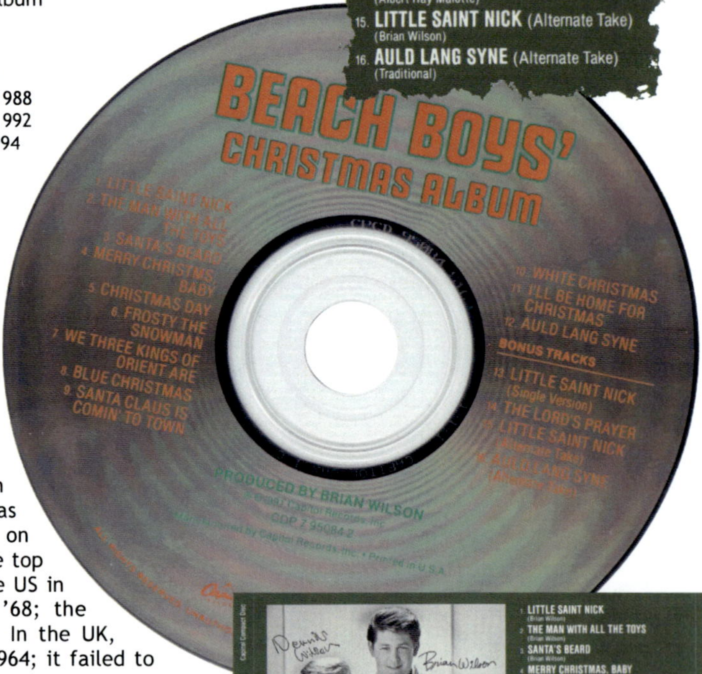
BEACH BOYS'
CHRISTMAS ALBUM
PRODUCED BY BRIAN WILSON

Album Notes:

The 'Christmas album' was the eighth Beach Boys album to enter the Billboard chart. The album entered the chart in the first week of Dec. 1964 and reach ed No.6 on the Billboard Xmas chart; it spent a total of 13 weeks on the charts. The album entered the top ten on the Christmas charts in the US in 1965 and again in '66 '67 and '68; the Beach Boys' seventh gold album. In the UK, the album was released in Nov. 1964; it failed to chart. The 7" single, 'Little St. Nick had been released in the US in 1963 and peaked at No.3 on the Christmas chart. 'The Man with All the Toys' reached No.3 on the US Christmas chart of 1964. This album is now updated as 'The Ultimate Christmas Album' The first CD release was in 1988 and was a replica of the album (No bonus tracks). The 1991/92 version included bonus tracks; the 1994 CD version had no bonus tracks - EMI Music for pleasure in the UK (I have not confirmed the 1994 US version details yet)

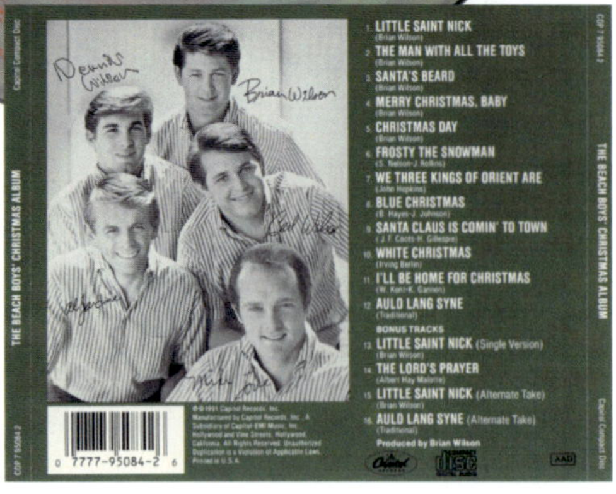
THE BEACH BOYS' CHRISTMAS ALBUM

The 1992 release

Title: The Beach Boys Ultimate Christmas
Release Date: Sept. 1998
Record Label: Capitol Records
CD Ref. No: 72434 95734 2 0
Country: US
No. of Disks: 1
Format: Audio CD
Audio: mono/stereo
Liner Notes: Brad Elliot

Album Notes:

This Christmas collection is called the 'Ultimate' collection, so with any luck there should be no more. The CD did reach No. 20 on the US Christmas chart in 2000. Brad Elliot provides the track notes in the Booklet. This album contains a number of tracks from the aborted 1977 Christmas album recorded at M.I.U. The Dennis Wilson song 'Morning Christmas' makes this CD worth buying; a previously unreleased track, it previously appeared on the 'Frontline' Christmas album bootleg.

1. Little Saint Nick
2. The Man With All The Toys
3. Santa's Beard
4. Merry Christmas, Baby
5. Christmas Day
6. Frosty The Snowman
7. We Three Kings Of Orient Are
8. Blue Christmas
9. Santa Claus Is Coming To Town
10. White Christmas
11. I'll Be Home For Christmas
12. Auld Lang Syne
13. Little Saint Nick (Single Version)
14. Auld Lang Syne (Alternate Mix)
15. Little Saint Nick (Alternate Version)
16. Child Of Winter (Christmas Song)
17. Santa's Got An Airplane
18. Christmas Time Is Here Again
19. Winter Symphony
20. (I Saw Santa) Rockin' Around The Christmas Tree
21. Melekalikimaka
22. Bells Of Christmas
23. Morning Christmas
24. Toy Drive Public Service Announcement
25. Dennis Wilson Christmas Message
26. Brian Wilson Christmas Interview

Christmas Album: 1988 release – front/back/disk

EMI Music for Pleasure Christmas Album: 1994 ?

Promo & Sampler releases

CD's in this category have a common characteristic; they are promotional CD's and were distributed on the advent of a major Beach Boys compilation release or event. I have detailed a number of these CD's, but there are many more in existence that should be catalogued (2nd edition?). I have detailed The Pet Sounds promotional CD's and CD sets in the Pet Sounds chapter.

Title & Notes: 14 Track Sampler; released in advance of the 1990 Twofer & Pet Sounds on CD event. Notice that the promo foldout shows the releases in 'long boxes. The 1990 Brother-Caribou single Album CD's, released in 1990, also appeared in long boxes for a short while.
Artist: The Beach Boys
Latest CD Release Date: 1990
Record Label: Capitol Records
CD Ref. No: DPRO 76168
Country: US
No. of Disks: 1
Format: Audio CD
Audio: mono/stereo

Title & Notes: Good Vibrations (30 Years of the Beach Boys). Release to promote the 30 Year box set, this CD contains 1/5th of the tracks on the box set and includes a short note by David Leaf
Artist: The Beach Boys
Latest CD Release Date: 1993
Record Label: Capitol Records
CD Ref. No: DPRO 79728
Country: US
No. of Disks: 1
Format: Audio CD
Audio: mono/stereo

Title: Good Vibrations; sort of promotes the 1995 Greatest Hits CD and doubles as a 'Tetra Pak' (the French carton Co.) promo
Artist: The Beach Boys
Latest CD Release Date: 1995
Record Label: EMI Electrola
CD Ref. No: 7243 8 82254 2 7
Country: Germany
No. of Disks: 1
Format: Audio CD
Audio: mono/stereo

Title: I Can Hear Music; A kind of single come promo for the 'Stars and Stripes Vol.1' album. Executive producer, Mike Love.
Latest CD Release Date: 1996
Record Label: River North (MCA)
CD Ref. No: MCD 80127
Country: US
No. of Disks: 1
Format: Audio CD
Audio: stereo

Title: Endless Harmony; Advanced listening CD from EMI UK. Released to promote the original 1998 release, The CD contains the entire Endless Harmony recording.
Artist: The Beach Boys
Latest CD Release Date: 1998
Record Label: EMI International
CD Ref. No: CDPP 077
Country: UK
No. of Disks: 1
Format: Audio CD
Audio: mono/stereo

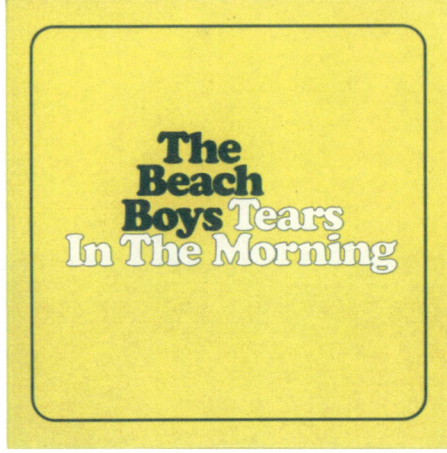

Title: Tears in The Morning; released to promote 'The Dutch Singles Collection'
Artist: The Beach Boys
Latest CD Release Date: 1998
Record Label: EMI
CD Ref. No: 7243 8 86082 2 0
Country: US
No. of Disks: 1
Format: Audio CD
Audio: stereo

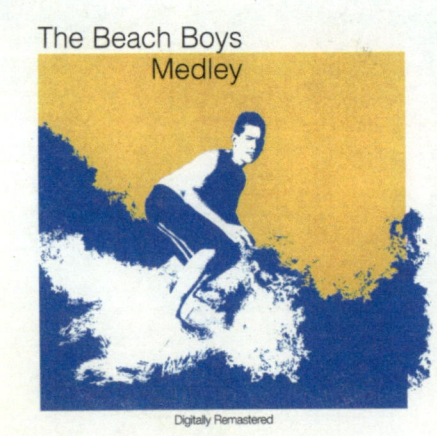

Title: Medley; Spanish release to promote the 'Very Best of The Beach Boys'
Artist: The Beach Boys
Latest CD Release Date: 2001
Record Label: EMI
CD Ref. No: PE 01074
Country: Spain
No. of Disks: 1
Format: Audio CD
Audio: mono/stereo

The Beach Boys on CD: Promos & Samplers

Title: Sounds of The Summer Singles; released to promote the 2003 'Sound of The Summer' compilation; includes a few singles and the Beach Boys Medley.
Artist: The Beach Boys
Latest CD Release Date: 2003
Record Label: Capitol Records
CD Ref. No: 7243 5 90000 2 2
Country: US
No. of Disks: 1
Format: Audio CD
Audio: mono/stereo

Title: Greatest Hits Volume 3: Best of the Brother Years; advance listening CD, released to promote the Brother Years compilation.
Artist: The Beach Boys
Latest CD Release Date: 2000
Record Label: Capitol Records
CD Ref. No: 7243 5 24511 2 BV
Country: US
No. of Disks: 1
Format: Audio CD
Audio: mono/stereo

pro-cd-9280

Title: Your Imagination; released to promote Brian 1998 solo album 'Imagination'
Artist: Brian Wilson
Latest CD Release Date: 1998
Record Label: Giant Records
CD Ref. No: pro cd 9280
Country: US
No. of Disks: 1
Format: Audio CD
Audio: mono/stereo

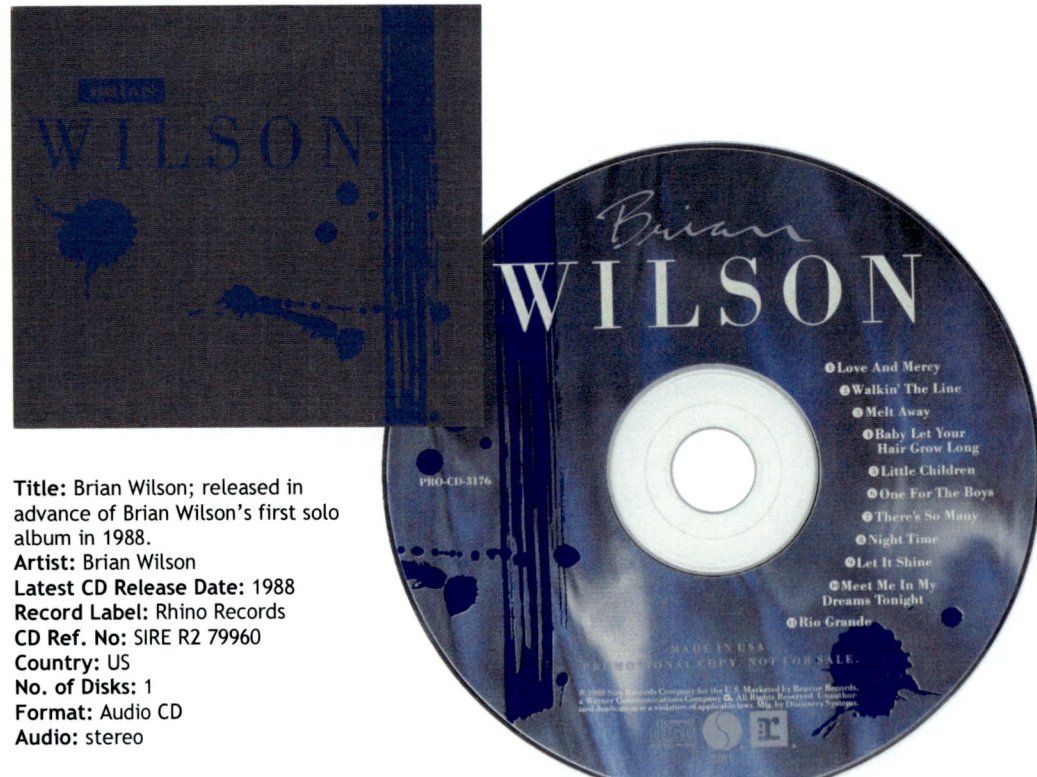

Title: Brian Wilson; released in advance of Brian Wilson's first solo album in 1988.
Artist: Brian Wilson
Latest CD Release Date: 1988
Record Label: Rhino Records
CD Ref. No: SIRE R2 79960
Country: US
No. of Disks: 1
Format: Audio CD
Audio: stereo

~ Japan ~ 日本
The Land of the Rising Song

Japanese Series

**Twofers
PastMasters
CoolPrice
Mini LP
Pet Sounds
Current + Miscellaneous releases**

The Beach Boys on CD: Japan

Japan - 1990 Twofers

Track Listing, Disk 1 (Titles & Time)...

1.	I Get Around (mono)	2:13
2.	All Summer Long (mono)	2:06
3.	Hushabye	2:39
4.	Little Honda	1:51
5.	We'll Run Away	1:59
6.	Carl's Big Chance (Instrumental)	2:24
7.	Wendy	2:14
8.	Do You Remember	1:37
9.	Girls On The Beach	2:22
10.	Drive-In	1:50
11.	Our Favorite Recording Sessions	1:58
12.	Don't Back Down	1:43

Total Playing time: 25:34

Title: Smiley Smile & Wild Honey
Release Date: 12 Dec. 1990
Record Label: Toshiba-EMI.
CD Ref. No: TOCP-6516
Country: Japan
No. of Disks: 1
Format: Audio CD
Audio: Mono/Stereo
Liner Notes: Song Lyrics & US Booklet

Album & Track Notes

The cover shows the displays images of the two original album front covers. This cover sleeve is a Japanese Jumper' and contains a fold out lyrics sheet in Japanese and English as well as a copy of the US twofer booklet (in English). These CD's and the series are in fact the same as the first 1990 US Capitol twofer releases The OBI strip provides general information in Japanese. Converted from analog to digital using 16 bit technology, the sound quality is inferior to the 2001 twofer release. This 1990 series was the only twofer series to be released in Japan. Detail of the complete twofer series is provided on the next page

Surfin' Safari/ Surfin' U.S.A.	TOCP-6511
Surfer Girl/ Shut Down Volume 2	TOCP-6512
Little Deuce Coupe/ All Summer Long	TOCP-6513
TODAY!/ Summer Days	TOCP-6514
Beach Boys' Party/ Stack-o-tracks	TOCP-6515
Smiley Smile/ Wild Honey	TOCP-6516
Friends20/20	TOCP-6517
Concert/69' (LIVE IN LONDON)	TOPC-6518

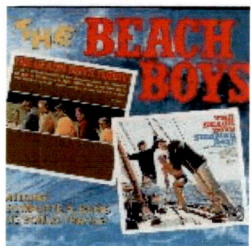

The Beach Boys on CD: Japan

PASTMASTERS

Track Listing; titles & times...

1.	Heroes and Villains	3:36
2.	Vegetables	2:06
3.	Fall Breaks and Back To Winter	2:15
4.	She's Going Bald	2:14
5.	Little Pad	2:30
6.	Good Vibrations	3:35
7.	With Me Tonight	2:16
8.	Wind Chimes	2:34
9.	Getting' Hungry	2:26
10.	Wonderful	2:21
11.	Whistle In	1:03

Total Playing time: 23:56

Title: Smiley Smile
Release Date: July 1990 (series)
Record Label: Toshiba-EMI
CD Ref. No: CP21 6012
Country: Japan
No. of Disks: 1
Format: Audio CD
Audio: mono/stereo (series)
Liner Notes: Song Lyrics

Album & Track Notes

The Japanese PastMasters series was released in 1990 and comprised the Capitol studio releases. These CD's (16 in all) are essentially re-mastered (to 16-bit digital) version of the original studio albums. Full detail of the PastMasters series is provided on the next page. These CD are now quite rare but can be found periodically on eBay

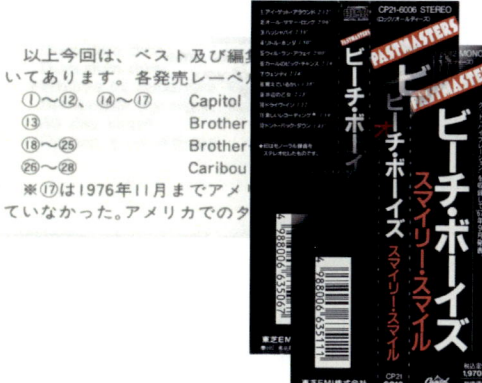

PASTMASTERS

Title	Catalog #
Surfin' Safari	CP21-6001
Surfin' U.S.A.	CP21-6002
Surfer Girl	CP21-6003
Little Deuce Coupe	CP21-6004
Shut Down Volume 2	CP21-6005
All Summer Long	CP21-6006
Beach Boys Concert	CP21-6007
TODAY!	CP21-6008
Summer Days (and Summer Nights!)	CP21-6009
Beach Boys Party	CP21-6010
Pet Sounds	CP21-6011
Smiley Smile	CP21-6012
Wild Honey	CP21-6013
Friends	CP21-6014
20/20	CP21-6015
Beach Boys '69	CP21-6016

Japan - Coolprice series 1997

Track Listing: titles & times...

#	Title	Time
1.	With a Little Help From My Friends	2:24
2.	The Letter	1:47
3.	I Was Made To Love Her	2:33
4.	You're Welcome	1:06
5.	The Lords Prayer	2:31
6.	Bluebirds Over The Mountain	2:50
7.	Celebrate The News	3:03
8.	Good Vibrations	3:33
9.	Land Ahoy	1:41
10.	In My Room (German Version)	2:15
11.	Cotton Fields	3:00
12.	All I Want To Do	1:37
13.	Auld Lang Syne (Burns)	1:18
14.	Medley #1	6:47
15.	Medley #2	9:36
16.	Medley #3	4:09

Title: Rarities
Release Date: 18th Sept. 1997
Record Label: Toshiba-EMI.
CD Ref. No: TOCP-3329
Country: Japan
No. of Disks: 1
Format: Audio CD
Audio: Mono/Stereo
Liner Notes: Song Lyrics

Album & Track Notes

The Japanese CoolPrice series was released in the months of September/October 1997 and comprised twenty CD's. The series included a CD release of the first Capitol Shutdown Album (a compilation including two Beach Boys tracks – 409 & Shut Down) and the well known Rarities CD (first released by capitol on Vinyl in 1983). The Rarities CD is readily available and has been re-released. The CD's of this series are now quite rare. For anyone looking for information on the genesis of the Rarities album, go here: http://www.surfsupcollectibles.com/rarities/

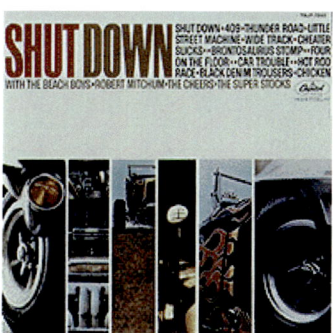

ShutDown, the first Capitol ShutDown album release and the reason the Beach Boys album was called Volume 2.

Japan - Coolprice series 1997

Title	Cat. No.	Rel. date
Surfin' Safari	TOCP-3311	18/9/1997
Surfin' U.S.A.	TOCP-3312	18/9/1997
ShutDown	tocp-3313	18/9/1997
Surfer Girl	tocp-3314	18/9/1997
Little Deuce Coupe	tocp-3315	18/9/1997
Shut Down Volume 2	tocp-3316	18/9/1997
All Summer Long	tocp-3317	18/9/1997
Beach Boys Concert	tocp-3318	18/9/1997
TODAY!	tocp-3319	18/9/1997
Summer Days...	tocp-3320	18/9/1997
Beach Boys Party	tocp-3321	16/10/1997
Pet Sounds	tocp-3322	16/10/1997
Smiley Smile	tocp-3323	16/10/1997
Wild Honey	tocp-3324	16/10/1997
Friends	tocp-3325	16/10/1997
Stack-o-tracks	tocp-3326	16/10/1997
20/20	tocp-3327	16/10/1997
Beach Boys '69	tocp-3328	16/10/1997
Rarities & Medley	tocp-3329	16/10/1997
Still Cruisin'	tocp-3330	16/10/1997
Christmas Party! + 5	tocp-3331	16/10/1997

The Beach Boys on CD: Japan Mini LP

Japanese mini LP CD series ~ 1998

Track Listing, Disk 1 (Titles & Time)...

1.	I Get Around (mono)	2:13
2.	All Summer Long (mono)	2:06
3.	Hushabye	2:39
4.	Little Honda	1:51
5.	We'll Run Away	1:59
6.	Carl's Big Chance (Instrumental)	2:24
7.	Wendy	2:14
8.	Do You Remember	1:37
9.	Girls On The Beach	2:22
10.	Drive-In	1:50
11.	Our Favorite Recording Sessions	1:58
12.	Don't Back Down	1:43

Total Playing time: 25:34

Title: All Summer Long
Release Date: 1998/2000 (latest series)
Record Label: Toshiba-EMI.
CD Ref. No: TOCP-50854 (CDP 7243 8 29631 2 7)
Country: Japan
No. of Disks: 1
Format: Audio CD
Audio: Mono/Stereo
Liner Notes: Song Lyrics

Album & Track Notes

The cover is a replica of the original album sleeve. The sleeve contains a fold out lyrics sheet in Japanese and English. Re-mastered to digital, all songs are as recorded on the original vinyl; in mono or stereo. The OBI strip provides general information in Japanese. The sound quality is excellent. Full detail of this mini LP series is provided on the next page. The series of 19 CD's was first released 1998, the current set was released in 2000. The 'Endless Summer' CD does not have 'Good Vibrations' as a 21st track

Japanese mini LP CD series ~ 1998

Surfin' Safari	TOCP-50849
Surfin' U.S.A.	TOCP-50850
Surfer Girl	TOCP-50851
Little Deuce Coupe	TOCP-50852
Shut Down Volume 2	TOCP-50853
All Summer Long	TOCP-50854
Beach Boys Concert	TOCP-50855
TODAY!	TOCP-50856
Summer Days (and Summer Nights!!)	TOCP-50857
Beach Boys' Party!	TOCP-50858
Smiley Smile	TOCP-50860
Wild Honey	TOCP-50861
Friends	TOCP-50862
Stack-o-tracks	TOCP-50863
20/20	TOCP-50864
Beach Boys 69' (live in London)	topc-50865
Endless Summer	TOPC-50866
Spirit of America	TOCP-50867
Made in U.S.A	tocp-50868

Japan - Pet Sounds

In 1988, Toshiba released the first CD version of Pet Sounds. Since then, eight other versions have been released – the detail is provided on the following pages

Title: Pet Sounds
Release Date: 19th June 2002
Record Label: Toshiba-EMI
CD Ref. No: TOCP-66031 (CDP 72435-26266-2-0)
Country: Japan
No. of Disks: 1
Format: Audio HDCD
Audio: Mono
Liner Notes: Song Lyrics & US Booklet

Track Listing...

1. Wouldn't It Be Nice
2. You Still Believe In Me
3. That's Not Me
4. Don't Talk (Put Your Head On My Shoulder)
5. I'm Waiting For The Day
6. Let's Go Away For Awhile
7. Sloop John B
8. God Only Knows
9. I Know There's An Answer
10. Here Today
11. I Just Wasn't Made For These Times
12. Pet Sounds
13. Caroline No

Album & Track Notes — TOSHIBA EMI

The cover shows the original Pet Sounds cover. This CD is the most recent release of Pet Sound by Toshiba-EMI and is the original Mono version of the album. The CD is re-mastered to HDCD format (24 bit). The CD is part of the Pet Sounds 2002 Series. Like the US/UK, there are many different releases of Pet Sound in Japan; on the following pages the detail of all known releases is provided, the CD's are depicted in reverse chronological order

Title: Pet Sounds
Release Date: 7th July 1999
Record Label: Toshiba-EMI
CD Ref. No: TOCP- 65255 (CDP 72435-21241-2-1)
Country: Japan
No. of Disks: 1
Format: Audio CD
Audio: Mono & Stereo
Liner Notes: Song Lyrics & US Booklet

Track Listing... (mono & stereo versions)

1. Wouldn't It Be Nice
2. You Still Believe In Me
3. That's Not Me
4. Don't Talk (Put Your Head On My Shoulder)
5. I'm Waiting For The Day
6. Let's Go Away For Awhile
7. Sloop John B
8. God Only Knows
9. I Know There's An Answer
10. Here Today
11. I Just Wasn't Made For These Times
12. Pet Sounds
13. Caroline No
14. Hang On To Your Ego - (bonus track mono)

Album & Track Notes

The cover shows the original Pet Sounds cover. This CD is the mono/stereo release; tracks 1 - 13 (mono) + Hang Onto Your Ego (track 14 mono) and tracks 15 -27 stereo. This CD is the equivalent of the US Capitol release and contains the US Booklet

The Beach Boys on CD: Japan, Pet Sounds

Track Listing...
1. Wouldn't It Be Nice
2. You Still Believe In Me
3. That's Not Me
4. Don't Talk (Put Your Head On My Shoulder)
5. I'm Waiting For The Day
6. Let's Go Away For Awhile
7. Sloop John B
8. God Only Knows
9. I Know There's An Answer
10. Here Today
11. I Just Wasn't Made For These Times
12. Pet Sounds
13. Caroline No

TOSHIBA EMI

Title: Pet Sounds
Release Date: 23rd July 1998
Record Label: Toshiba-EMI
CD Ref. No: TOCP-50859 (CDP 7243 8 37666 2 8)
Country: Japan
No. of Disks: 1
Format: Audio CD
Audio: Mono
Liner Notes: Song Lyrics

Album & Track Notes

The cover shows the original Pet Sounds cover and is identical to the original LP release; the CD is part of the 1998 Toshiba mini LP CD series.

Track Listing...
1. Wouldn't It Be Nice
2. You Still Believe In Me
3. That's Not Me
4. Don't Talk (Put Your Head On My Shoulder)
5. I'm Waiting For The Day
6. Let's Go Away For Awhile
7. Sloop John B
8. God Only Knows
9. I Know There's An Answer
10. Here Today
11. I Just Wasn't Made For These Times
12. Pet Sounds
13. Caroline No
14. Unreleased Backgrounds
15. Hang On To Your Ego
16. Trombone Dixie

Title: Pet Sounds
Release Date: 16th Oct. 1997
Record Label: Toshiba-EMI
CD Ref. No: TOCP-3322 (CDP 7 48421 2)
Country: Japan
No. of Disks: 1
Format: Audio CD
Audio: Mono
Liner Notes: Song Lyrics

Album & Track Notes

The cover shows the original Pet Sounds cover and is identical to the original LP release; the CD is part of the 1998 Toshiba 'Beach Boys Original Albums' series. Contains three bonus tracks and is the equivalent of the US Capitol release: CDP 548421 released in 1990

Track Listing...

1. Wouldn't It Be Nice
2. You Still Believe In Me
3. That's Not Me
4. Don't Talk (Put Your Head On My Shoulder)
5. I'm Waiting For The Day
6. Let's Go Away For Awhile
7. Sloop John B
8. God Only Knows
9. I Know There's An Answer
10. Here Today
11. I Just Wasn't Made For These Times
12. Pet Sounds
13. Caroline No
14. Unreleased Backgrounds
15. Hang On To Your Ego
16. Trombone Dxie

Title: Pet Sounds
Release Date: 28th June 1995
Record Label: Toshiba-EMI
CD Ref. No: TOCP-3018
Country: Japan
No. of Disks: 1
Format: Audio CD
Audio: Mono
Liner Notes: Song Lyrics

Album & Track Notes

The cover shows the original Pet Sounds cover and is identical to the original LP release; the CD is part of the 1995 Toshiba 'CoolPrice' series. Contains three bonus tracks and is the equivalent of the US Capitol release: CDP 548421 released in 1990

Track Listing...

1. Wouldn't It Be Nice
2. You Still Believe In Me
3. That's Not Me
4. Don't Talk (Put Your Head On My Shoulder)
5. I'm Waiting For The Day
6. Let's Go Away For Awhile
7. Sloop John B
8. God Only Knows
9. I Know There's An Answer
10. Here Today
11. I Just Wasn't Made For These Times
12. Pet Sounds
13. Caroline No
14. Unreleased Backgrounds
15. Hang On To Your Ego
16. Trombone Dxie

Title: Pet Sounds
Release Date: 12th Dec. 1990
Record Label: Toshiba-EMI
CD Ref. No: TOCP-6519
Country: Japan
No. of Disks: 1
Format: Audio CD
Audio: Mono
Liner Notes: Song Lyrics

Album & Track Notes

The cover shows the original Pet Sounds cover and is identical to the original LP release; the CD is part of the 1990 release of the Japanese twofer series. The CD contains three bonus tracks and is the equivalent of the US Capitol release: CDP 548421 released in 1990

Track Listing...

1. Wouldn't It Be Nice
2. You Still Believe In Me
3. That's Not Me
4. Don't Talk (Put Your Head On My Shoulder)
5. I'm Waiting For The Day
6. Let's Go Away For Awhile
7. Sloop John B
8. God Only Knows
9. I Know There's An Answer
10. Here Today
11. I Just Wasn't Made For These Times
12. Pet Sounds
13. Caroline No

Title: Pet Sounds
Release Date: 28th July 1989
Record Label: EMI.
CD Ref. No: CP21-6011
Country: Japan
No. of Disks: 1
Format: Audio CD
Audio: Mono
Liner Notes: Song Lyrics

Album & Track Notes

The cover shows the original Pet Sounds cover and is identical to the original LP release; the CD is part of the 1989 EMI 'Pastmasters' series, the first Japanese release series of the Beach Boys back catalogue. This CD is the poorer sound quality cousin to the current Capitol release: CDP 7243 5 27319-2-3 and the Japan 2002 Pet Sounds CD (above)

Track Listing...

1. Wouldn't It Be Nice
2. You Still Believe In Me
3. That's Not Me
4. Don't Talk (Put Your Head On My Shoulder)
5. I'm Waiting For The Day
6. Let's Go Away For Awhile
7. Sloop John B
8. God Only Knows
9. I Know There's An Answer
10. Here Today
11. I Just Wasn't Made For These Times
12. Pet Sounds
13. Caroline No
14. Unreleased Backgrounds
15. Hang On To Your Ego - (bonus track mono)

Title: Pet Sounds
Release Date: 21st Dec. 1988
Record Label: Toshiba-EMI
CD Ref. No: CP28-1003
Country: Japan
No. of Disks: 1
Format: Audio CD
Audio: Mono
Liner Notes: Song Lyrics

Album & Track Notes

The cover shows the original Pet Sounds cover and is identical to the original LP release; the CD is part of the 1988 release of the Japanese 'GreenLine' series. The CD contains two bonus tracks.

The Beach Boys on CD: Japan, Pet Sounds

Japan - Current releases

The current Japanese single album CD releases are the year 2001, 24 bit HDCD versions created for the 2001 Capitol twofer series. The CD's contain bonus tracks. The bonus tracks are the same tracks that appear on the current Capitol twofer releases (2001). The bonus tracks are detailed on the following pages. The post Capitol CD's (LP's) were released in the year 2000 and are 24 bit remasters and not HDCD products. These CD's can be bought online via a number of Japanese CD shops...
http://www.cdjapan.co.jp

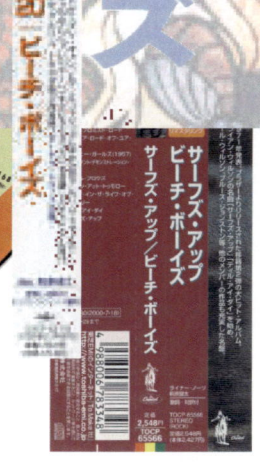

The Beach Boys on CD: Japan, Current releases

サーフィン・サファリ
Bonus Tracks
1. Cindy, Oh Cindy
2. Land Ahoy

Title: Surfin' Safari
Release Date: 16th June 2001
Record Label: Toshiba-EMI
CD Ref. No: TOCP-53161
Country: Japan
No. of Disks: 1
Format: Audio CD
Audio: HDCD mono
Liner Notes: Song Lyrics

サーフィン U.S.A.
Bonus Tracks
1. The Baker Man

Title: Surfin' U.S.A.
Release Date: 16th June 2001
Record Label: Toshiba-EMI
CD Ref. No: TOCP-53162
Country: Japan
No. of Disks: 1
Format: Audio CD
Audio: HDCD stereo
Liner Notes: Song Lyrics

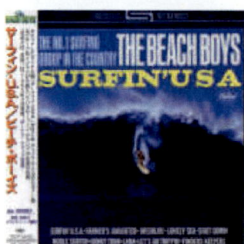

サーファー・ガール
Bonus Tracks
1. In My Room (German version)
2. I Do

Title: Surfer Girl
Release Date: 16th June 2001
Record Label: Toshiba-EMI
CD Ref. No: TOCP-53163
Country: Japan
No. of Disks: 1
Format: Audio CD
Audio: HDCD stereo
Liner Notes: Song Lyrics

リトル・デュース・クーペ
Bonus Tracks
1. Be True To Your School (single version)

Title: Little Deuce Coupe
Release Date: 16th June 2001
Record Label: Toshiba-EMI
CD Ref. No: TOCP-53164
Country: Japan
No. of Disks: 1
Format: Audio CD
Audio: HDCD mono/stereo
Liner Notes: Song Lyrics

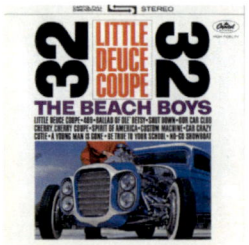

シャット・ダウン VOLUME 2
Bonus Tracks
1. Fun, Fun, Fun (single version)

Title: SHUT DOWN Volume 2
Release Date: 16th June 2001
Record Label: Toshiba-EMI
CD Ref. No: TOCP-53165
Country: Japan
No. of Disks: 1
Format: Audio CD
Audio: HDCD mono/stereo
Liner Notes: Song Lyrics

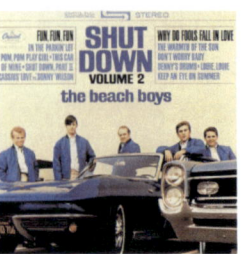

The Beach Boys on CD: Japan, Current releases

オール・サマー・ロング
ALL SUMMER LONG

Bonus Tracks
1. All Dressed Up For School
2. Little Honda (alterative take)
3. Don't Back Down (alternative take)

Title: All Summer Long
Release Date: 16th June 2001
Record Label: Toshiba-EMI
CD Ref. No: TOCP-53166
Country: Japan
No. of Disks: 1
Format: Audio CD
Audio: HDCD mono/stereo
Liner Notes: Song Lyrics

ビーチ・ボーイズ・クリスマス・アルバム（完全版）
ULTIMATE CHRISTMAS

Title: Ultimate Christmas
Release Date: 19th Nov. 2002
Record Label: Toshiba-EMI
CD Ref. No: TOCP-65006
Country: Japan
No. of Disks: 1
Format: Audio CD
Audio: HDCD mono/stereo
Liner Notes: Song Lyrics

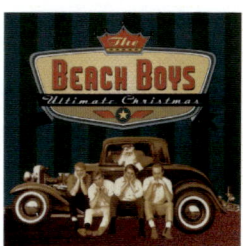

ビーチ・ボーイズ・コンサート
BEACH BOYS CONCERT

Title: Concert
Release Date: 9th April 2001
Record Label: Toshiba-EMI
CD Ref. No: TOCP-53167
Country: Japan
No. of Disks: 1
Format: Audio CD
Audio: HDCD stereo
Liner Notes: Song Lyrics

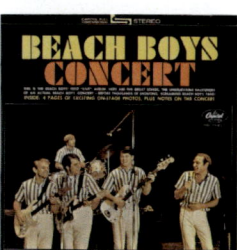

ビーチ・ボーイズ・トゥデイ
BEACH BOYS TODAY!

Bonus Tracks
1. Dance, Dance, Dance (alternative take
2. I'm So Young (alternative take)

Title: TODAY!
Release Date: 16th June 2001
Record Label: Toshiba-EMI
CD Ref. No: TOCP-53168
Country: Japan
No. of Disks: 1
Format: Audio CD
Audio: HDCD mono/stereo
Liner Notes: Song Lyrics

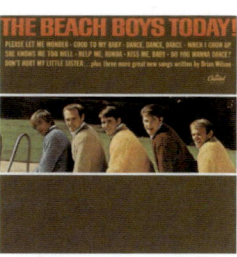

サマー・デイズ...
###

Bonus Tracks
6. The Little Girl I Once Knew (single version)
7. Let Him Run Wild (alternative take)
8. Graduation Day (Studio version)

Title: Summer Days (And Summer Nights!!)
Release Date: 27th June 2001
Record Label: Toshiba-EMI
CD Ref. No: TOCP-53169
Country: Japan
No. of Disks: 1
Format: Audio CD
Audio: HDCD mono/stereo
Liner Notes: Song Lyrics

The Beach Boys on CD: Japan, Current releases

ビーチ・ボーイズ・パーティ
BEACH BOYS' PARTY!

Title: Party
Release Date: 27th June 2001
Record Label: Toshiba-EMI
CD Ref. No: TOCP-53170
Country: Japan
No. of Disks: 1
Format: Audio CD
Audio: HDCD
Liner Notes: Song Lyrics

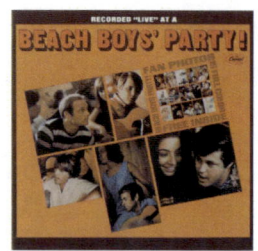

ペット・サウンズ
PET SOUNDS

Title: Pet Sounds
Release Date: 27th June 2001
Record Label: Toshiba-EMI
CD Ref. No: TOCP-3322
Country: Japan
No. of Disks: 1
Format: Audio CD
Audio: HDCD mono
Liner Notes: Song Lyrics

スマイリー・スマイル
SMILEY SMILE

Bonus Tracks
1. Heroes & Villains (alternative take)
2. Good Vibrations (various sessions)
3. Good Vibrations (earlt take)
4. You're Welcome
5. Can't Wait Too Long

Title: Smiley Smile
Release Date: 27th June 2001
Record Label: Toshiba-EMI
CD Ref. No: TOCP-53171
Country: Japan
No. of Disks: 1
Format: Audio CD
Audio: HDCD mono/stereo
Liner Notes: Song Lyrics

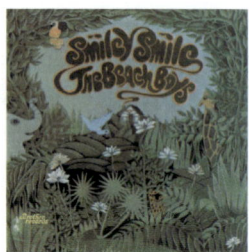

ワイルド・ハニー
WILD HONEY

Bonus Tracks
1. Their Hearts Were Full Of Spring

Title: Wild Honey
Release Date: 27th June 2001
Record Label: Toshiba-EMI
CD Ref. No: TOCP-53172
Country: Japan
No. of Disks: 1
Format: Audio CD
Audio: HDCD stereo
Liner Notes: Song Lyrics

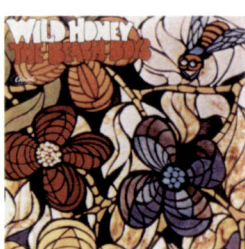

フレンズ
FRIENDS

Bonus Tracks
1. We're Together Again
2. Walk On By
3. Old Folks At Home/Ol' Man River

Title: Friends
Release Date: 27th June 2001
Record Label: Toshiba-EMI
CD Ref. No: TOCP-53173
Country: Japan
No. of Disks: 1
Format: Audio CD
Audio: HDCD mono/stereo
Liner Notes: Song Lyrics

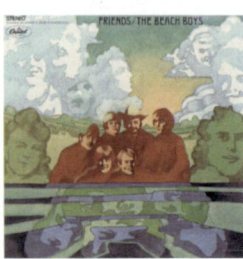

The Beach Boys on CD: Japan, Current releases

Bonus Tracks

1. Help Me Rhonda
2. California Girls
3. Our Car Club

Title: Stack-O-Tracks
Release Date: 27th June 2001
Record Label: Toshiba-EMI
CD Ref. No: TOCP-53174
Country: Japan
No. of Disks: 1
Format: Audio CD
Audio: HDCD mono/stereo
Liner Notes: Song Lyrics

Bonus Tracks

1. Breakaway
2. Celebrate The News

Title: 20/20
Release Date: 27th June 2001
Record Label: Toshiba-EMI
CD Ref. No: TOCP-53175
Country: Japan
No. of Disks: 1
Format: Audio CD
Audio: HDCD stereo
Liner Notes: Song Lyrics

Bonus Tracks

1. Heroes & Villains

Title: Beach Boys 69'
Release Date: 27th June 2001
Record Label: Toshiba-EMI
CD Ref. No: TOCP-53176
Country: Japan
No. of Disks: 1
Format: Audio CD
Audio: HDCD stereo
Liner Notes: Song Lyrics

Title: Sunflower
Release Date: 30th Aug. 2000
Record Label: Toshiba-EMI
CD Ref. No: TOCP-65565
Country: Japan
No. of Disks: 1
Format: Audio CD
Audio: stereo
Liner Notes: Song Lyrics

Title: Surf's Up
Release Date: 30th Aug. 2000
Record Label: Toshiba-EMI
CD Ref. No: TOCP-65566
Country: Japan
No. of Disks: 1
Format: Audio CD
Audio: stereo
Liner Notes: Song Lyrics

The Beach Boys on CD: Japan, Current releases

カール&ザ・パッションズ～ソー・タフ
CARL & THE PASSIONS ~ SO TOUGH

Title: Carl & The Passions
Release Date: 27th Sept. 2000
Record Label: Toshiba-EMI
CD Ref. No: TOCP-65567
Country: Japan
No. of Disks: 1
Format: Audio CD
Audio: stereo
Liner Notes: Song Lyrics

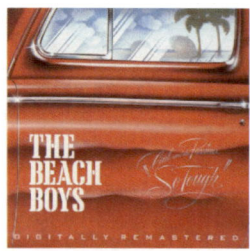

オランダ
HOLLAND

Title: Holland
Release Date: 27th Sept. 2000
Record Label: Toshiba-EMI
CD Ref. No: TOCP-65568
Country: Japan
No. of Disks: 1
Format: Audio CD
Audio: stereo
Liner Notes: Song Lyrics

ビーチ・ボーイズ・イン・コンサート
BEACH BOYS IN CONCERT

Title: In Concert
Release Date: 30th Aug, 2000
Record Label: Toshiba-EMI
CD Ref. No: TOCP-65569
Country: Japan
No. of Disks: 1
Format: Audio CD
Audio: stereo
Liner Notes: Song Lyrics

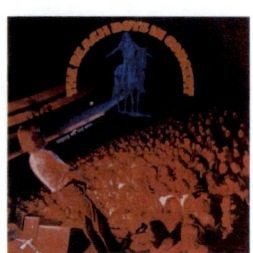

15ビッグ・ワンズ
15 BIG ONES

Title: 15 Big Ones
Release Date: 27th Sept. 2000
Record Label: Toshiba-EMI
CD Ref. No: TOCP-65570
Country: Japan
No. of Disks: 1
Format: Audio CD
Audio: stereo
Liner Notes: Song Lyrics

ラヴ・ユー
LOVE YOU

Title: Love You
Release Date: 27th Sept. 2000
Record Label: Toshiba-EMI
CD Ref. No: TOCP-65571
Country: Japan
No. of Disks: 1
Format: Audio CD
Audio: stereo
Liner Notes: Song Lyrics

The Beach Boys on CD: Japan, Current releases

M.I.U.アルバム
M.I.U. ALBUM

Title: M.I.U.
Release Date: 27th Sept.. 2000
Record Label: Toshiba-EMI
CD Ref. No: TOCP-65572
Country: Japan
No. of Disks: 1
Format: Audio CD
Audio: stereo
Liner Notes: Song Lyrics

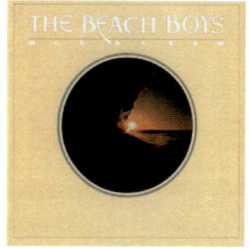

L.A.(ライト・アルバム)
L.A. (LIGHT ALBUM)

Title: L.A. (Light Album)
Release Date: 27th Sept. 2000
Record Label: Toshiba-EMI
CD Ref. No: TOCP-65573
Country: Japan
No. of Disks: 1
Format: Audio CD
Audio: stereo
Liner Notes: Song Lyrics

キーピン・ザ・サマー・アライヴ
KEEPIN' THE SUMMER ALIVE

Title: Keepin' The Summer Alive
Release Date: 27th Sept. 2000
Record Label: Toshiba-EMI
CD Ref. No: TOCP-65574
Country: Japan
No. of Disks: 1
Format: Audio CD
Audio: stereo
Liner Notes: Song Lyrics

ザ・ビーチ・ボーイズ '85
THE BEACH BOYS '85

Title: The Beach Boys
Release Date: 27th Sept 2000
Record Label: Toshiba-EMI
CD Ref. No: TOCP-65575
Country: Japan
No. of Disks: 1
Format: Audio CD
Audio: stereo
Liner Notes: Song Lyrics

スティル・クルージン
STILL CRUISIN'

Title: Still Cruisin'
Release Date: 17th Oct. 1997
Record Label: Toshiba-EMI
CD Ref. No: TOCP-3330
Country: Japan
No. of Disks: 1
Format: Audio CD
Audio: stereo
Liner Notes: Song Lyrics

The Beach Boys on CD: Japan, Current releases

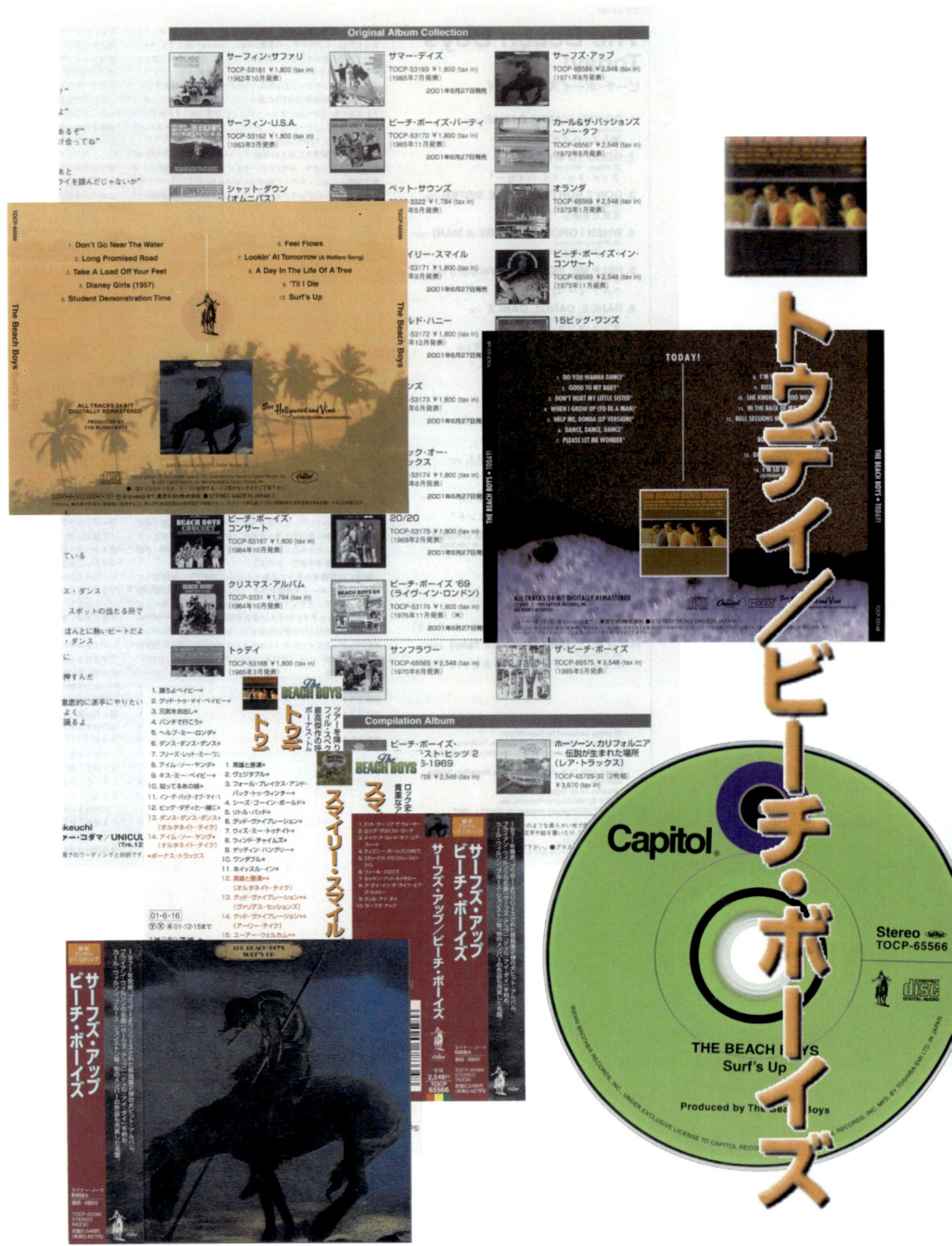

Japan - Greatest Hits

Track Listing, Greatest Hits II 1962~1965

#	Title	Time
1.	Surfin' Safari (mono)	2:05
2.	409 (mono)	1:58
3.	Surfin' (mono)	2:09
4.	Surfin' U.S.A.	2:27
5.	Shut Down	1:49
6.	Surfer Girl	2:26
7.	Little Deuce Coupe	1:37
8.	In My Room	2:11
9.	Be True To Your School (mono)	2:06
10.	Cherry, Cherry Coupe	1:47
11.	Spirit of America	2:23
12.	Fun, Fun, Fun (mono)	2:18
13.	Why Do Fools Fall In Love (mono)	1:57
14.	Don't Worry Baby (mono)	2:42
15.	The Warmth of the Sun	2:53
16.	I Get Around (mono)	2:10
17.	All Summer Long (mono)	2:06
18.	Little Honda	1:51
19.	Girls on the Beach	2:23
20.	Dance, Dance, Dance (mono)	1:58
21.	Do You Wanna Dance (mono)	2:17
22.	She Knows Me Too Well (mono)	2:28
23.	Please Let Me Wonder (mono)	2:44
24.	Kiss Me, Baby (mono)	2:33
25.	Help Me, Rhonda (mono)	2:45
26.	California Girls (mono)	2:36
27.	Girl Don't Tell Me (mono)	2:18
28.	The Little Girl I Once Knew	2:35
29.	There's No Other (like my baby) (mono)	3:00
30.	Barbara Ann (mono)	2:05

Title: Greatest Hits 1 1962-1965
Release Date: (I & II – Apr. 2000 & June 2001)
Record Label: Toshiba-EMI.
CD Ref. No: Vol.I TOCP-65727 (orig. TOCP-0201)
Vol.II TOCP-65728 (orig. TOCP-0202)
Vol.III TOCP-65457 (June, 2000)
Country: Japan
No. of Disks: 1
Format: Audio CD
Audio: Mono/stereo
Liner Notes: Song Lyrics

Album & Track Notes

Originally a two CD set, the Greatest Hits series was originally released in 2000 and subsequently re-released as a three CD set (with additional tracks on Vols. I & II) in 2001. The third disk contains tracks from 'The Brother Years". This is a great series and the three CD set contains over 80 tracks, great value. Each CD contains an extensive booklet containing song lyrics but once again it's a pity that the liner notes are only provided in Japanese. The OBI strips provide general information in Japanese

The Beach Boys on CD: Japan, Greatest Hits

Track Listing, Greatest Hits II 1966-1969

1. WOULDN'T IT BE NICE
2. YOU STILL BELIEVE IN ME
3. DON'T TALK (Put Your Head On My Shoulder)
4. SLOOP JOHN B.
5. GOD ONLY KNOWS
6. I JUST WASN'T MADE FOR THERE TIMES
7. CAROLINE, NO
8. GOOD VIBRATIONS
9. HEROES AND VILLAINS
10. YOU'RE WELCOME
11. GETTIN' HUNGRY
12. THEIR HEARTS WERE FULL OF SPRING
13. WILD HONEY
14. I WAS MADE TO LOVE HER
15. DARLIN'
16. HERE COMES THE NIGHT
17. FRIENDS
18. BE HERE IN THE MORNING
19. WAKE THE WORLD
20. BUSY DOIN' NOTHIN'
21. DO IT AGAIN
22. BLUEBIRDS OVER THE MOUNTAIN
23. I CAN HEAR MUSIC
24. ALL I WANT TO DO
25. COTTON FIELDS (THE COTTON SONG)
26. IME TO GET ALONE
27. ELEBRATE THE NEWS
28. BREAKAWAY

Track Listing, Greatest Hits III 1970-1986

1. ADD SOME MUSIC TO YOUR DAY
2. SUSIE CINCINNATI
3. THIS WHOLE WORLD
4. TEARS IN THE MORNING
5. LONG PROMISED ROAD
6. TIL I DIE
7. SURF'S UP
8. MARCELLA
9. SAIL ON, SAILOR
10. THE TRADER
11. CALIFORNIA SAGA (On My Way to Sunny - California)
12. ROCK AND ROLL MUSIC
13. IT'S O.K.
14. HONKIN' DOWN THE HIGHWAY
15. PEGGY SUE
16. HERE COMES THE NIGHT
17. GOOD TIMIN'
18. SUMAHAMA
19. GOIN' ON
20. OME GO WITH ME
21. GETCHA BACK
22. CALIFORNIA DREAMIN'

グレイテスト・ヒッツ

Back Cover: TOCP-0202

Beach Boys on CD: I Can Hear Music + Others

Track Listing, Disk 1 (Titles & Time)...

#	Title	Time
1.	I Can Hear Music	2:37
2.	Sweet Sunday Kinda Love	2:42
3.	The Trader	5:04
4.	Livin' With A Heartache	4:05
5.	Girl Can't Tell Me (mono)	2:19
6.	Marcella	3:53
7.	God Only Knows	2:53
8.	San Miguel	2:25
9.	Only With You	2:58
10.	Darlin' (mono)	2:12
11.	This Whole World	1:56
12.	Full Sail	2:56
13.	Palisades Park	2:28
14.	Long Promised Road	3:29
15.	Good Timin'	2:11
16.	The Night Was So Young	2:13
17.	Wild Honey (mono)	2:38
18.	Good Vibrations (mono)	3:36
19.	Steamboat	4:33
20.	She Believes In Love Again	3:29
21.	I'll Bet He's Nice	2:35
22.	Goin' South	3:15

Total Playing time: 25:34

Title: I Can Hear Music
Release Date: 26th July 2002
Record Label: Toshiba-EMI.
CD Ref. No: TOCP-66035
Country: Japan
No. of Disks: 1
Format: Audio CD
Audio: Mono/Stereo
Liner Notes: Song Lyrics

Album & Track Notes

Every Beach Boys fan should own this album. Released only in Japan, the CD contains a great selection of songs with Carl Wilson on lead vocals and the sound quality of the re-mastering is excellent. The CD contains 22 of Carl's greatest contributions on record and blasts of with one of his finest, "I Can Hear Music". The CD contains an extensive booklet containing song lyrics; it's a pity that the liner notes are only provided in Japanese. The OBI strip provides general information in Japanese. This CD is part of the Pet Sounds 2002 series released by Toshiba-EMI

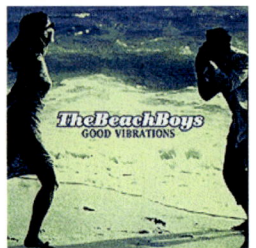

Title: Good Vibrations (The Beach Boys)
Release Date: August 8th, 1997
Record Label: Toshiba-EMI.
CD Ref. No: TOCP-50135
Country: Japan
No. of Disks: 1
Format: Audio CD
Audio: Mono/Stereo
Liner Notes: Song Lyrics

Title: Super Now (The Beach Boys)
Release Date: Dec. 10th, 1997
Record Label: Toshiba-EMI.
CD Ref. No: TOCP-51001
Country: Japan
No. of Disks: 1
Format: Audio CD
Audio: Mono/Stereo
Liner Notes: Song Lyrics

Title: The California Dream (Best of The Beach Boys)
Release Date: Dec. 4th, 1996
Record Label: Toshiba-EMI.
CD Ref. No: TOCP-50107-8
Country: Japan
No. of Disks: 2
Format: Audio CD
Audio: Mono/Stereo
Liner Notes: Song Lyrics

Title: The Beach Boys Greatest
Release Date: Mar. 30th, 1998
Record Label: Toshiba-EMI.
CD Ref. No: TOCP-51076
Country: Japan
No. of Disks: 1
Format: Audio CD
Audio: Mono/Stereo
Liner Notes: Song Lyrics

Title: For The Girls
Release Date: 1993
Record Label: Toshiba-EMI.
CD Ref. No: TOCP-7870
Country: Japan
No. of Disks: 1
Format: Audio CD
Audio: Mono/Stereo
Liner Notes: Song

Bootleg Sounds
(unofficial releases of Beach Boys music)

The issue of bootlegs releases (of any artist) will provide opposing argument and heated discussion. Since the central purpose of this book is to present information on the availability of Beach Boys music on CD, it is unavoidable that 'non official' (and usually widely available) releases would be detailed. Non-official releases fall into two categories; CD's of Studio based work and unofficial recording of live concerts. With that said, in the following pages I shall present the detail of the most (in)famous non official releases of the Beach Boys music, including 'The Unsurpassed Masters Series,' 'The VIGOtone (Spank & Pegboy) releases, The Dumb Angel Rarities series, Deep Sea Treasures and certain other known unofficial studio and live CD releases. I shall illustrate/detail only those CD's which I have personally had experience of hearing. For a fuller examination of 'non official' releases, I would point the reader to the following Web sites for further information: www.cabinessence.com/brian & http://www.vigotone.com/ & http://dauber.www3.50megs.com/index.html

The pastiche below illustrates an assortment of available CD releases. The quality of the sound and packaging varies from bootleg issue to issue. It is also important not to judge the book by its cover; if you are considering the purchase of an unofficial release, do some research first; some of the stuff out there is just awful and lends weight to the anti-bootleg argument.

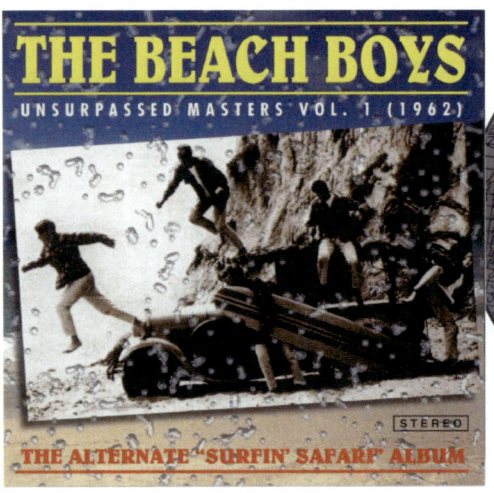

Title: UM Vol. 1, The Alternative Surfin' Safari
Release Date: 1997
Record Label: Sea of Tunes
CD ref. No: C 9703
Country: World
No. of Disks: 1
Format: Audio CD
Audio: mono/stereo
Liner Notes: N/A

Title: UM Vol. 2, The Alternative "Surfin' USA".
Release Date: 1997
Record Label: Sea of Tunes
CD ref. No: C 9704
Country: World
No. of Disks: 1
Format: Audio CD
Audio: mono/stereo
Liner Notes: N/A

Title: UM Vol. 3, The Alternative "Surfer Girl"
Release Date: 1997
Record Label: Sea of Tunes
CD ref. No: C 9705
Country: World
No. of Disks: 1
Format: Audio CD
Audio: mono/stereo
Liner Notes: N/A

Title: UM Vol. 4, Miscellaneous Trax
Release Date: 1997
Record Label: Sea of Tunes
CD ref. No: C 9706 & C 9707
Country: World
No. of Disks: 2
Format: Audio CD
Audio: mono/stereo
Liner Notes: N/A

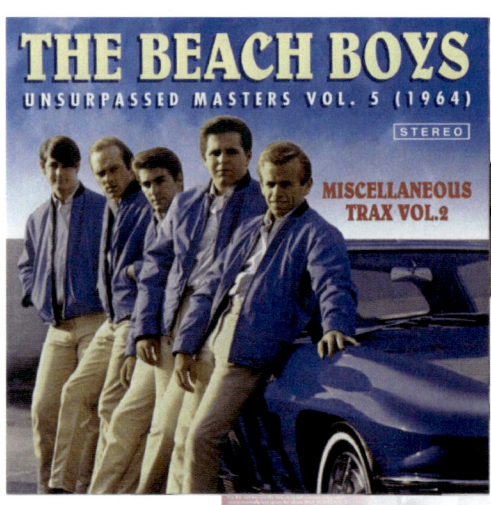

Title: UM Vol. 5, Miscellaneous Trax Vol. 2
Release Date: 1998
Record Label: Sea of Tunes
CD ref. No: C 9711
Country: World
No. of Disks: 2
Format: Audio CD
Audio: mono/stereo
Liner Notes: N/A

Title: UM Vol. 6, The Alternative "All Summer Long"
Release Date: 1998
Record Label: Sea of Tunes
CD ref. No: C 9712/13/14
Country: World
No. of Disks: 3
Format: Audio CD
Audio: mono/stereo
Liner Notes: N/A

Bootleg Sounds
(unofficial releases of Beach Boys music)

The issue of bootlegs releases (of any artist) will provide opposing argument and heated discussion. Since the central purpose of this book is to present information on the availability of Beach Boys music on CD, it is unavoidable that 'non official' (and usually widely available) releases would be detailed. Non-official releases fall into two categories; CD's of Studio based work and unofficial recording of live concerts. With that said, in the following pages I shall present the detail of the most (in)famous non official releases of the Beach Boys music, including 'The Unsurpassed Masters Series, 'The VIGOtone (Spank & Pegboy) releases, The Dumb Angel Rarities series, Deep Sea Treasures and certain other known unofficial studio and live CD releases. I shall illustrate/detail only those CD's which I have personally had experience of hearing. For a fuller examination of 'non official' releases, I would point the reader to the following Web sites for further information: www.cabinessence.com/brian & http://www.vigotone.com/ & http://dauber.www3.50megs.com/index.html

The pastiche below illustrates an assortment of available CD releases. The quality of the sound and packaging varies from bootleg issue to issue. It is also important not to judge the book by its cover; if you are considering the purchase of an unofficial release, do some research first; some of the stuff out there is just awful and lends weight to the anti-bootleg argument.

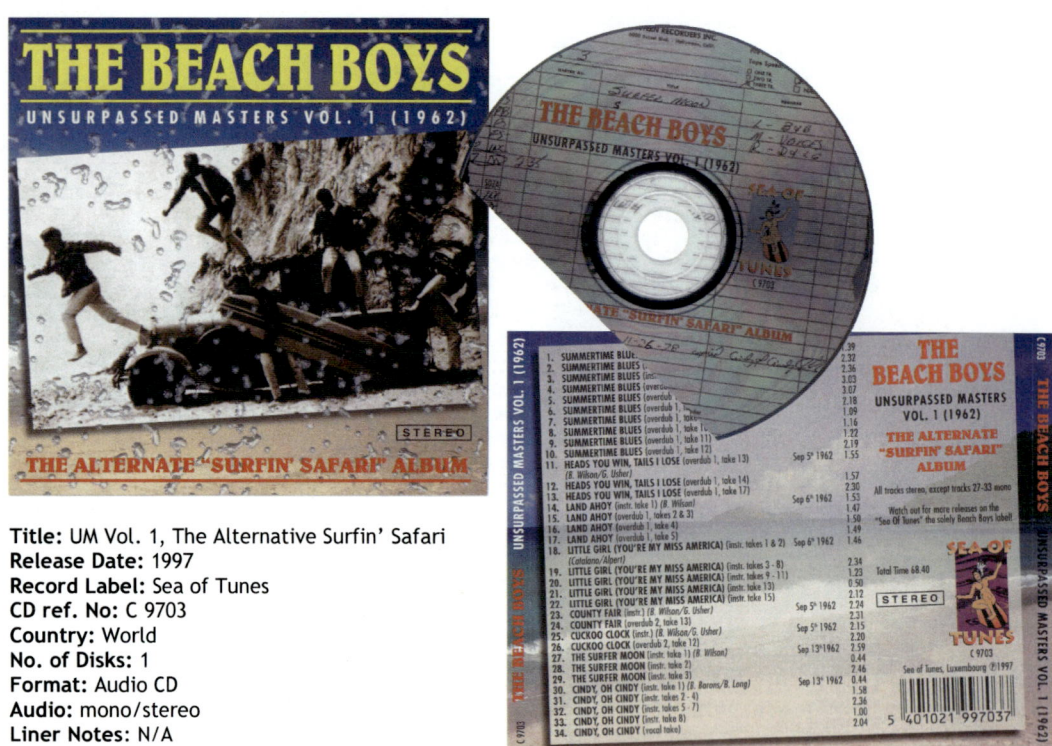

Title: UM Vol. 1, The Alternative Surfin' Safari
Release Date: 1997
Record Label: Sea of Tunes
CD ref. No: C 9703
Country: World
No. of Disks: 1
Format: Audio CD
Audio: mono/stereo
Liner Notes: N/A

Title: UM Vol. 2, The Alternative "Surfin' USA".
Release Date: 1997
Record Label: Sea of Tunes
CD ref. No: C 9704
Country: World
No. of Disks: 1
Format: Audio CD
Audio: mono/stereo
Liner Notes: N/A

Title: UM Vol. 3, The Alternative "Surfer Girl"
Release Date: 1997
Record Label: Sea of Tunes
CD ref. No: C 9705
Country: World
No. of Disks: 1
Format: Audio CD
Audio: mono/stereo
Liner Notes: N/A

Title: UM Vol. 4, Miscellaneous Trax
Release Date: 1997
Record Label: Sea of Tunes
CD ref. No: C 9706 & C 9707
Country: World
No. of Disks: 2
Format: Audio CD
Audio: mono/stereo
Liner Notes: N/A

Title: UM Vol. 5, Miscellaneous Trax Vol. 2
Release Date: 1998
Record Label: Sea of Tunes
CD ref. No: C 9711
Country: World
No. of Disks: 2
Format: Audio CD
Audio: mono/stereo
Liner Notes: N/A

Title: UM Vol. 6, The Alternative "All Summer Long"
Release Date: 1998
Record Label: Sea of Tunes
CD ref. No: C 9712/13/14
Country: World
No. of Disks: 3
Format: Audio CD
Audio: mono/stereo
Liner Notes: N/A

The Beach Boys on CD: Bootlegs

Title: UM Vol. 7, The Alternative "Today"
Release Date: 1998
Record Label: Sea of Tunes
CD ref. No: C 9715/16/17/18
Country: World
No. of Disks: 4
Format: Audio CD
Audio: mono/stereo
Liner Notes: N/A

Title: UM Vol. 8, The Alternative "Today" Vol. 2
Release Date: 1998
Record Label: Sea of Tunes
CD ref. No: C 9719/20/21/22
Country: World
No. of Disks: 4
Format: Audio CD
Audio: mono/stereo
Liner Notes: N/A

The Beach Boys on CD: Bootlegs

Title: UM Vol. 9, The Alternative "Summer Days (and Summer Nights)"
Release Date: 1998
Record Label: Sea of Tunes
CD ref. No: C 9723/24/25/26
Country: World
No. of Disks: 4
Format: Audio CD
Audio: mono/stereo
Liner Notes: N/A

THE BEACH BOYS — UNSURPASSED MASTERS VOL. 9 (1965) DISC 1

Feb 24th 1965	1. HELP ME, RHONDA (take 1) (B. Wilson)	stereo	4.45
	2. HELP ME, RHONDA (takes 2-5)	stereo	2.08
	3. HELP ME, RHONDA (take 6)	stereo	3.34
	4. HELP ME, RHONDA (1st vocal overdub)	mono	3.38
	5. HELP ME, RHONDA (2nd vocal overdub)	stereo	3.09
March 29th 1965	6. SANDY (rehearsals) (B. Wilson)	mono	2.48
	7. SANDY (track only)	mono	3.07
	8. SANDY (rehearsals)	mono	2.40
	9. SANDY (instrumental insert)	stereo	2.51
	10. SANDY (chorus rehearsal)	mono	0.43
	11. SANDY (instrumental insert)	stereo	2.46
	12. SANDY (1st vocal overdub)	stereo	7.46
	13. SANDY (2nd vocal overdub)	stereo	2.48
March 30th 1965	14. LET HIM RUN WILD (take 16) (B. Wilson)	mono	2.54
	15. LET HIM RUN WILD (instrumental insert)	stereo	2.48
	16. LET HIM RUN WILD (1st vocal overdub 1 & 2)	mono	2.24
	17. LET HIM RUN WILD (1st vocal overdub 3)	mono	2.22
	18. LET HIM RUN WILD (2nd vocal overdub 1-8)	mono	8.49
	19. LET HIM RUN WILD (mono mix)	mono	2.18

[Total time: 59.43]

DISC 2

March 30th 1965	1. SALT LAKE CITY (rehearsals) (B. Wilson)	stereo	10.47
	2. SALT LAKE CITY (takes 1-3)	stereo	3.59
	3. SALT LAKE CITY (takes 4-8)	stereo	4.13
	4. SALT LAKE CITY (intro rehearsals)	stereo	4.41
	5. SALT LAKE CITY (take 9)	stereo	2.17
April 6th 1965	6. CALIFORNIA GIRLS (takes 5 & 6) (B. Wilson)	stereo	1.44
	7. CALIFORNIA GIRLS (take 7)	stereo	3.06
	8. CALIFORNIA GIRLS (rehearsals)	stereo	3.29
	9. CALIFORNIA GIRLS (takes 8-14)	stereo	3.13
	10. CALIFORNIA GIRLS (take 15)	stereo	2.58
	11. CALIFORNIA GIRLS (takes 16-38)	stereo	17.00
	12. CALIFORNIA GIRLS (takes 39 & 40)	stereo	3.06
	13. CALIFORNIA GIRLS (take 41)	stereo	3.20
	14. CALIFORNIA GIRLS (takes 42-44)	stereo	4.03

[Total time: 68.13]

DISC 3

April 30th 1965	1. GIRL DON'T TELL ME (rehearsals) (B. Wilson)	mono	3.59
	2. GIRL DON'T TELL ME (takes 1-6)	mono	7.18
	3. GIRL DON'T TELL ME (take 7)	mono	3.20
	4. GIRL DON'T TELL ME (takes 8-10)	mono	4.06
	5. GIRL DON'T TELL ME (takes 11-16)	mono	4.40
	6. GIRL DON'T TELL ME (take 16)	mono	3.1
	7. GIRL DON'T TELL ME (instrumental insert)	stereo	2.5
	8. GIRL DON'T TELL ME (vocal overdub)	stereo	2.5
May 3rd 1965	9. THEN I KISSED HER (rehearsals) (P. Spector/E. Greenwich/J. Barry)	mono	3.2
	10. THEN I KISSED HER (takes 1 & 2)	mono	2.4
	11. THEN I KISSED HER (takes 3-12)	mono	8.4
	12. THEN I KISSED HER (takes 13-15)	mono	2.0
	13. THEN I KISSED HER (take 16)	mono	2.2
	14. THEN I KISSED HER (1st instrumental insert)	stereo	2.2
	15. THEN I KISSED HER (2nd instrumental insert)	stereo	2.2
	16. THEN I KISSED HER (1st vocal overdub)	stereo	2.3
	17. THEN I KISSED HER (2nd vocal overdub)	stereo	2.3

[Total time: 62.3]

DISC 4

May 5th 1965	1. GRADUATION DAY (vocal rehearsals) (J. Sherman/N. Sherman)	stereo	7.11
	2. GRADUATION DAY (vocal take)	stereo	3.11
	3. GRADUATION DAY (vocal take)	stereo	2.17
	4. GRADUATION DAY (vocal overdub)	stereo	2.21
May 5th 1965	5. AMUSEMENT PARK USA (take 9) (B. Wilson)	mono	3.02
	6. AMUSEMENT PARK USA (1st vocal overdub)	stereo	3.01
	7. AMUSEMENT PARK USA (2nd vocal overdub)	stereo	3.01
May 24th 1965	8. YOU'RE SO GOOD TO ME (rehearsal) (B. Wilson)	mono	2.34
	9. YOU'RE SO GOOD TO ME (takes 1-6)	mono	5.07
	10. YOU'RE SO GOOD TO ME (take 7a)	mono	1.04
	11. YOU'RE SO GOOD TO ME (take 7b)	mono	0.59
	12. YOU'RE SO GOOD TO ME (takes 8-16)	mono	4.14
	13. YOU'RE SO GOOD TO ME (take 17)	mono	3.30
	14. YOU'RE SO GOOD TO ME (takes 18-23)	mono	1.55
	15. YOU'RE SO GOOD TO ME (take 24)	mono	2.23
	16. YOU'RE SO GOOD TO ME (instrumental insert)	stereo	2.25
May 24th 1965	17. THE GIRL FROM NEW YORK CITY (take 1) (B. Wilson)	mono	1.33
	18. THE GIRL FROM NEW YORK CITY (take 2)	mono	1.00
	19. THE GIRL FROM NEW YORK CITY (takes 3-13)	mono	7.05
	20. THE GIRL FROM NEW YORK CITY (take 15)	mono	1.30
	21. THE GIRL FROM NEW YORK CITY (take 16)	mono	2.37
	22. THE GIRL FROM NEW YORK CITY (take 17)	mono	2.34
	23. THE GIRL FROM NEW YORK CITY (vocal overdub)	stereo	2.26
	24. THE GIRL FROM NEW YORK CITY (vocal overdub)	stereo	2.24

[Total time: 70.06]

The Beach Boys on CD: Bootlegs

Title: UM Vol. 10, The Alternative "Beach Boys Party|
Release Date: 1998
Record Label: Sea of Tunes
CD ref. No: C 9727/28/29/30
Country: World
No. of Disks: 4
Format: Audio CD
Audio: stereo
Liner Notes: N/A

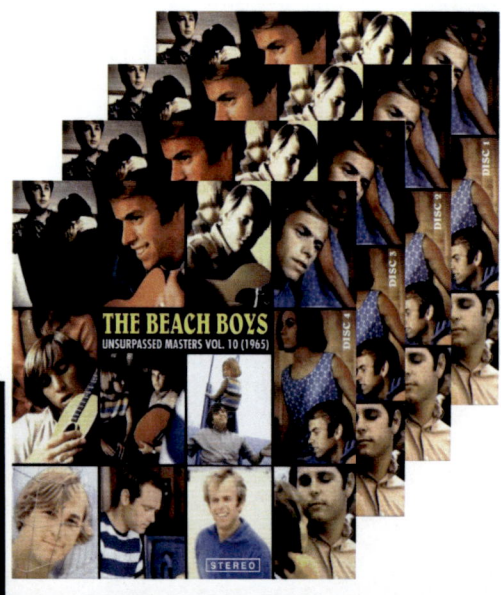

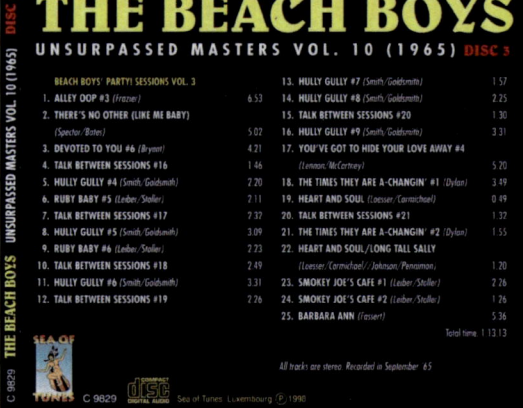

Title: UM Vol. 11 (1965)
Release Date: 1998
Record Label: Sea of Tunes
CD ref. No: C 9731/32
Country: World
No. of Disks: 2
Format: Audio CD
Audio: mono/stereo
Liner Notes: N/A

The Beach Boys on CD: Bootlegs

Title: UM Vol. 12, Sloop Joh B Sesson + Radio Spots
Release Date: 1998
Record Label: Sea of Tunes
CD ref. No: C 9733/34
Country: World
No. of Disks: 2
Format: Audio CD
Audio: mono/stereo
Liner Notes: N/A

Title: UM Vol. 13, The Alternative "Pet Sound" Vol.1
Release Date: 1998
Record Label: Sea of Tunes
CD ref. No: C 9735/36/37/38
Country: World
No. of Disks: 4
Format: Audio CD
Audio: mone/stereo
Liner Notes: N/A

Title: UM Vol. 14, The Alternative "Pet Sound" Vol. 2
Release Date: 1998
Record Label: Sea of Tunes
CD ref. No: C 9739/40/41/42
Country: World
No. of Disks: 4
Format: Audio CD
Audio: mono/stereo
iner Notes: N/A

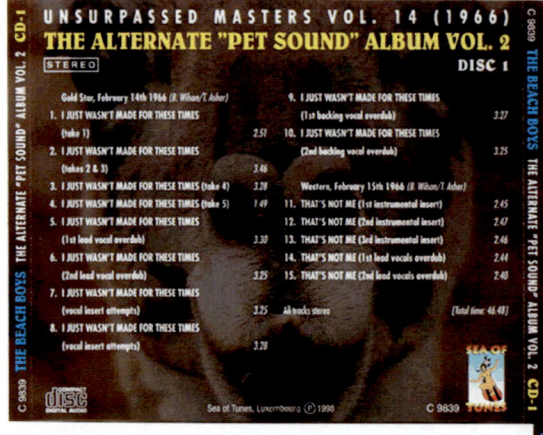

Title: UM Vol. 15, Good Vibrations
Release Date: 1999
Record Label: Sea of Tunes
CD ref. No: C 9946/47/48
Country: World
No. of Disks: 3
Format: Audio CD
Audio: mono/stereo
iner Notes: N/A

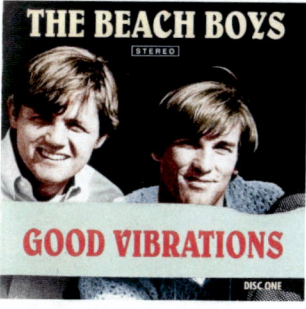

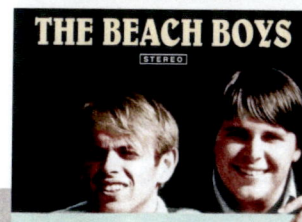

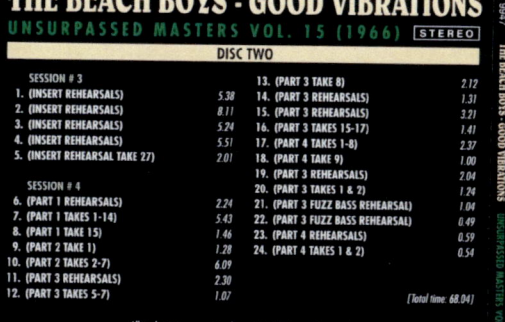

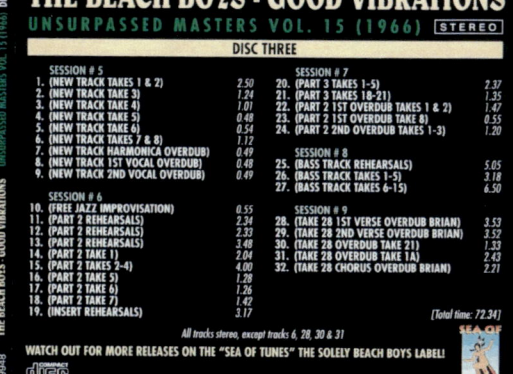

Title: UM Vol. 16, "SMiLE"
Release Date: 1999
Record Label: Sea of Tunes
CD ref. No: C 9949
Country: World
No. of Disks: 1
Format: Audio CD
Audio: mono/stereo
Liner Notes: N/A

CD & Track Notes

Pretty good sound quality, some background talking and noises; overall, a great introduction to the music of SMiLE. This CD is almost impossible to obtain.

The Beach Boys on CD: Bootlegs

Title: UM Vol. 17, "Smile Sessions"
Release Date: 1999
Record Label: Sea of Tunes
CD ref. No: C 9950/51/52
Country: World
No. of Disks: 3
Format: Audio CD
Audio: mono/stereo
Liner Notes: N/A

CD & Track Notes

Disk 1 - poor sound quality; an awful lot of background noise ("pitsville...") on most of the tracks...drive you nuts after 10 minutes. I would not rush out and buy this, even if it is a bootleg. Another argument against bootlegs...you are not protected from a QA standpoint. Disk 3 is great, fascinating to hear Brian Wilson conducting things...very lucid and very much in control. Sound quality on disk 3 is much better, no 'noise'.

The Beach Boys on CD: Bootlegs

Title: UM Vol. 18, The Alternative "Smiley Smile"
Release Date: 1999
Record Label: Sea of Tunes
CD ref. No: C 9953
Country: World
No. of Disks: 1
Format: Audio CD
Audio: stereo
Liner Notes: N/A

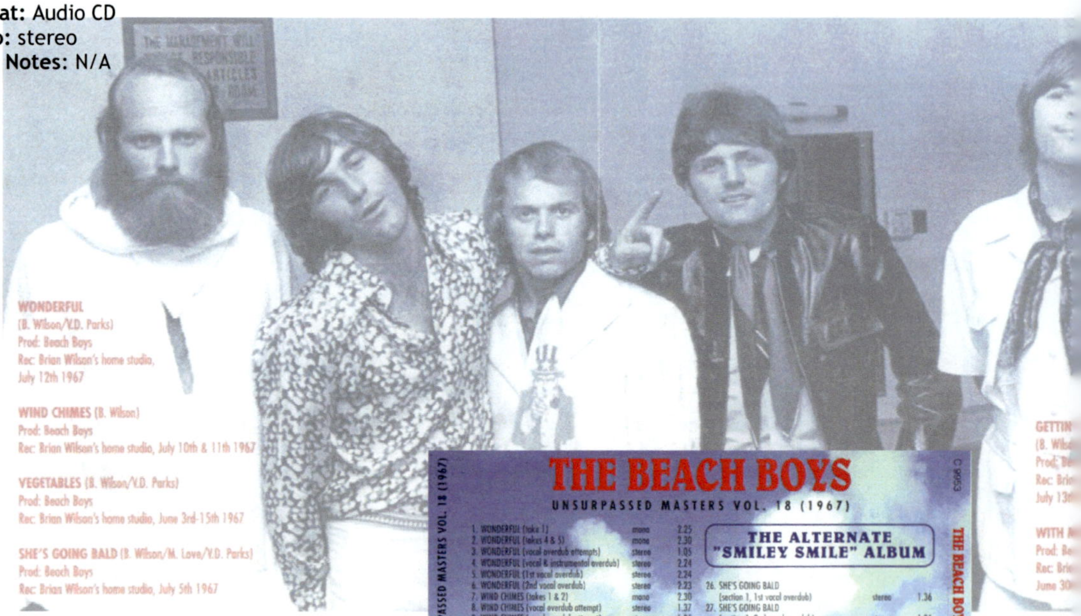

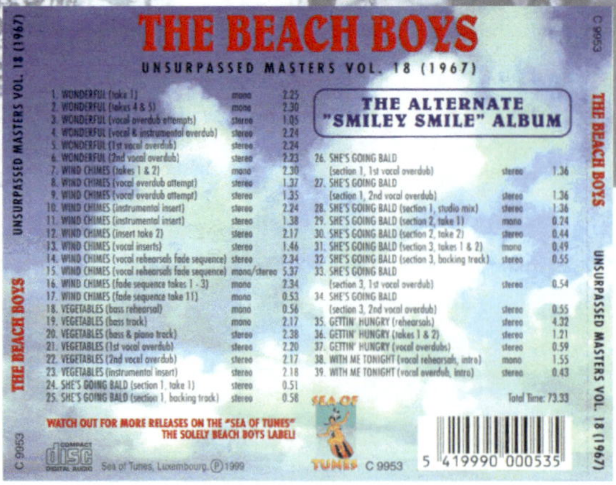

The Beach Boys on CD: Bootlegs

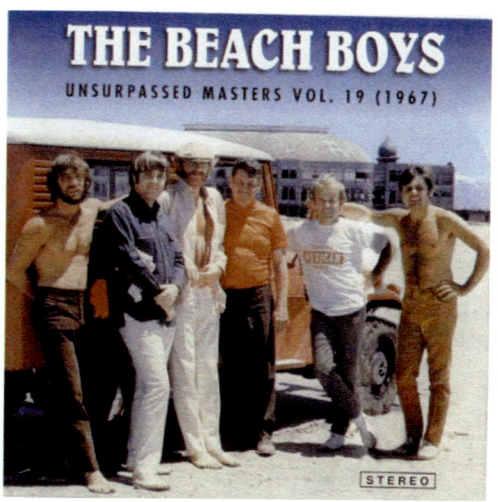

Title: UM Vol. 19, The Alternative "Wild Honey"
Release Date: 1999
Record Label: Sea of Tunes
CD ref. No: C 9954/55
Country: World
No. of Disks: 2
Format: Audio CD
Audio: mono/stereo
Liner Notes: N/A

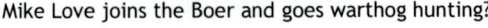

Mike Love joins the Boer and goes warthog hunting?

Title: UM Vol. 20, "Odds & Ends"
Release Date: 1999
Record Label: Sea of Tunes
CD ref. No: C 9956/57
Country: World
No. of Disks: 2
Format: Audio CD
Audio: mono/stereo
Liner Notes: N/A

The Beach Boys on CD: Bootlegs

Title: UM "Live in Sacramento"
Release Date: 1997
Record Label: Sea of Tunes
CD ref. No: C 9701
Country: World
No. of Disks: 1
Format: Audio CD
Audio: mono/stereo
Liner Notes: N/A

Title: UM "Live in Sacramento, 2nd Concert"
Release Date: 1997
Record Label: Sea of Tunes
CD ref. No: C 9702
Country: World
No. of Disks: 1
Format: Audio CD
Audio: mono/stereo
Liner Notes: N/A

Title: UM The Alternative "Beach Boys Christmas"
Release Date: 1997
Record Label: Sea of Tunes
CD ref. No: C 9708/9/10
Country: World
No. of Disks: 3
Format: Audio CD
Audio: mono/stereo
Liner Notes: N/A

CD & Track Notes

Not Heard

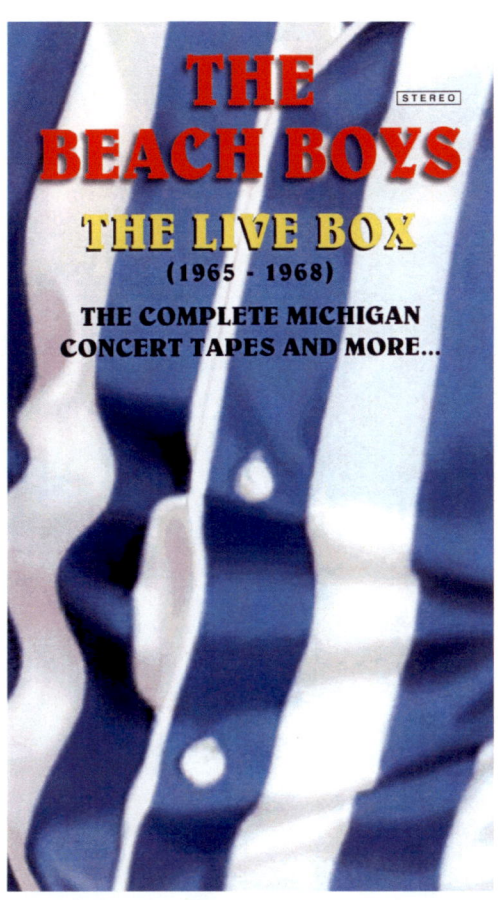

Title: UM "The Live Box"
Release Date: 1998
Record Label: Sea of Tunes
CD ref. No: C 9843/4/5
Country: World
No. of Disks: 3
Format: Audio CD
Audio: mono/stereo
Liner Notes: N/A

Album & Track Notes:

Not heard.

The Beach Boys on CD: Bootlegs

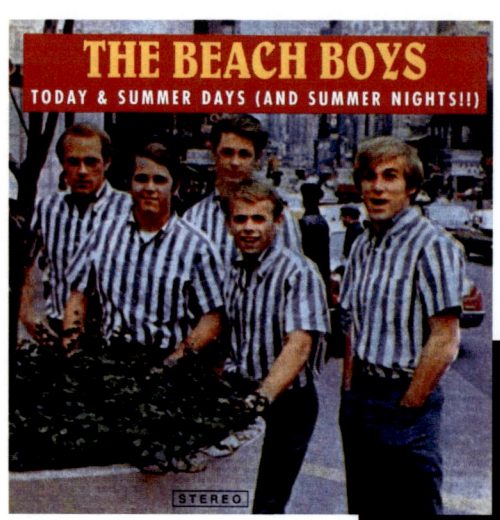

Title: UM Vol. 21, "Today & SD&SN)
Release Date: 1999
Record Label: Sea of Tunes
CD ref. No: C 9958
Country: World
No. of Disks: 1
Format: Audio CD
Audio: stereo
Liner Notes: N/A

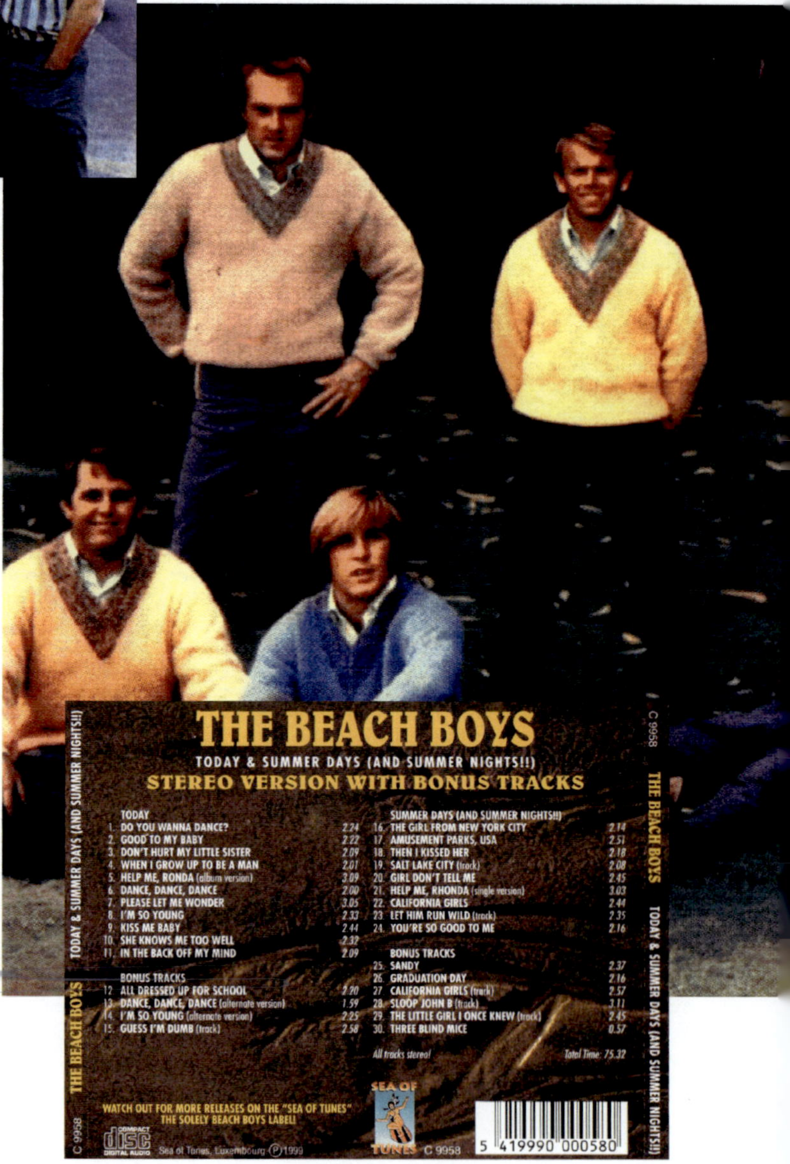

Title: Rarities Vol. 1: The Beach Boys 1962-1968
Release Date: 2001
Record Label: Dumb Angel
CD ref. No: DA 002
Country: World
No. of Disks: 1
Format: Audio CD
Audio: mono/stereo
Liner Notes: Booklet Photographs

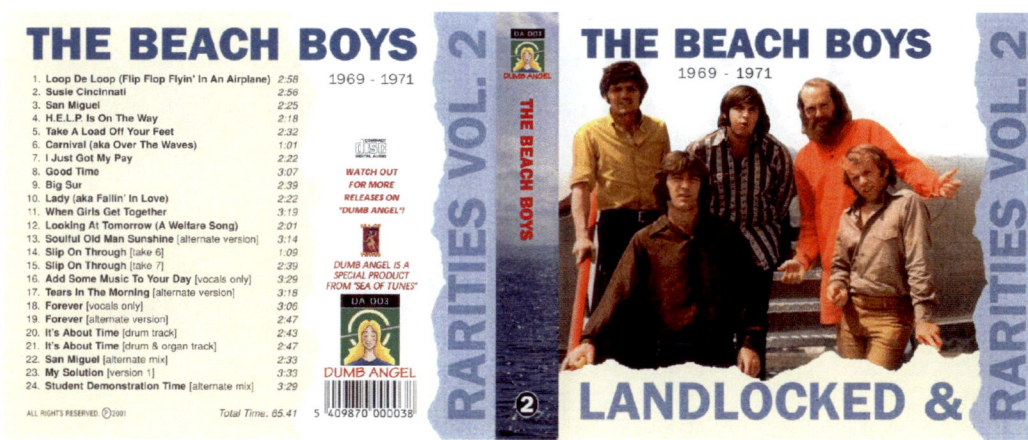

Title: Rarities Vol. 2: Landlocked & The Beach Boys 1969-1971
Release Date: 2001
Record Label: Dumb Angel
CD ref. No: DA 003
Country: World
No. of Disks: 1
Format: Audio CD
Audio: mono/stereo
Liner Notes: Booklet Photographs

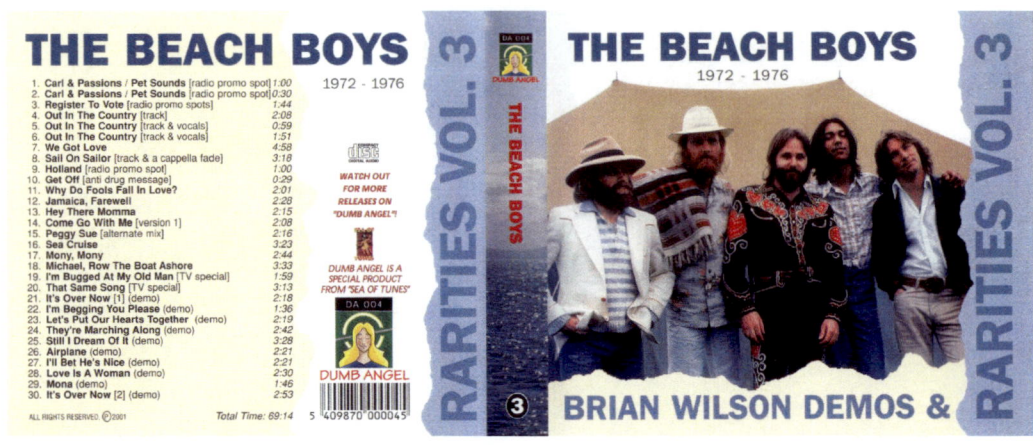

Title: Rarities Vol. 3: Brian Wilson Demos & The Beach Boys 1972-1976
Release Date: 2001
Record Label: Dumb Angel
CD ref. No: DA 004
Country: World
No. of Disks: 1
Format: Audio CD
Audio: mono/stereo
Liner Notes: Booklet Photographs

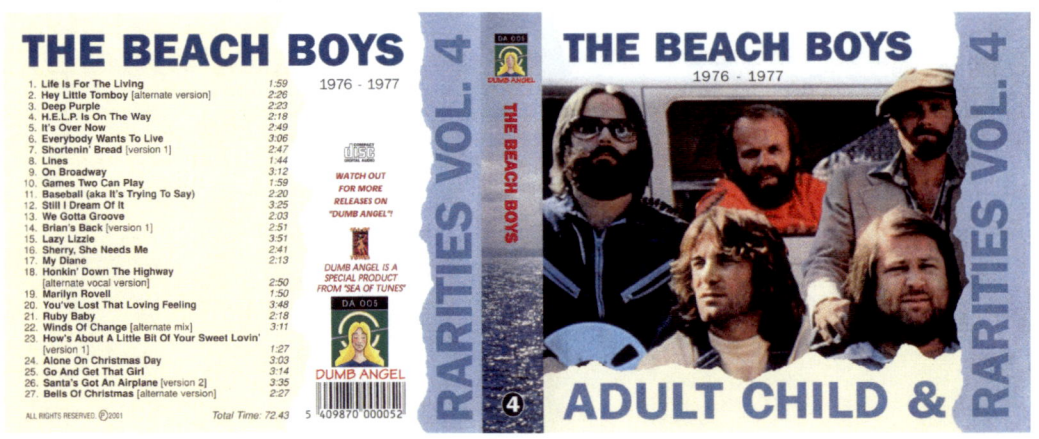

Title: Rarities Vol. 4: Adult Child & The Beach Boys 1976-1977
Release Date: 2001
Record Label: Dumb Angel
CD ref. No: DA 005
Country: World
No. of Disks: 1
Format: Audio CD
Audio: mono/stereo
Liner Notes: Booklet Photographs

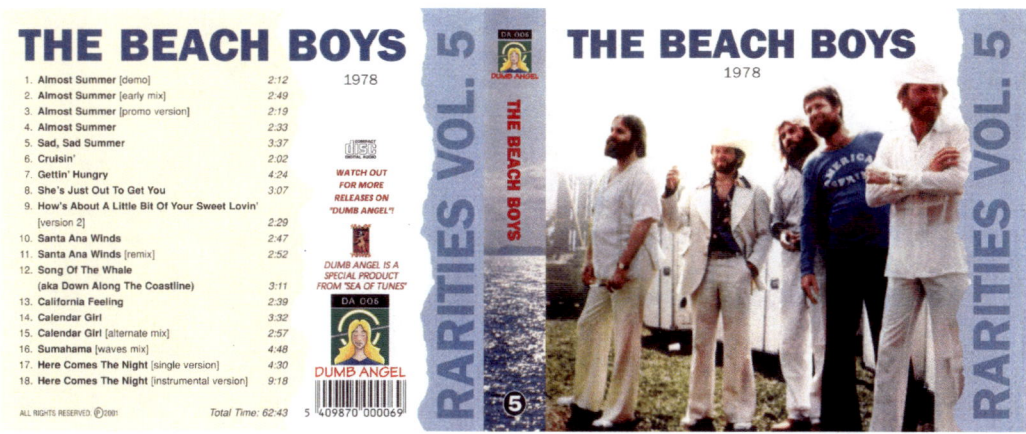

Title: Rarities Vol. 5: The Beach Boys 1978
Release Date: 2001
Record Label: Dumb Angel
CD ref. No: DA 006
Country: World
No. of Disks: 1
Format: Audio CD
Audio: mono/stereo
Liner Notes: Booklet Photographs

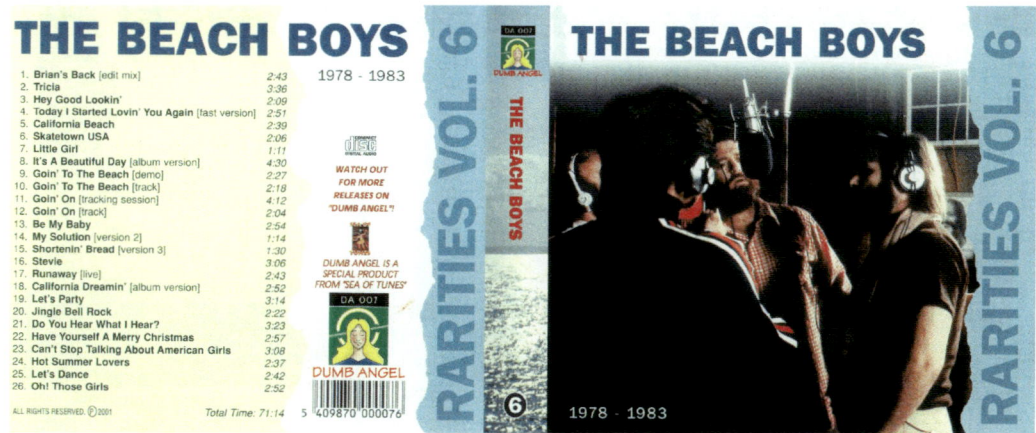

Title: Rarities Vol. 6: The Beach Boys 1978-1983
Release Date: 2001
Record Label: Dumb Angel
CD ref. No: DA 007
Country: World
No. of Disks: 1
Format: Audio CD
Audio: mono/stereo
Liner Notes: Booklet Photographs

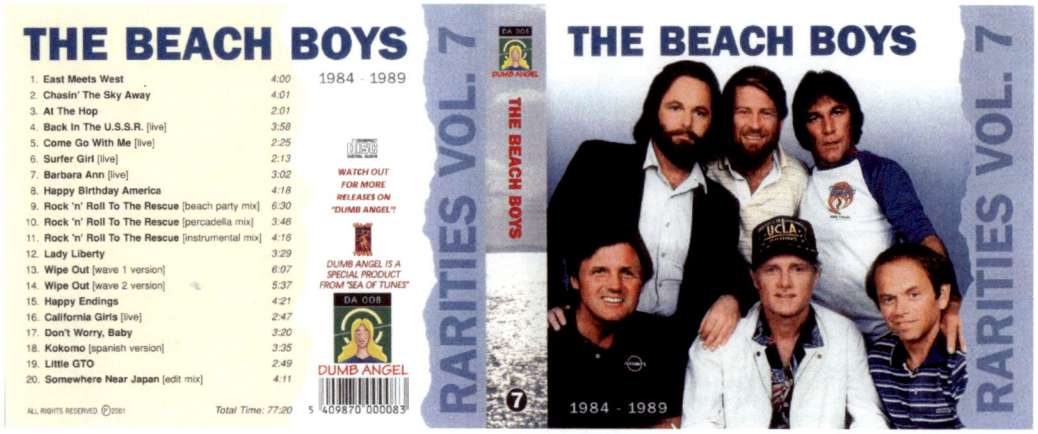

Title: Rarities Vol. 7: The Beach Boys 1984 - 1998
Release Date: 2001
Record Label: Dumb Angel
CD ref. No: DA 008
Country: World
No. of Disks: 1
Format: Audio CD
Audio: mono/stereo
Liner Notes: Booklet Photographs

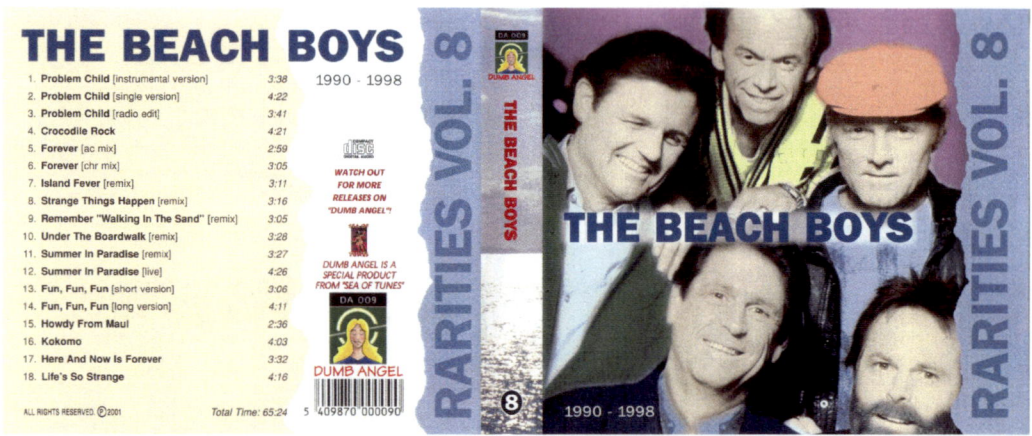

Title: Rarities Vol. 8: The Beach Boys 1990 - 1998
Release Date: 2001
Record Label: Dumb Angel
CD ref. No: DA 009
Country: World
No. of Disks: 1
Format: Audio CD
Audio: mono/stereo
Liner Notes: Booklet Photographs

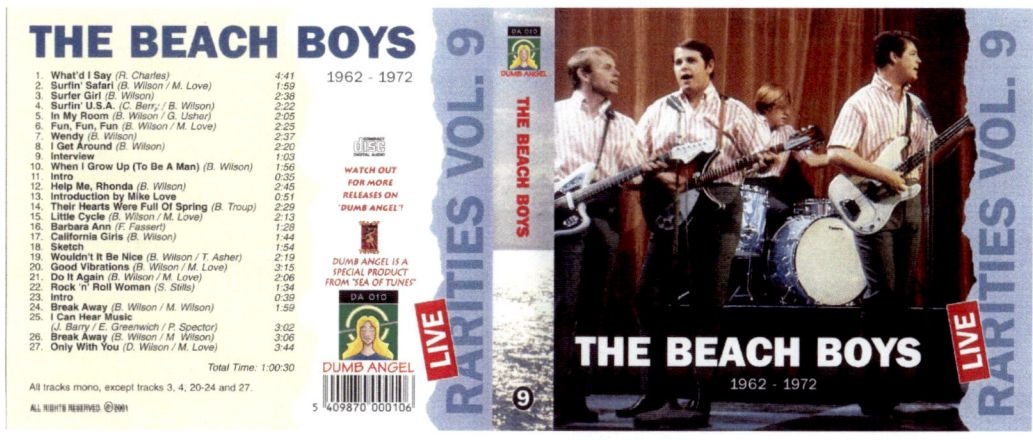

Title: Rarities Vol. 9: The Beach Boys Live 1962 - 1972
Release Date: 2001
Record Label: Dumb Angel
CD ref. No: DA 010
Country: World
No. of Disks: 1
Format: Audio CD
Audio: mono/stereo
Liner Notes: Booklet Photographs

Title: Rarities Vol. 10: The Beach Boys Live; Washington DC 1967, Lost Concert 1964
Release Date: 2001
Record Label: Dumb Angel
CD ref. No: DA 011
Country: World
No. of Disks: 1
Format: Audio CD
Audio: mono
Liner Notes: Booklet Photographs

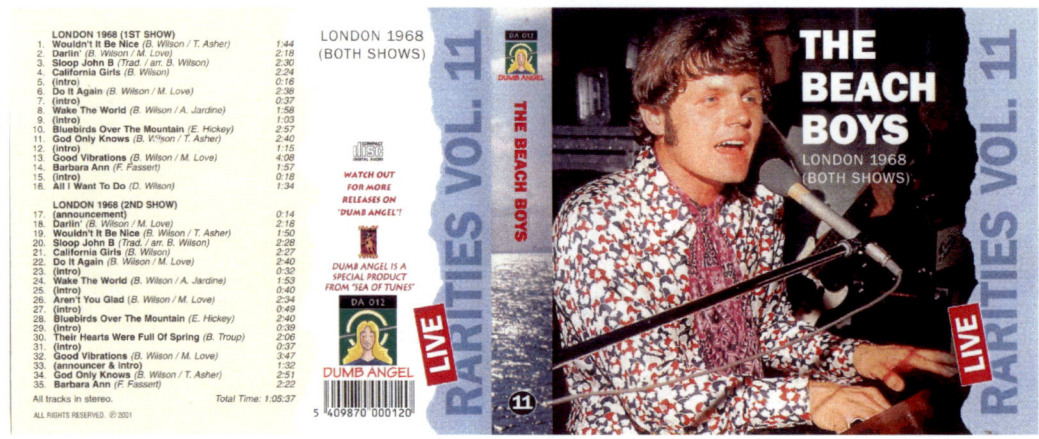

Title: Rarities Vol. 11: The Beach Boys Live; London 1968 (both shows)
Release Date: 2001
Record Label: Dumb Angel
CD ref. No: DA 012
Country: World
No. of Disks: 1
Format: Audio CD
Audio: stereo
Liner Notes: Booklet Photographs

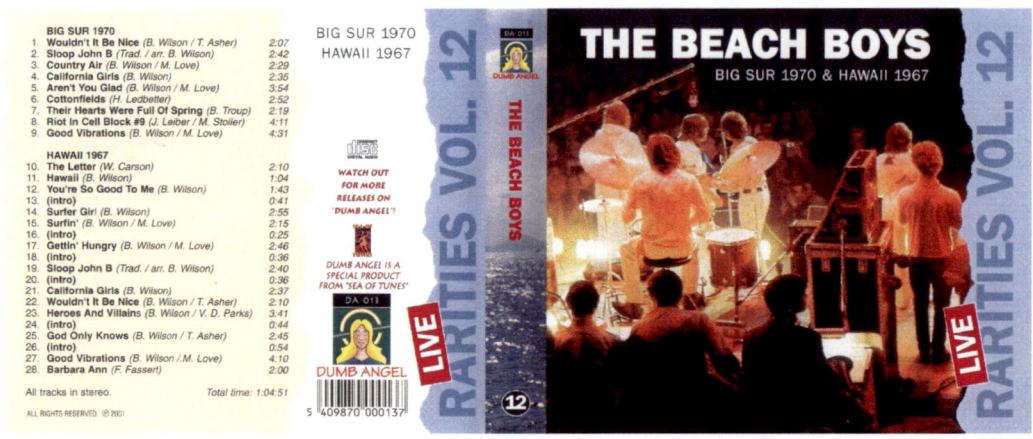

Title: Rarities Vol. 12: The Beach Boys Live; Big Sur 1970, Hawaii 1967
Release Date: 2001
Record Label: Dumb Angel
CD ref. No: DA 013
Country: World
No. of Disks: 1
Format: Audio CD
Audio: mono/stereo
Liner Notes: Booklet Photographs

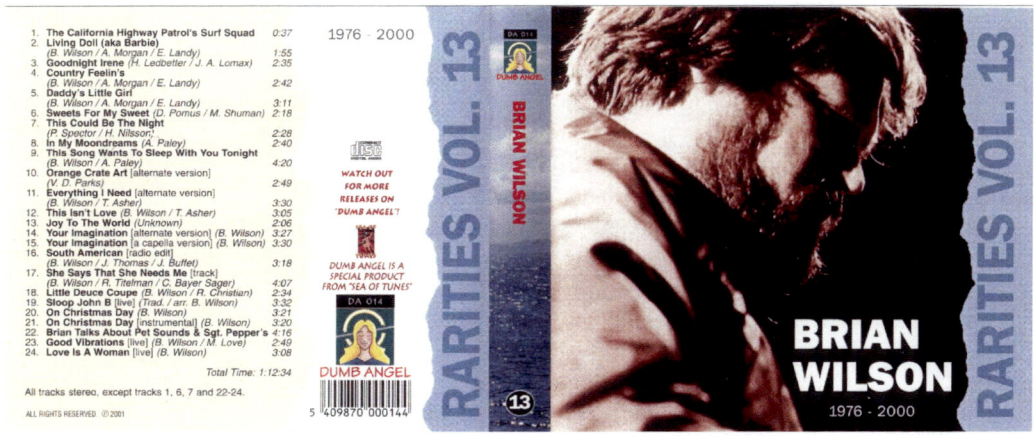

Title: Rarities Vol. 13: Brian Wilson 1976 - 2000
Release Date: 2001
Record Label: Dumb Angel
CD ref. No: DA 014
Country: World
No. of Disks: 1
Format: Audio CD
Audio: mono/stereo
Liner Notes: Booklet Photographs

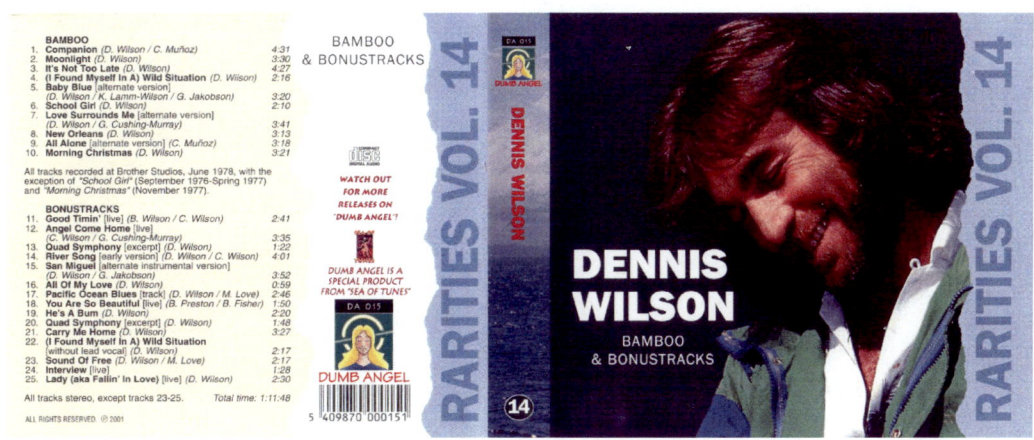

Title: Rarities Vol. 14: Dennis Wilson; Bamboo & Bonus Tracks
Release Date: 2001
Record Label: Dumb Angel
CD ref. No: DA 015
Country: World
No. of Disks: 1
Format: Audio CD
Audio: mono/stereo
Liner Notes: Booklet Photographs

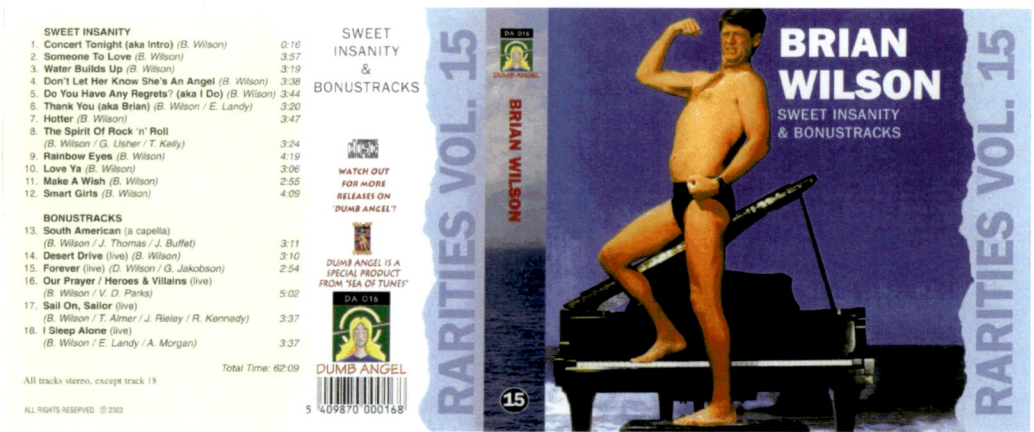

Title: Rarities Vol. 15: Sweet Insanity & Bonus Tracks
Release Date: 2001
Record Label: Dumb Angel
CD ref. No: DA 016
Country: World
No. of Disks: 1
Format: Audio CD
Audio: mono/stereo
Liner Notes: Booklet Photographs

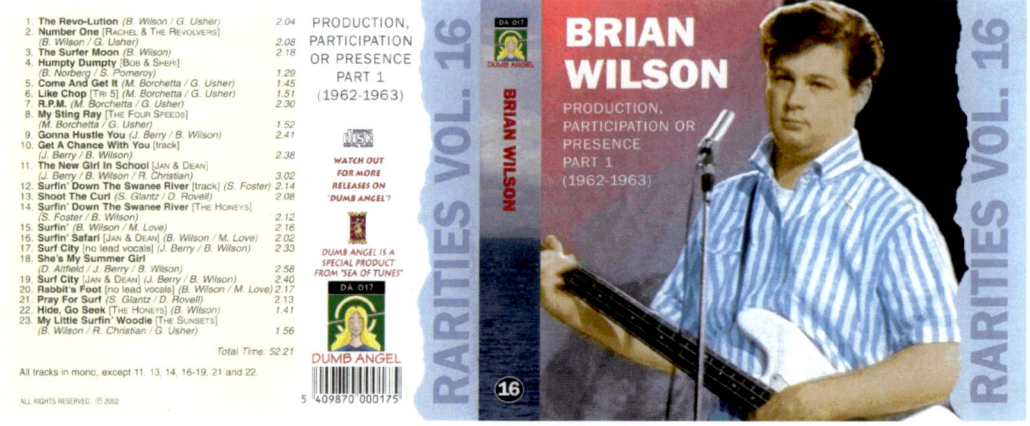

Title: Rarities Vol. 16: Brian Wilson; Production Participation or Presence, Part 1 (1962 – 1963)
Release Date: 2001
Record Label: Dumb Angel
CD ref. No: DA 017
Country: World
No. of Disks: 1
Format: Audio CD
Audio: mono/stereo
Liner Notes: Booklet Photographs

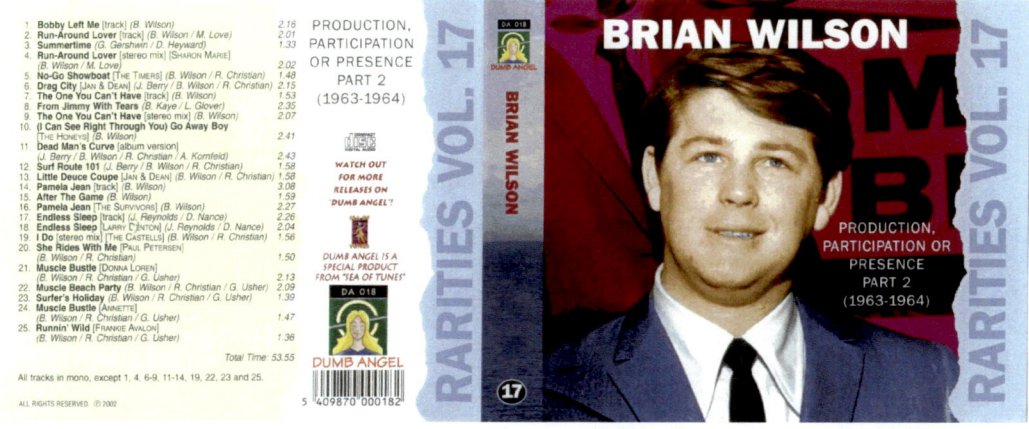

Title: Rarities Vol. 17: The Brian Wilson; Production Participation or Presence, Part 2 (1963 – 1964)
Release Date: 2001
Record Label: Dumb Angel
CD ref. No: DA 018
Country: World
No. of Disks: 1
Format: Audio CD
Audio: mono/stereo
Liner Notes: Booklet Photographs

Title: Rarities Vol. 18: Brian Wilson; Production Participation or Presence, Part 3 (1964 – 1965)
Release Date: 2001
Record Label: Dumb Angel
CD ref. No: DA 019
Country: World
No. of Disks: 1
Format: Audio CD
Audio: mono/stereo
Liner Notes: Booklet Photographs

Title: SMiLE
Release Date: 1993
Record Label: Vigotone
CD ref. No: VIGO 110 & 111
Country: World
No. of Disks: 2
Format: Audio CD
Audio: mono/stereo
Liner Notes: Fold out Poster

Title: Lei'd In Hawaii - Rehearsal
Release Date: 1994
Record Label: Vigotone
CD ref. No: VIGO 133
Country: World
No. of Disks: 2
Format: Audio CD
Audio: mono/stereo
Liner Notes: N/A

Title: Heroes & Vibrations
Release Date: 1998
Record Label: Vigotone
CD ref. No: VIGO 163
Country: World
No. of Disks: 1
Format: Audio CD
Audio: mono/stereo
Liner Notes: N/A

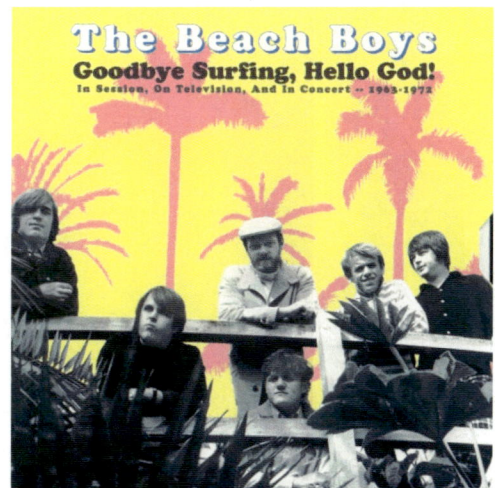

Cover Sleeve Front

Title: Goodbye Surfing, Hello God!
Release Date: 2001
Record Label: Vigotone
CD ref. No: VT 238/239/240/241/242
Country: World
No. of Disks: 5
Format: Audio CD
Audio: mono/stereo
Liner Notes: Booklet

The Beach Boys on CD: Bootlegs

Booklet Cover

Cover Sleeve Back

Disk 1 (front & back)

The Beach Boys on CD: Bootlegs

Disk 2 (front & back)

Disks 3 & 4 (front & back)

The Beach Boys on CD: Bootlegs

Disk 5 (front & back)

Title: Mike Love, Not War
Release Date: 1994
Record Label: Spank Records
CD ref. No: SP 108
Country: World
No. of Disks: 1
Format: Audio CD
Audio: mono/stereo
Liner Notes: N/A

Title: Lego My Ego
Release Date: 1995
Record Label: Spank Records
CD ref. No: SP 140/141/142
Country: World
No. of Disks: 1
Format: Audio CD
Audio: mono/stereo
Liner Notes: Booklet

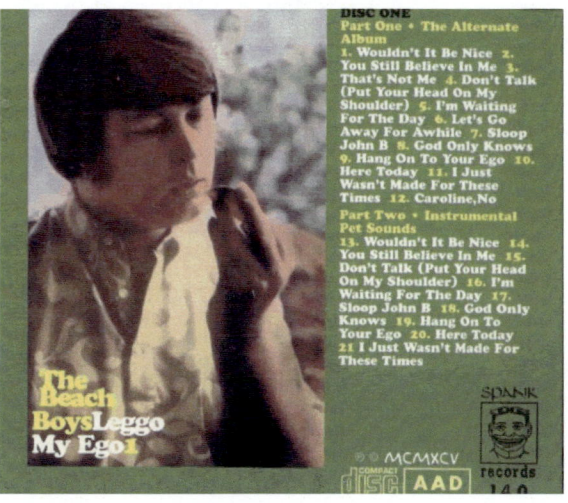

The Beach Boys on CD: Bootlegs

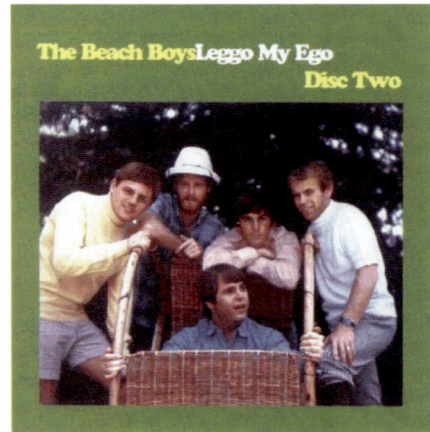

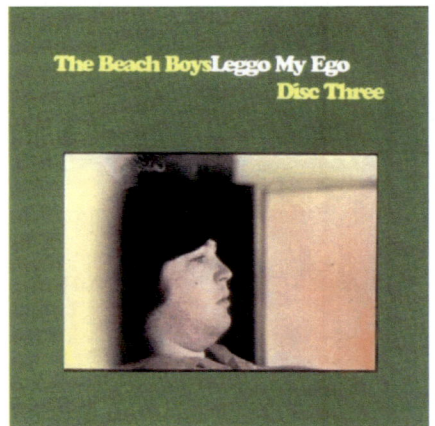

Title: Capitol Punishment
Release Date: 1995
Record Label: Spank Records
CD ref. No: SP 143/144
Country: World
No. of Disks: 2
Format: Audio CD/CD-R
Audio: mono/stereo
Liner Notes: Booklet

Booklet

Title: Aloha From Hawaii
Release Date: 2001
Record Label: Spank Records
CD ref. No: SP 147
Country: World
No. of Disks: 1
Format: Audio CD/CD-R
Audio: mono/stereo
Liner Notes: N/A

The Beach Boys on CD: Bootlegs

Sleeve Cover & Back

Title: Landlocked/Adult Child Hawaii
Release Date: 1997
Record Label: PegBoy
CD ref. No: PB 1009
Country: World
No. of Disks: 1
Format: Audio CD-R
Audio: mono/stereo
Liner Notes: N/A

Booklet

Disk Cover & Back

247

The Beach Boys on CD: Bootlegs

1. **Sail On Sailor 1973 Instruments only** - The majestic track uncovered. Featuring an a cappella vocal fade.
2. **Add Somme music To Your Day 1970 Vocal Only** - An unbelievably rich vocal display. The perfect Beach Boys harmonies are allowed to shine without instrumental competition.
3. **Slip On through 1970 alternate mix** - Dennis and Carl are heard vigorously discussing their work. A truly revealing process.
4. **Forever 1970 Vocal only** - Spectacular harmonies unimpaired by Instruments. Brian's closing falsetto extends far beyond the released version.
5. **Forever 1970 Alternate mix** - An entirely different mix complete with Instruments.
6. **Student Demonstration Time 1970 Alternate mix** - Mike's wonderful rocker has a very different sound here. Include in the mix are alternate sound effects.
7. **San Miguel 1970 Alternate mix** - Carl's false start kicks off this unique Session mix.
8. **Murray The K 1963 Station promo** - Murry Wilson leads his boys to harmony glory.
9. **Little Girl I Once Knew 1965 Sessions** - Brian challenges the Wrecking Crew to play it warm and romantic.
10. **Barbara Ann 1965 Concert promo** - Carl and Dennis having some fun.
11. **We Blew It 1965 Sessions** - Dean Torrance shows up and all hell breaks loose.
12. **Good Vibrations 1966 Sessions** - Brian's masterpiece like you've never heard it.
13. **Unknown Harmony 1968 Unreleased recording** - Originally intended for the friends LP this ethereal track never saw the light of day until now.
14. **Breakaway 1969 Alternate version** - A completely different vocal take gives this song a fresh sound.
15. **Surfin' U.S.A. 1963 Instruments only** - the original Beach Boys surfing guitar sound.
16. **I Get Around 1964 Instruments only** - Inside the head of Brian Wilson.
17. **All Summer long 1964 Instruments only** - Xylophone and trumpets harmonies clearly revealed.
18. **She Knows Me Too Well 1965 No Lead vocal** - Fantastic backing harmonies clearly revealed.
19. **I'm So young 1965 Alternate mix** - A perfect stereo mix.
20. **In The Back Of My Mind 1965 Instruments only** - Evidence that perhaps this should have been released as an instrumental.

Title: Deep Sea Treasures
Release Date: 2000
Record Label: Polar Bear
CD ref. No: PB 062
Country: World
No. of Disks: 1
Format: Audio CD
Audio: mono/stereo
Liner Notes: N/A

Title: Harmony Friends
Release Date: unknown
Record Label: unknown
CD ref. No: BB 676869 1/2
Country: World
No. of Disks: 2
Format: Audio CD
Audio: mono/stereo
Liner Notes: N/A

51 Big Ones-Outtakes, Oddities and Alternatives 1967-1969

CD 1
1. Harmony friends
2. Fall breaks and back to winter
3. Here comes the night
4. Can't wait too long
5. God only knows
6. California girls
7. You're so good to me
8. Help me Rhonda
9. Little bird
10. Friends
11. Be with me
12. Never learn not to love
13. Never learn not to love
14. Bluebirds over the mountain
15. Bluebirds over the mountain
16. The nearest faraway place
17. Break away
18. Break away
19. With a little help from my friends
20. Time to get alone

*For more track information see the Booklet

CD 2
1. Wonderfull
2. Wonderfull
3. Wind chimes
4. She's going bald
5. Gettin' hungry
6. With me tonight
7. She's going bald
8. Vegetables
9. Cool, cool water
10. I was made to love her
11. I was made to love her
12. Here comes the night
13. A thing or two
14. The letter
15. Darlin'
16. Darlin'
17. Wild honey
18. Wild honey
19. Friends
20. Friends
21. Do it again
22. Do it again
23. We're together again
24. Walk on by
25. I can hear music
26. I can hear music
27. Instrumental
28. Time to get alone
29. Break away
30. Steve Desper: America, I love you
31. Redwood: Time to get alone

The Beach Boys on CD: Bootlegs

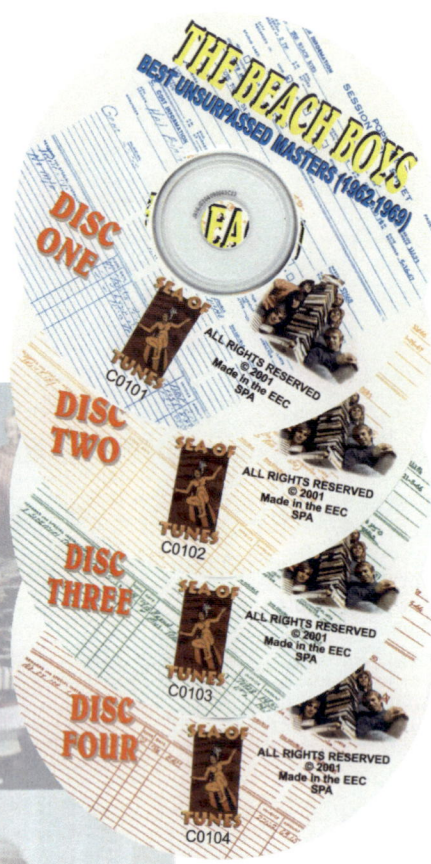

Title: Best of Unsurpassed Masters
Release Date: 2003
Record Label: Sea of Tunes ???
CD ref. No: C 0101/0102/0103/0104
Country: World
No. of Disks: 4
Format: Audio CD
Audio: mono/stereo
Liner Notes: Booklet

The Beach Boys on CD: Bootlegs

Title: Do It Again
Release Date: 1990
Record Label: Triangle
CD ref. No: PYCD 054
Country: Italy
No. of Disks: 1
Format: Audio CD
Audio: mono/stereo
Liner Notes: N/A

CD & Track notes

A bootleg of the concert at Syracuse University, New York, May 1st 1971

Title: Twofer
Release Date: 2002
Record Label: Unknown
CD ref. No: -
Country: Russia
No. of Disks: 1
Format: Audio CD
Audio: mono/stereo
Liner Notes: N/A

CD & Track Notes

These CD's come from the Russian Federation. They bear no marking and the bootlegger manages to confuse the Brother twofer background with the Capitol releases. I have seen the whole twofer series in this form being sold on the internet. The sound quality is astonishing and exactly mimics the current EMI-Capitol releases.

Title: Long Lost Surf Songs Vol.2
Release Date: 1995
Record Label: Silver Rarities
CD ref. No: -
Country: Germany
No. of Disks: 1
Format: Audio CD
Audio: mono/stereo
Liner Notes: N/A

CD Notes: There are 5 volumes in this series

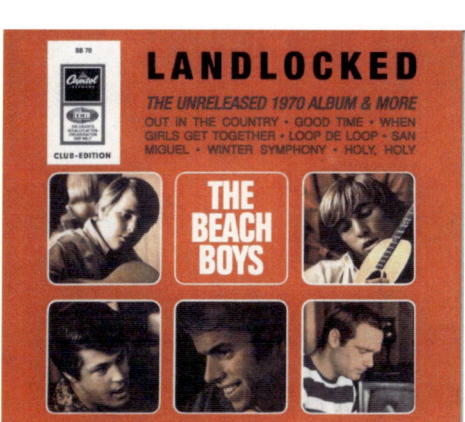

Title: Landlocked + (other tracks)
Release Date: unknown
Record Label: Odeon
CD ref. No: BB 70
Country: Germany
No. of Disks: 1
Format: Audio CD
Audio: mono/stereo
Liner Notes: N/A

CD Notes: An absolutely superb CD, one of the most interesting CD's in my collection!!

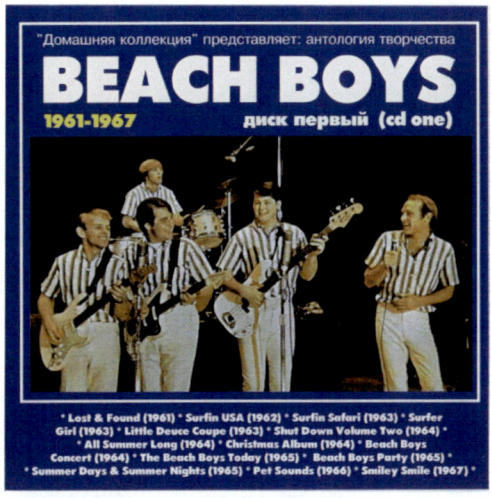

CD Listing, Disk 1

01 Lost & Found (1961)
02 Surfin USA (1962)
03 Surfin Safari (1963)
04 Surfer Girl (1963)
05 Little Deuce Coupe (1963)
06 Shut Down Volume Two (1964)
07 All Summer Long (1964)
08 Christmas Album (1964)
09 Beach Boys Concert (1964)
10 The Beach Boys Today (1965)
11 Summer Days and Summer Nights (1965)
12 Beach Boys Party (1965)
13 Pet Sounds (1966)
14 Smiley Smile (1967)

Title: Beach Boys 1961-1967 Disk 1
Release Date: 2000
Record Label: Delta MM Corp.
CD Ref. No: Disk 1
Country: Russian Federation
No. of Disks: 1
Format: Audio CD
Audio: Mono/Stereo
Liner Notes: Multimedia Windows: track listings, pictures, biographies, etc.,

Album & Track Notes

This series of disks contains volumes of Beach Boys Albums; Bootlegs in mp3 format on a single CD. The software provided on each CD provides a user friendly interface and access to music, data & picture files. These CD are designed to be played in a PC, but can also be played on CD & DVD players which support mp3 format. There are 8 CD in the series, full details are provided on the following pages.

PC User Interface

CD 1: contents…

Lost & Found (1961)
Surfin USA (1962)
Surfin Safari (1963)
Surfer Girl (1963)
Little Deuce Coupe (1963)
Shut Down Volume Two (1964)
All Summer Long (1964)
Christmas Album (1964)
Beach Boys Concert (1964)
The Beach Boys Today (1965)
Summer Days and Summer Nights (1965)
Beach Boys Party (1965)
Pet Sounds (1966)
Smiley Smile (1967)

Disk 2: Contents…

Smile (unreleased album) (1966)
Smile Sessions CD1 (1966)
Smile Sessions CD2 (1966)
Smile Sessions CD3 (1966)
Wild Honey (1967)
Wally Heider Studios (1967)
Friends (1968)
Stack-O-Track (1968)
20-20 (1968)
Live In London (1969)

 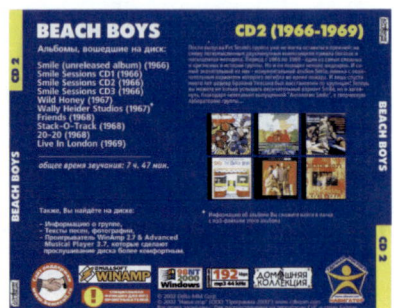

Disk 3: contents…

1. Sunflower (1970)
2. Surf's Up (1971)
3. Landlocked (Unreleased Album) (1971)
4. Carl And The Passions - So Tough (1972)
5. Holland - Mt Vernon And Fairway (A Fairy Tale) (1973)
6. The Beach Boys In Concert (1973)
7. 15 Big Ones (1976)
8. The Beach Boys Love You (1977)
9. The M.I.U. Alburn (1978)
10. L.A. (Light Alburn) (1979)
11. Jan & Dean - Greatest Hits Live (1993)

The Beach Boys on CD: Russian Bootlegs

Disk 4: contents...

1. Keepin The Summer Alive (1980)
2. Ten Years of Harmony (2CD) (1981)
3. The Beach Boys (1985)
4. Made In USA (1986)
5. Still Cruisin' (1987)
6. Summer in Paradise (1992)
7. Greatest Hits Live (1993)
8. Endless Harmony [Soundtrack] (1998)

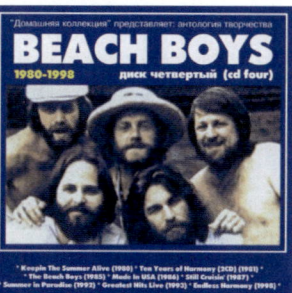

Disk 5: contents...

1. Good Vibrations (CD1) (1993)
2. Good Vibrations (CD2) (1993)
3. Good Vibrations (CD3) (1993)
4. Good Vibrations (CD4) (1993)
5. Good Vibrations (CD5) (1993)
6. The Brother Years (2000)

Disk 6: contents...

1. Pet Sounds Sessions CD1 - The Stereo Mix - 1993
2. Pet Sounds Sessions CD2 - Sessions - 1993
3. Pet Sounds Sessions CD3 - Stack-O-Vocal - 1993
4. Pet Sounds Sessions CD4 - The Mono Mix - 1993
5. Archaeology - Lost Recording Sessions (CD1) - 2001
6. Archaeology - Lost Recording Sessions (CD2) - 2001
7. Hawthorne, CA (CD1) - 2001
8. Hawthorne, CA (CD2) - 2001

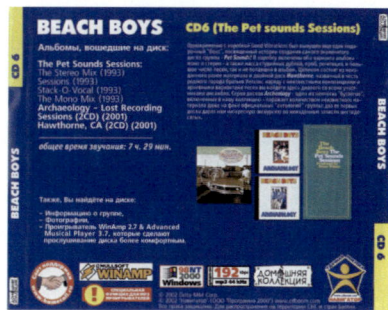

Disk 7: contents…

1. Brian Wilson
2. Adult Child (Unreleased Album) - 1976
3. Brian Wilson (Deluxe Edition) - 1988
4. Sweet Insanity - Sessions - 1991
5. I Just Wasn't Made For These Times - 1995
6. Orange Crate Art - 1995
7. Imagination - 1999
8. Brian Wilson Live at the Roxy Theatre (CD1) - 2000
9. Brian Wilson Live at the Roxy Theatre (CD2) - 2000
10. The Beach Boys
11. Ultimate Christmas - 1998

Disk 8: contents…

1. Carl Wilson
2. Carl Wilson - 1981
3. Youngblood - 1983
4. Like A Brother - 2000
5. Dennis Willson
6. Pacific Ocean Blue - 1977
7. Bamboo (Unreleased Second Album) - 1978
8. Bruce Johnston
9. Going Public - 1977
10. The Wilsons
11. The Wilsons - 1997
12. Wilson Phillips
13. Wilson Phillips - 1990
14. Shadows And Light - 1992

 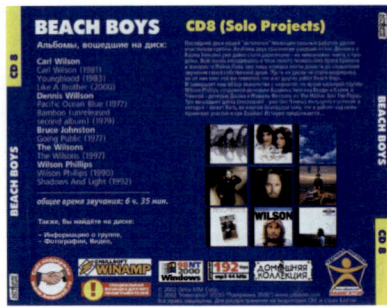

I'm A Cork On The Ocean - solo projects

This section deals with the CD output of the various members of the Beach Boys as solo performers. Each member of the Beach Boys has at one time or another produced solo material, the list below provides some historical detail.

Brian Wilson:	Adult Child (unreleased)	1976
	Brian Wilson	1988
	I Just Wasn't Made For These Times	1995
	Orange Crate Art	1995
	The Wilsons (4 tracks by BW)	1997
	Imagination	1998
	Live At the Roxy	2000
	Pet Sounds Live	2002
Carl Wilson:	Carl Wilson	1981
	Youngblood	1983
	Like A Brother	2001
Dennis Wilson:	Pacific Ocean Blue	1977
	Bamboo (unreleased)	1979
Bruce Johnston:	Going Public	1977
Mike Love:	Looking Back With Love	1881
Alan Jardine:	Live in Las Vegas	2001

The solo recording career of the Beach Boys began with the release of Brian Wilson and the Pet Sounds' single 'Caroline No'. Recorded for the Beach boys new label CBS (Caribou), Dennis Wilson began his solo career in 1977 with 'Pacific Ocean Blue'. Released in September 1977, the album charted at No. 96 the following month, and spent eight weeks in the charts. The CD version of this album is very difficult to obtain, and today will cost you $70+; rumours persist regarding a re-release, the problem seems to be an ownership issue. Bruce Johnston released 'Going Public' in 1977. Having left the Beach boys in 1972, Bruce Johnston would return to the fold for the completion of the L.A. (Light Album). In 1979, Dennis' second solo project 'Bamboo' failed to make it to vinyl. In 1981, just before he left the Beach Boys for a short spell, Carl Wilson released his first solo album, 'Carl Wilson'; the album reaching the lowly spot of No.185 in May 1981. In November 1981, Mike Love released his only solo effort to date; it failed miserably and did not make the record books never mind the charts. In 1981, the Beach Boys were in complete disarray. In February 1983, Carl Wilson released 'Youngblood', but it failed to make the charts. On December 28th 1883, Dennis Wilson died after a drowning accident. In 1988, Brian Wilson released his first solo album; titled 'Brian Wilson', the album reached No.54 on the Billboard chart and stayed for thirteen weeks. In 1995, Brian Wilson sang vocals on the Van Dyke Parks project 'Orange Crate art' – Sire 54272-8. Brian Wilson did not have another CD success until 1998, when 'Imagination' peaked at No.88 and spent two weeks on the US charts. Carl Wilson died on February 6th, 1998. In 2001, Al Jardine released his only solo album to date, 'Live at Las Vegas'; it features Al's sons and Brian Wilson's daughters Carnie and Wendy. Since 1998, Brian has released 'Live at The Roxy' and 'Pet Sounds Live', both CD's have accompanying DVD's of the live concerts. Brian Wilson continuous to record, his new album is due for release in early 2004 and in Feb. 2004 Brian Wilson will tour Europe and present 'SMiLE', live for the first time. The following pages provide some detail of the Beach Boys solo releases. All of the above recordings are available on CD (officially or unofficially). I would recommend 'Pacific Ocean Blue', 'Live at The Roxy' - two great albums.

The Beach Boys on CD: Solo Projects

Title & Notes: Pacific Ocean Blue
Artist: Dennis Wilson
Latest CD Release Date: Mar, 1991/Sept. 1977(LP)
Record Label: Caribou
CD Ref. No: Caribou ZK 34354/074643435420
       Europe/UK: EPC (CR) 4683512
Country: US
No. of Disks: 1
Format: Audio CD
Audio: stereo

Original SONY CD back

Title & Notes: Carl Wilson
Artist: Carl Wilson
Latest CD Release Date: Mar. 1981 (LP)
Record Label: Caribou
CD Ref. No: Caribou NJZ 37010(LP)
       Sony SRCS6102 (CD)
Country: US/Japan
No. of Disks: 1
Format: Audio CD (bootleg or SONY)
Audio: stereo
CD Note: Briefly released on CD by SONY Music in Japan, the two Carl Wilson solo albums are now OOP. The CD cover (right) is 'unofficial', the official SONY CD back cover is shown above

The Beach Boys on CD: Solo Projects

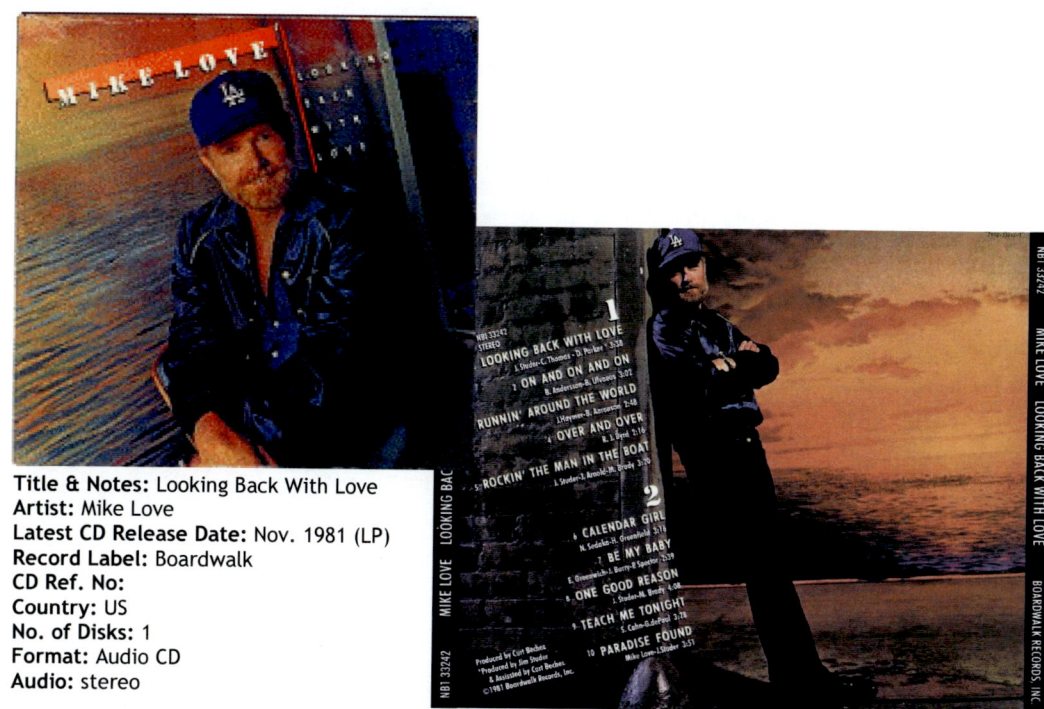

Title & Notes: Looking Back With Love
Artist: Mike Love
Latest CD Release Date: Nov. 1981 (LP)
Record Label: Boardwalk
CD Ref. No:
Country: US
No. of Disks: 1
Format: Audio CD
Audio: stereo

Title & Notes: Youngblood
Artist: Carl Wilson
Latest CD Release Date: Feb. 1983 (LP)
Record Label: Caribou
CD Ref. No: Caribou BFZ 37970 (LP)
SONY SRCS6103 (CD)
Country: US/Japan
No. of Disks: 1
Format: Audio CD (bootleg or SONY)
Audio: stereo

CD Note: Briefly released on CD by SONY Music in Japan, the two Carl Wilson solo albums are now OOP. The CD cover (right) is 'unofficial', the official SONY CD back cover is shown above

The Beach Boys on CD: Solo Projects

Title & Notes: Brian Wilson
Artist: Brian Wilson
Latest CD Release Date: 2000 (latest)
Record Label: Warner/Rhino
CD Ref. No: UK: July 7th, 1988 SIRE 925669 2
US: July 12th, 1988 SIRE 25669
UK: Sept. 18th, 2000 Rhino 8122 79960 2
US: Sept. 5th, 2000 Rhino/Warner R2 79960
Country: US
No. of Disks: 1
Format: Audio CD
Audio: stereo.
CD Notes: The 2000 re-issue produced by Mark Linett & David Leaf and contained many bonus tracks

Title & Notes: I Just Wasn't Made For These Times
Artist: Brian Wilson
Latest CD Release Date: 1995
Record Label: MCA Records
CD Ref. No: MCD 111 270 2
Country: US
No. of Disks: 1
Format: Audio CD
Audio: stereo

Title & Notes: Brian Wilson
Artist: Imagination
Latest CD Release Date: July 1998
Record Label: Paladin
CD Ref. No:
 UK: Jan. 21st, 2000 RCA 74321573032
 US: June 16th, 1998 Giant/Warner 9 24703 2
 US: DTS 5.1 mix Aug. 26th, 1998 Giant/DTS 71021-51018-2-8
Country: US
No. of Disks: 1
Format: Audio CD
Audio: stereo

Title & Notes: Live At The Roxy
Artist: Brian Wilson
CD Release Date: US, June 2001
Record Label: BriMel Records
CD Ref. No: There are four (UK, US(2) and Japan) versions of this CD available.

1st US: May 1st, 2000 BriMel Records - 1001
2nd US: June 19th, 2001 Oglio Records - OGL82012 (2 bonus tracks+interview)
Europe: Jan. 21st, 2002 Sanctuary - SANDD 107(4 bonus tracks+interview)
Japan: Mar. 19th, 2002 Victor Ent. - VICP-617889(5 bonus tracks+interview)

Country: US
No. of Disks: 1
Format: Audio CD
Audio: stereo

The Beach Boys on CD: Solo Projects

Track Listing...

1. Show Inro
2. Wouldn't It Be Nice
3. You Still Believe In Me
4. That's Not Me
5. Don't Talk (Put Your Head On My Shoulder)
6. I'm Waiting For The Day
7. Let's Go Away For Awhile
8. Sloop John B
9. God Only Knows
10. I Know There's An Answer
11. Here Today
12. I Just Wasn't Made For These Times
13. Pet Sounds
14. Caroline No

Title: Brian Wilson Presents Pet Sounds Live
Release Date: 2002
Record Label: Sanctuary/BriMel Records
CD Ref. No:

Pet Sounds (Brian Wilson presents live UK) June 3rd, 2002 Sanctuary	SANCD118
UK Promo	SANPR118
Pet Sounds (Brian Wilson presents live US) June 11th, 2002 Sanctuary	84556
Pet Sounds (Brian Wilson presents live, Japan+) Aug. 5th, 2002 Toshiba-EMI	TOCP-66088

Country: US
No. of Disks: 1
Format: Audio CD
Audio: stereo
Liner Notes: David Leaf

Album & Track Notes

Brian Wilson and his band (Jeffrey Foskett & The Wondermints, Darian Sahanaja et al) peformed Pet Sounds live at the Royal Festival Hall, London in late January 2002. The concert was recorded and then mixed in the studio by Mark Linett; the result is this CD. The booklet (hard to read) has notes by David Leaf and provides the background and sets the scene for the live performances. A really great CD! The promo version serial number is SANPR118. On the Japanese version of this CD, there are two bonus tracks; 'Meant For You' & 'Friends' – released by Toshiba-EMI; TOCP-66088 - **strange but true!**

The Beach Boys on CD: Solo Projects

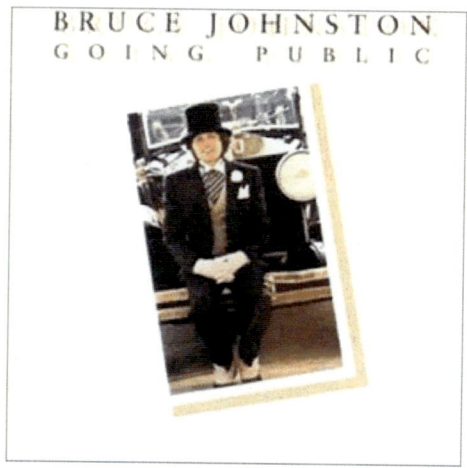

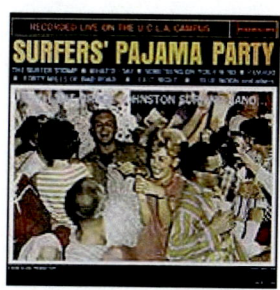

Also available on CD: Bruce Johnston – latest release 1995, a bunch of surf songs from the early 60's – available from CDuniverse

Title & Notes: Going Public
Artist: Bruce Johnston
Latest CD Release Date: Nov/Dec 2000
Record Label: Edsel Records (UK)
CD Ref. No: EDCD697
Country: US
No. of Disks: 1
Format: Audio CD
Audio: stereo

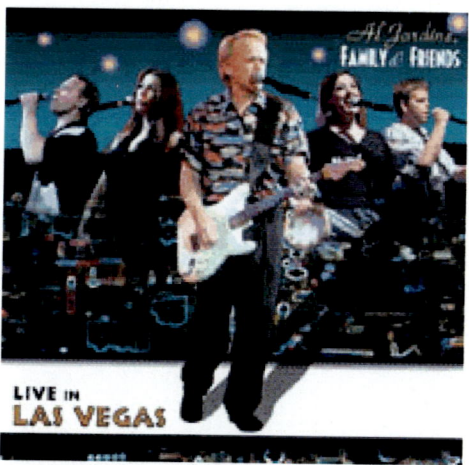

Title & Notes: Live in Las Vegas
Artist: Al Jardine
Latest CD Release Date: 2001
Record Label: Available via Al's website
CD Ref. No:
Country: US
No. of Disks: 1
Format: Audio CD
Audio: stereo

The Beach Boys on CD: Solo Projects

Title & Notes: Like A Brother: Carl teams up with Robert Lamm of Chicago and Gerry Beckley of America and was recorded between 1993 and 1995. VD Parks lends a hand on the recordings. There is a Japanese version (Victor Entertainment) of this CD, it include three extra tracks - 1. Standing at Your Door/2. Blue after All /3. In The Dark
Artist: Carl Wilson
Latest CD Release Date: June 20th, 2000
Record Label: Transparent Music
CD Ref. No: US/UK: 1221829
Japan: VICP-61387
Country: US/Europe/Japan
No. of Disks: 1
Format: Audio CD
Audio: stereo

Artist: Dennis Wilson
Latest CD Release Date:
Record Label: Vigotone (bootleg)
CD Ref. No: VIGO 144
Country: World
No. of Disks: 1
Format: Audio CD
Audio: stereo

CD Notes: His last solo recordings. This is not an actual Vigotone creation. It a bootleg using the now defunct Vigotone bootleg label.

The Beach Boys on CD: Solo Projects

Title: Summer Cruisin'
Artist: Mike Love & Bruce Johnston
Latest CD Release Date: Sept. 2001
Record Label: EMI Music Canada/Capitol
CD Ref. No: -
Country: North America
No. of Disks: 1
Format: Audio CD
Audio: stereo

CD Notes: A release by Chrysler Motor Company. Mike Love and Bruce Johnston redo Beach Boys classic songs. Mike adds two new unreleased recordings to the disk

Title: Salute NASCAR
Artist: Mike & Bruce & David Marks
Latest CD Release Date: 1998
Record Label: Tosko Marketing
CD Ref. No: n/a
Country: North America
No. of Disks: 1
Format: Audio CD
Audio: stereo

The Beach Boys on CD: Solo Projects

The Vigotone Company also produced three Brian Wilson bootleg CD's These are illustrated below.

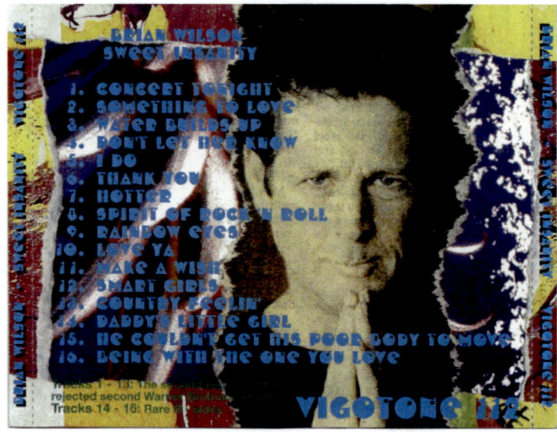
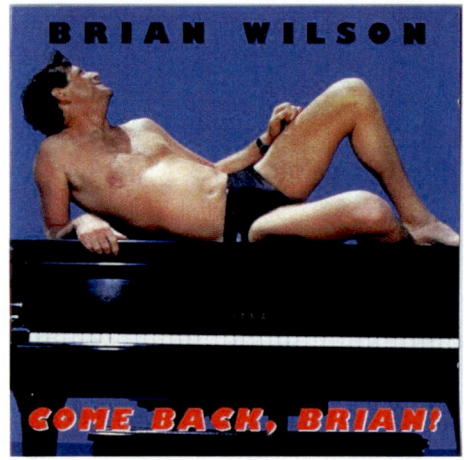

Appendices

Appendix I

Beach Boys Associates

Murry Wilson

The father of the Wilson brother's and Mike Love's uncle, Murry Wilson managed the Beach Boys from 1961 until he was fired in April 1994. Murry Wilson was a strict disciplinarian and was an oppressive force in the life of his sons and in particular Brian Wilson. Murry Wilson maintained his relationship with the Beach Boys until 1969 and was The Beach Boys publishing manager until he sold the 'Sea of Tunes Publishing' and Brian Wilson's' entire catalogue to A & M Record in late 1969; he neglected to tell Brian Wilson. Murry Wilson (Reggie Dunbar) co-wrote the Beach Boys last Capitol single, the superb 'Breakaway'. Murry Wilson died in 1973.

David Leaf

David Leaf is the pre-eminent Beach Boys historian and author of 'The Beach Boys and the Californian Myth'. David Leaf has also written the liner notes/booklets on the following CD releases:

1986	Made in USA (Capitol, Beach Boys 25th Anniversary compilation)
1990	Capitol Beach Boys twofer CD liner notes
1990	Pet Sounds CD release and subsequent versions
1993	Good Vibrations: 30 Years of The Beach Boys Box Set Booklet
1997	Pet Sounds Sessions: Contributed to Booklet Notes
2002	Wrote the liner notes for Brian Wilson presents 'Pet Sounds Live'

Chuck Britz

Engineer and studio mentor to Brian Wilson on The Beach Boys early recordings. Chuck Britz engineered the majority of the Capitol albums. He died in 2000

Jack Reilly

Jack Rieley was The Beach Boys Manager in the early 70's. He wrote a number of songs on 'C&TP' and 'Holland'. Jack Rieley was influential in moving the Beach Boys to Holland in 1972 for the creation of the Holland album. He asked Ricky Fataar and Blondie Chaplin to join the Beach Boys. He co-wrote a number of songs for the band, including; 'Long Promised Road' and 'Trader' (with Carl Wilson), Marcella (with Brian Wilson) and 'Sail on, Sailor' and performed the vocal for the 'Surf's Up' track, 'A Day in the Life of a Tree', he also narrated, 'Mount Vernon and Fairway' (A Fairy Tale): A Fairy Tale in Several Parts.

Mark Linnet

Has worked extensively with the Beach Boys and Brian Wilson since 1988, he has been involved in the following projects:

1988	Brian Wilson solo album and it's re-release in 2000
1990	Pet Sound first release on CD
1990	Engineered (Digitally remastered, compiled & coordinated) the Capitol twofer releases and re-mixed some of the bonus material
2001	Produced and coordinated the 2001 Capitol 24 bit HDCD twofer re-issues
2002	Recorded and mixed Brian Wilson presents 'Pet Sounds Live'
2002	Produced, mixed and mastered the 2002/3 CD release 'The Beach Boy' live at Knebworth'
2003	Re-engineered 'Pet Sounds' to Pet Sounds DVD audio 5.1

Appendix II

Beach Boys Composers, Co-lyricists

Gary Usher

Gary Usher and Brian Wilson met in early 1962, became friends and co-wrote some of the Beach Boys early songs, including; '409', 'In My room' and 'Lonely Sea'. The Brian Wilson-Gary Usher compositions appear across the first six Beach Boys albums. In mid 1986, the proposed 'Wilson Project', the Brian Wilson-Gary Usher (producer) collaboration began. The project was aborted in early 1987, Eugene Landy is 'credited' with the blame. Gary Usher died in 1990

Roger Christian

In 1962, Brian teamed up with Roger Christian and together they wrote a number of the famous car song including; 'Little Deuce Coupe', 'Spirit of America', 'Shut Down' and the wonderful ballad, 'Don't Worry Baby'. With Brian Wilson, he co-wrote seven of the tracks that appear on 'Little Deuce Coupe', and a couple on 'Shut Down Vol.2'. Roger Christian died in 1991.

Tony Asher

Tony Asher worked in the advertising industry in 1966. For a short period (a few weeks) in 1966, he joined Brian Wilson and together they crafted the lyrics for the album 'Pet Sounds'. It is remarkable that the lyricist for one of the greatest albums of all simply went back to his 'normal' job and into the pages of Rock history.

Van Dyke Parks

Van Dyke Parks is a musician (multi instrumentalist), composer, arranger, producer, and lyricist; has worked with everyone and 'his granny'. Van Dyke Parks has released nine LP's/CD' since 1967. He joined Brian Wilson in the autumn of 1966 to act a collaborator on the Beach Boys new album 'Smile'. A number of negative forces led the project being abandoned in early 1971 and after Van Dyke Parks had removed himself after disagreements with Mike Love and adverse reaction to his lyrics. Ironically the drama surrounding the collapse of Smile has made it 'infamous' and Smile and V.D. Parks remains at the forefront of current Beach Boys folklore. In 1995, Brian Wilson and V.D. Parks re-united and collaborated on the CD, 'Orange Crate Art', Brian Wilson provided vocals and vocal arrangements. Today, Smile is available on bootleg and time has vindicated Brian Wilson and Van Dyke Parks; the musical and lyrical content of Smile is well established and acclaimed. Brian Wilson will tour with 'Smile', live in 2004.

Gregg Jakobson

Gregg Jakobson co-wrote with Dennis Wilson in the 70's, his songs include; 'Clebrate the News', 'Forever', 'Baby Blue' and the brilliant 'San Miguel'.

Others

Other co-writers over the years 1962-1993 include: Terry Melcher (mainly with Mike Love, later recordings), Daryl Dragon (of 'Captain & Tennille'), Steve Kalinich, Dr. E. Landy, Randy Bachman (with Carl Wilson on KTSA), G. Cushing-Murray (with Carl Wilson on L.A.)

Appendix III

CD Discography (alpha order)

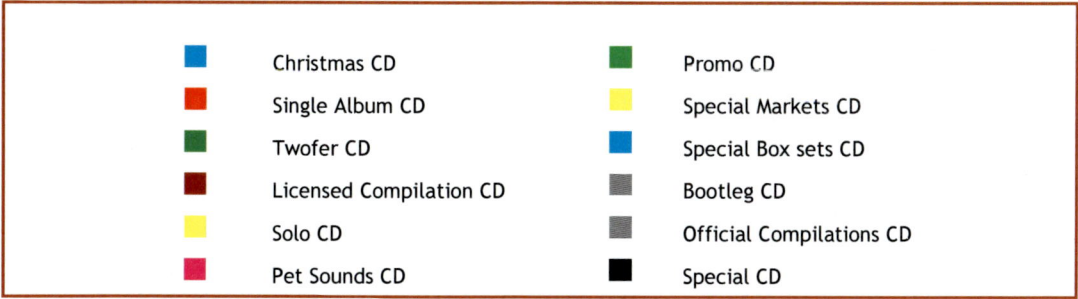

CD Title	Page	Release Date	Label	CD Ref No
'69 Live in London (Japan - Coolprice)	p185	Oct., 1997	Toshiba-EMI	TOCP-3328
'69 Live in London (Japan - Mini LP series)	p187	1998 & 2000	Toshiba-EMI	TOCP-50865
'69 Live in London (Japan - PastMasters)	p183	June, 1990	Toshiba-EMI	CP21-6016
'69 Live in London (Japan + bonus tracks)	p199	June 27th, 2001	Toshiba-EMI	TOCP-53176
'69 Live in London	p.31	July 26th, 1994	Capitol	CDP 724382963424
15 Big Ones (UK)	p.37	unknown	Caribou	EPC 4638482
15 Big Ones (US)	p.37	Jan. 15th, 1991	Caribou	ZK 46955
15 Big Ones	p.200	Sept. 27th, 2000	Toshiba-EMI	TOCP-65570
15 Big Ones/Love You	p.62	Aug. 15th, 2000	Capitol	724352794522
16 Superhits	p.151	1988	Duchesse	CD 352020
20 All Time Greats (Australia)	App.6	1991	Capitol/EMI	CDP 791013
20 Golden Greats	p.100	1987	EMI	CDP 7467282
20 Good Vibrations (The Greatest Hits Vol.1)	p.118	1999	Capitol/EMI	724352186020
20 Good Vibrations	p.111	1995	Capitol	724382941828
20 Great Love Songs	p.145	1996	Disky	7243 8 63072 8
20 More Good Vibrations (The Greatest Hits Vol.2)	p.119	1999	Capitol/EMI	724352023820
20/20 (Japan - Coolprice)	p.185	Oct., 1997	Toshiba-EMI	TOCP-3327
20/20 (Japan - Mini LP series)	p.187	1998 & 2000	Toshiba-EMI	TOCP-50864
20/20 (Japan - PastMasters)	p.184	June, 1990	Toshiba-EMI	CP21-6015
20/20 (Japan + bonus tracks)	p.199	June 27th, 2001	Toshiba-EMI	TOCP-53175
20/20	p.30	July 26th, 1994	Capitol	CDP 724382963820
21 Little Ones (bootleg)	p.268	1995	Vigotone	VIGO 151
32 Great Songs	p.157	unknown	StarLife	CD 91011
36 All Time Greatest Hits Long Box (Spec. Mkts.)	p.138	2000	EMI/Capitol SM	S23 18607
36 All Time Greatest Hits/Classics (Special Markets)	p.141	2000	EMI/Capitol SM	S23 18607
Absolute Best of Vol. 1	p.105	1991	Capitol	CDP 7967952
Absolute Best of Vol. 2	p.105	1991	Capitol	CDP 7967962
All Summer Long (Japan - Coolprice)	p.185	Sept., 1997	Toshiba-EMI	TOCP-3317
All Summer Long (Japan - Mini LP series)	p.187	1998 & 2000	Toshiba-EMI	TOCP-50854
All Summer Long (Japan - PastMasters)	p.183	June, 1990	Toshiba-EMI	CP21-6006
All Summer Long (Japan + bonus tracks)	p.197	June 16th, 2001	Toshiba-EMI	TOCP-53166
All Summer Long (Special Markets)	p.135	1992	CEMA	S21 57639
All Summer Long	p.144	1997	Disky	DC 878682
All Summer Long	p.19	June 28th, 1994	Capitol	CDP 724382963127
All Time Greatest Hits (Special Markets)	p.135	1990	CEMA	CDL 57355
Aloha From Hawaii	p.244	2001	Spank Records	SP 147
Beach Boys 1961-1967 (Russia)	p.256	2000	Delta MM Corp.	Disk #1
Beach Boys 1966-1969 (Russia)	p.256	2000	Delta MM Corp.	Disk #2
Beach Boys 1970-1979 (Russia)	p.256	2000	Delta MM Corp.	Disk #3
Beach Boys 1980-1998 (Russia)	p.257	2000	Delta MM Corp.	Disk #4
Beach Boys Brian Wilson Solo (Russia)	p.258	2000	Delta MM Corp.	Disk #7
Beach Boys Christmas	p.169	unknown	CEMA	S21 17417
Beach Boys Good Vibrations (Russia)	p.257	2000	Delta MM Corp.	Disk #5
Beach Boys Party! (Japan - Coolprice)	p.185	Oct., 1997	Toshiba-EMI	TOCP-3321

The Beach Boys on CD: Appendices

Appendix III

CD Discography (alpha order)

CD Title	Page	Release Date		Label	CD Ref No
Beach Boys Party! (Japan – current)	p.198	June 27th, 2001	■	Toshiba-EMI	TOCP-53170
Beach Boys Party! (Japan - PastMasters)	p.183	June, 1990	■	Toshiba-EMI	CP21-6010
Beach Boys Party!	P.24	July 26th, 1994	■	Capitol	CDP 724382964025
Beach Boys Party!/Stack-o-Tracks (Canada)	p.67	1990	■	Capitol	C2 ?????
Beach Boys Party!/Stack-O-Tracks (UK)	p.66	1990	■	Capitol	CZ 325
Beach Boys Party!/Stack-O-Tracks	p.181	Dec. 12th, 1990	■	Toshiba-EMI	TOCP-6515
Beach Boys Party!/Stack-O-Tracks	p.57	2001	■	Capitol	724353164126
Beach Boys Party!/Stack-O-Tracks	p.65	1990	■	Capitol	CDP 7 93697 2
Beach Boys Party!/Stack-O-Tracks	p.68	1990	■	BMG	D 100450
Beach Boys Party!/Stack-O-Tracks	p.68	2001	■	BMG	D 1400639
Beach Boys Pet Sounds Sessions (Russia)	p.257	2000	■	Delta MM Corp.	Disk #6
Beach Boys Solo Projects (Russia)	p.257	2000	■	Delta MM Corp.	Disk #8
Beach Party (Live in Montego Bay -26/6/82	p.167	1992	■	Intl. Broadcast	IRB 2025
Best of The Beach Boys 1970-1986 Broth. Years (UK)	p.121	2000	■	Capitol/EMI	724352451428
Best of Unsurpassed Masters (4 disks)	p.250	2003	■	Sea of Tunes?	C 0101/02/03/04
Brian Wilson (1st release - Brian Wilson solo UK)	p.262	July 7th, 1988	■	SIRE	925669 2
Brian Wilson (1st release - Brian Wilson solo US)	p.262	July 12th, 1988	■	SIRE	925669 2
Brian Wilson (2nd release - Brian Wilson solo UK)	p.262	Sept. 18th, 2000	■	Rhino	8122 79960 2
Brian Wilson (2nd release - Brian Wilson solo US)	p.262	Sept. 5th, 2000	■	Rhino/Warner	R2 79960
Brian Wilson (BW promo)	p.178	1988	■	Rhino	SIRE R2 79960
California Dream (Best of The Beach Boys)	p.206	Dec. 4th, 1996	■	Toshiba-EMI	TOCP-50107-8
California Dreamin'	p.144	1998	■	Disky	7243 8 53422 4
California Dreamin'	p.152	1992	■	BR Music	BX 402-2
California Feelin' (Classics selected by B. Wilson)	n/a	June 21st, 2002	■	Toshiba-EMI	TOCP-66030
California Girls	p.161	1997	■	EuroSound	3309
California Girls	p.163	2001	■	Universe (FNM)	3309
California Girls	p.47	1987	■	Capitol	CDP 7480462
California Gold	p.104	1990	■	Capitol	7965492
Capitol Punishment (2 disks)	p.243	1995	■	Spank Records	SP 143/144
Carl & the Passions	p.200	Sept. 27th, 2000	■	Toshiba-EMI	TOCP-65567
Carl & the Passions	p.34	Feb. 26th, 1991	■	Caribou	ZK 46953
Carl and the Passions "So Tough"/Holland	p.62	Aug. 15th, 2000	■	Capitol	724352569427
Carl Wilson (Carl Wilson solo)	p.260	1881	■	SONY	SRCS6102
Catch a Wave (Box Set) (Special Markets)	p.140	2001	■	EMI/Capitol SM	CDP 7243 5 36171 2 7
Christmas Album (+5 Bonus tracks)	p.21	Sept 8th, 1992	■	Capitol	CDP 7950842
Christmas Album (10 tracks)	p.169	1991	■	EMI/Capitol SM	CDL 9012
Christmas Album (1988, no bonus tracks)	p.21	unknown	■	BMG	D 133854
Christmas Album (1st release 1988 CD))	p.21	1988	■	Capitol	CDP 07777910082
Christmas Album (Australia, 1990's)	App.6	1990's	■	AXIS/EMI	CDAX 701413
Christmas Album (No bonus tracks)	p.21	1994	■	Capitol	CDP 724383072927
Christmas Album+5 (Japan - Coolprice)	p.185	Oct., 1997	■	Toshiba-EMI	TOCP-3331
Christmas Hits	p.185	unknown	■	Universe	UN 3 160
Christmas Songs	p.169	unknown	■	Duchesse	352094
Classics selected by Brian Wilson	p.125	2002	■	Capitol/EMI	724354008726
Come Back Brian (bootleg)	p.268	1994	■	Vigotone	VIGO 125
Concert (Japan - Coolprice)	p.185	Sept., 1997	■	Toshiba-EMI	TOCP-3318
Concert (Japan - Mini LP series)	p.187	1998 & 2000	■	Toshiba-EMI	TOCP-50855
Concert (Japan - PastMasters)	p.183	June, 1990	■	Toshiba-EMI	CP21-6007
Concert	p.197	Apr. 9th, 2001	■	Toshiba-EMI	TOCP-53167
Concert	p.20	July 26th, 1994	■	Capitol	CDP 077779042722
Concert/Live in London (Beach Boys '69) (Canada)	p.67	1990	■	Capitol	C2 ?????
Concert/Live in London (Beach Boys '69) (UK)	p.66	1990	■	Capitol	CZ ???
Concert/Live in London (Beach Boys '69)	p.181	Dec. 12th, 1990	■	Toshiba-EMI	TOCP-6518
Concert/Live in London (Beach Boys '69)	p.55	2001	■	Capitol	724353186128
Concert/Live in London (Beach Boys '69)	p.65	1990	■	Capitol	CDP 7 93695 2
Concert/Live in London (Beach Boys '69)	p.68	1990	■	BMG	D ?????
Concert/Live in London (Beach Boys '69)	p.68	2001	■	BMG	D 1400670
Deep Sea Treasures, Vol.1	p.248	2000	■	Polar Bear	PB 062
Do It Again	p.251	1990	■	Triangle	PYCD 054
Endless Harmony (1998)	p.115	1998	■	Capitol/EMI	724349639126
Endless Harmony (2000)	p.122	2000	■	Capitol/EMI	724352400225
Endless Harmony (Advance Listening Promo)	p.175	1998	■	EMI Inter.	CDPP 077
Endless Harmony	p.122	1998	■	Toshiba-EMI	TOCP-50720

The Beach Boys on CD: Appendices

Appendix III

CD Discography (alpha order)

CD Title	Page	Release Date		Label	CD Ref No
Endless Harmony	p.122	June 29th, 2002	■	Toshiba-EMI	TOCP-66032
Endless Summer (Japan - Mini LP series)	p.187	1998 & 2000	■	Toshiba-EMI	TOPC-50866
Endless Summer	p.96	1987	■	Capitol	CDP 7464672
Endless Summer	p.98	1996	■	DCC	GZS-1076
For the Girls	p.206	1993	■	Toshiba-EMI	TOCP-7870
Forever Surfin'	p.161	1997	■	A PRIORI	791303
Friends (Japan - Coolprice)	p.185	Oct., 1997	■	Toshiba-EMI	TOCP-3325
Friends (Japan - Mini LP series)	p.187	1998 & 2000	■	Toshiba-EMI	TOCP-50862
Friends (Japan - PastMasters)	p.183	June, 1990	■	Toshiba-EMI	CP21-6014
Friends (Japan + bonus tracks)	p.198	June 27th, 2001	■	Toshiba-EMI	TOCP-53173
Friends	p.28	July 26th, 1994	■	Capitol	CDP 724382963721
Friends/20/20	p.65	1990	■	Capitol	CDP 7 93697 2
Friends/20/20 (Canada)	p.67	1990	■	Capitol	C2 ?????
Friends/20/20 (UK)	p.66	1990	■	Capitol	CZ 341
Friends/20/20	p.181	Dec. 12th, 1990	■	Toshiba-EMI	TOCP-6517
Friends/20/20	p.59	2001	■	Capitol	724353163822
Friends/20/20	p.68	1990	■	BMG	D ??????
Friends/20/20	p.68	2001	■	BMG	D 1400621
Fun, Fun, Fun (Beach Boys Best)	p.163	1990	■	EMI-Electrola	CDF 670 573
Fun, Fun, Fun (live)	p.151	1989	■	LazerLight	15164
Fun, Fun, Fun (live, Australia)	p.157	unknown	■	Rainbow	RCD 5703
Going Public (Bruce Johnston solo)	p.265	2000	■	EDSEL	EDCD697
Gold Collection	p.159	1991	■	ALEX	CD 050
Good Vibrations (30 Year Box set Selection, Promo)	p.174	1993	■	Capitol	DPRO 79728
Good Vibrations (30 Years of Beach Boys # 6(UK)	*p.129*	*June, 1993*	■	*EMI / Capitol*	*CDP 0777 789927 2 8*
Good Vibrations (30 Years of Beach Boys bonus)	*p.129*	*June, 1993*	■	*Capitol*	*CDP 0777 781299 2 9*
Good Vibrations (30 Years of Beach Boys Box)	*p.129*	*June, 1993*	■	*Capitol*	*CDP 0777 781294 2 4*
Good Vibrations (30 Years of Beach Boys Box)	*p.129*	*June, 1993*	■	*Toshiba-EMI*	**TOCP-8021~26**
Good Vibrations (30 Years of Beach Boys disk #1)	*p.129*	*June, 1993*	■	*Capitol*	*CDP 0777 781295 2 3*
Good Vibrations (30 Years of Beach Boys disk #2)	*p.129*	*June, 1993*	■	*Capitol*	*CDP 0777 781296 2 2*
Good Vibrations (30 Years of Beach Boys disk #3)	*p.129*	*June, 1993*	■	*Capitol*	*CDP 0777 781297 2 1*
Good Vibrations (30 Years of Beach Boys disk #4)	*p.129*	*June, 1993*	■	*Capitol*	*CDP 0777 781298 2 0*
Good Vibrations (Beach Boys live)	p.165	1983	■	Fabbri Edit.	MRL 060
Good Vibrations (German Greatest Hits Promo)	p.174	1995	■	EMI Electrola	7243 8 82254 2 7
Good Vibrations (Special Markets)	p.137	2000	■	EMI/SUGO music	CDP 7243 5 28228 2 9
Good Vibrations (The Beach Boys)	p.206	August 8th, 1997	■	Toshiba-EMI	TOCP-50135
Good Vibrations Vol. 2	p.164	2001	■	Music Collect.	GPH 73002
Good Vibrations	p.160	1994	■	Cedar (Charly)	CRB 505
Goodbye Surfin', Hello God! (5 disks)	p.239	2001	■	Vigotone	VIT238/39/240/41/42
Greatest Car Song (Special Markets)	p.136	1990	■	CEMA	S21 57241
Greatest Hits (29 Classics)	p.117	1999	■	Capitol/EMI	724352164820
Greatest Hits (Germany)	App.6		■	Starlight	
Greatest Hits (Hollywood)	p.150	1987	■	Hollywood	HCD-109
Greatest Hits (Prime Cuts - Canada)	p.154	1994	■	Retro Music	SLD 13332
Greatest Hits 1 (1962-1965)	p.203	April 24th, 2000	■	Toshiba-EMI	TOPC-0201
Greatest Hits 1 (1962-1965)	p.203	June 16th, 2001	■	Toshiba-EMI	TOPC-65727
Greatest Hits 2 (1966-1969)	p.203	April 24th, 2000	■	Toshiba-EMI	TOPC-0202
Greatest Hits 2 (1966-1969)	p.203	June 16th, 2001	■	Toshiba-EMI	TOPC-65728
Greatest Hits 3 (1970-1986)	p.203	June 28th, 2000	■	Toshiba-EMI	TOPC-65457
Greatest Hits Vol.3 Best of the Brother Years (US)	p.121	2000	■	Capitol/EMI	724352500024
Greatest Hits	p.114	1998	■	Capitol/EMI	72434956962
Greatest Surfin Songs (Special Markets)	p.136	1992	■	CEMA	S21 57240
Harmony Friends (2 disks)	p.249	unknown	■	unknown	BB 676869 _
Hawthorn CA	p.124	June 16th, 2001	■	Toshiba-EMI	TOCP-65729~30
Hawthorn CA	p.124	2001	■	Capitol/EMI	724353158323
Heroes & Vibrations	p.239	1998	■	Vigotone	VIGO 163
Heroes & Villains (live)	p.154	1995	■	Smart Art	WZ 98003
Hits of the Beach Boys	p.125	2002	■	EMI	724354007224
Holland (Japan – current)	p.200	Sept. 27th, 2000	■	Toshiba-EMI	TOCP-65568
Holland (UK)	p.35	unknown	■	Caribou	EPC 4678372
Holland (US)	p.35	Oct. 23rd, 1990	■	Caribou	ZK 46952
I Can Here Music (Carl Wilson - Japan)	p.205	July 26th, 2002	■	Toshiba-EMI	TOPC-66035
I Can Here Music (Stars and Stripes Promo)	p.175	1996	■	River North	MCD 80127

The Beach Boys on CD: Appendices

Appendix III

CD Discography (alpha order)

CD Title	Page	Release Date		Label	CD Ref No
I Get Around	p.150	unknown	■	Comet	43448
I just Wasn't Made For These Times (BW solo)	p.262	Sept. 1995	■	MCA records	MCD 111 270 2
I Love You	p.107	1993/1999	■	EMI	07777895762
Imagination (BW promo - blue)	App.6	1998	■	Giant	27703
Imagination (BW solo UK)	p.263	Jan. 21st, 2000	■	RCA	74321573032
Imagination (BW solo US DTS 5.1 mix)	p.263	Aug. 26th, 1998	■	Giant/DTS	71021-51018-2-8
Imagination (BW solo US)	p.263	June 16th, 1998	■	Giant/Warner	9 24703 2
In Concert (Japan – current)	p.200	Feb. 25th, 2002	■	Toshiba-EMI	TOCP-65569
In Concert (UK)	p.36	unknown	■	Caribou	EPC 4683452
In Concert (US)	p.36	Oct. 23rd, 1990	■	Caribou	ZK 46954
In Concert	p.36	July 18th 2000	■	Capitol	CDP 724382963226
Instrumental Hits	n/a	June 19th, 2002	■	Toshiba-EMI	TOCP-66033
Keepin' the Summer Alive (Japan – current)	p.201	Sept. 27th, 2000	■	Toshiba-EMI	TOCP-65574
Keepin' the Summer Alive (UK)	p.41	unknown	■	Caribou	EPC 4683501
Keepin' the Summer Alive (US)	p.41	Feb. 26th, 1991	■	Caribou	ZK 46959
Keepin' the Summer Alive/The Beach Boys	p.64	Aug. 15th, 2000	■	Capitol	724352569427
L.A. (Light Album) (Japan – current)	p.201	Sept. 27th, 2000	■	Toshiba-EMI	TOCP-65573
L.A. (Light Album) (UK Collectors Choice)	p.40	unknown	■	Caribou	9021272
L.A. (Light Album) (US)	p.40	Oct. 24th, 1989	■	Caribou	ZK 46958
L.A. (Light Album) (US)	p.40	unknown	■	Caribou	ZK 35752
Landlocked	p.253	unknown	■	Odeon	BB 70
Landlocked/Adult Child	p.247	1997	■	PegBoy	PB 1009
Le Meilleur Des Beach Boys	p.120	1999	■	EMI France	5214292
Lego My Ego (The alternative Pet Sounds, 3 disks)	p.243	1995	■	Spank Records	SP 140/141/142
Lei'd in Hawaii	p.238	1994	■	Vigotone	VIGO 133
Let's Go Surfin'	p.108	1994	■	EMI-Australia	8144372
Like a Brother (Carl Wilson + others solo)	p.266	June 20th, 2000	■	Transparent	1221829
Like a Brother (Japan + three tracks)	p.266	June 26th, 2001	■		VICP-61387
Little Deuce Coupe (Japan - Coolprice)	p.185	Sept., 1997	■	Toshiba-EMI	TOCP-3315
Little Deuce Coupe (Japan - Mini LP series)	p.187	1998 & 2000	■	Toshiba-EMI	TOCP-50852
Little Deuce Coupe (Japan - PastMasters)	p.143	June, 1990	■	Toshiba-EMI	CP21-6004
Little Deuce Coupe (Japan + bonus track– current)	p.196	June 16th, 2001	■	Toshiba-EMI	TOCP-53164
Little Deuce Coupe	p.134	1989	■	CEMA	CDL 57241
Little Deuce Coupe (CEMA Canada)	p.17	1992	■	CEMA	S21-57682
Little Deuce Coupe	p.17	June 28th, 1994	■	Capitol	CDP 724382966128
Little Deuce Coupe - Volume 3	p.168	1993	■	Duchesse	CD 352143
Little Deuce Coupe/All Summer Long - 2nd	p.68	2001	■	BMG	D 1387802
Little Deuce Coupe/All Summer Long - 1st	p.65	1990	■	BMG	D 100446
Little Deuce Coupe/All Summer Long (2001)	p.54	2001	■	Capitol	724353151622
Little Deuce Coupe/All Summer Long	p.65	1990	■	Capitol	CDP 7 93693 2
Little Deuce Coupe/All Summer Long (Canada)	p.67	1990	■	Capitol	C2 ?????
Little Deuce Coupe/All Summer Long (Japan)	p.181	Dec. 12th, 1990	■	Toshiba-EMI	TOCP-6513
Little Deuce Coupe/All Summer Long (UK)	p.66	1990	■	Capitol	CZ 320
Live at Knebworth	p.45	Oct., 2002	■	Eagle	ER 200022
Live at The Roxy (B. Wilson live 1st US)	p.263	May 1st, 2000	■	BriMel Records	1001
Live at The Roxy (B. Wilson live, 2nd US, 3 bonus)	p.263	June 19th, 2001	■	Oglio Records	OGL82012
Live at The Roxy (Europe, 5 bonus (4 songs))	p.263	Jan. 21st, 2002	■	Sanctuary	SANDD 107
Live at The Roxy (Japan, 6 bonus (5 songs))	p.263	Mar. 19th, 2002	■	Victor Ent.	VICP-617889
Live Hits Collection	p.167	unknown	■	Acd	CD 154.151
Live in Las Vegas (Al Jardine live solo)	p.265	2001	■		HV100
Long Lost Surf Songs Vol. 1	p.253	1995	■	Silver Rarities	
Long Lost Surf Songs Vol. 2	p.253	1995	■	Silver Rarities	
Long Lost Surf Songs Vol. 3	p.253	1995	■	Silver Rarities	
Long Lost Surf Songs Vol. 4	p.253	1995	■	Silver Rarities	
Long Lost Surf Songs Vol. 5	p.253	1995	■	Silver Rarities	
Long Promised Road	p.128	1998	■	Capitol/EMI	DPRO12138
Looking Back with Love (Mike Love solo)	p.261	unknown	■	Boardwalk	
Lost and Found	p.48	1991	■	DCC	DZS 054
Love You (UK)	p.38	unknown	■	Caribou	EPC 4638472
Love You (US)	p.38	Jan. 15th, 1991	■	Caribou	ZK 46956
Love You	p.200	Sept. 27th, 2000	■	Toshiba-EMI	TOCP-65571
M.I.U Album (Japan – current)	p.201	Sept. 27th, 2000	■	Toshiba-EMI	TOCP-65572
M.I.U Album	p.39	Feb. 26th, 1991	■	Caribou	ZK 46957

Appendix III

CD Discography (alpha order)

CD Title	Page	Release Date	Label	CD Ref No
M.I.U. Album/L.A. (Light Album)	p.63	Aug. 15th, 2000	Capitol	724352795024
Made in the U.S.A. (Japan - Mini LP series)	p.187	1998 & 2000	Toshiba-EMI	TOCP-50868
Made in U.S.A	p.102	July, 1986	Capitol	CDP 7463242
Medley (Spanish Very Best Promo)	p.176	2001	EMI	PE 01074
Merry Christmas From...	p.169	2001	CEMA	0777 7 56620 2 3
Merry Christmas From...	p.169	Oct. 15th, 1997	LazerLight	7243 5 27702 2 9
Merry Christmas From...	p.169	unknown	Frontline	FLCD 14
Mike Love, Not war	p.242	1994	Spank Records	SP 108
Most of The Beach Boys	p.106	1992	EMI-Australasia	4380012
Orange Crate Art	p.259	Nov. 14th, 1995	Sire Records	54272-8
Original Gold (Box Set disk #1)	*p.143*	*1999*	*Disky*	*7243 8 57892 1*
Original Gold (Box Set disk #2)	*p.143*	*1999*	*Disky*	*7243 8 57902 7*
Original Gold (Box Set)	*p.143*	*1999*	*Disky*	*HR 857712*
Original Surfin' Hits	p.156	1995	Curb Records	D2 77747
Pacific Ocean Blue (Dennis Wilson solo)	p.260	Mar, 1991	Caribou	ZK34354/074643435420
Pacific Ocean Blue (DW solo, Euro release)	p.260	Mar, 1991	Caribou	EPC 4683512
Perfect Harmony	p.113	1997	EMI	724382127727
Pet Sound Sessions (Advance Listening disk #1)	*p.76*	*1996*	*EMI (UK)*	*CDPP 025*
Pet Sound Sessions (Advance Listening disk #2)	*p.76*	*1996*	*EMI (UK)*	*CDPP 026*
Pet Sound Sessions (Advance Listening disk #3)	*p.76*	*1996*	*EMI (UK)*	*CDPP 027*
Pet Sound Sessions (Advance Listening disk #4)	*p.76*	*1996*	*EMI (UK)*	*CDPP 028*
Pet Sounds (Audio DVD 5.1 Surround mix US)	p.83	July 22nd, 2003	Capitol	7243 4 77937 9 0
Pet Sounds (Audio DVD 5.1 Surround mix UK)	p.83	Sept. 8th, 2003	EMI	EMI 4779369
Pet Sounds (Brian Wilson presents live UK promo)	p.264	2002	Sanctuary	SANPR118
Pet Sounds (Brian Wilson presents live UK)	p.82	June 3rd, 2002	Sanctuary	SANCD118
Pet Sounds (Brian Wilson presents live US)	p.82	June 11th, 2002	Sanctuary	84556
Pet Sounds (Brian Wilson presents live), Japan+	p.82	Aug. 5th, 2002	Toshiba-EMI	TOCP-66088
Pet Sounds (Gold)	p.74	Mar. 20th, 1993	DCC	GZS 1035
Pet Sounds (HDCD 24 bit mono)	p.80	Sept 4th, 2000	Capitol	7243 5 27319 2 3
Pet Sounds (Japan - CoolPrice)	p.185	June 28th, 1995	Toshiba-EMI	TOCP-3018
Pet Sounds (Japan - Greenline)	p.193	Dec. 21st, 1988	Toshiba-EMI	CP28-1003
Pet Sounds (Japan - Mini LP series)	p.187	2000	Toshiba-EMI	TOCP-50859
Pet Sounds (Japan - PastMasters)	p.183	July 28th, 1989	Toshiba-EMI	CP21-6011
Pet Sounds (Japan)	p.192	Dec. 12th, 1990	Toshiba-EMI	TOCP-6519
Pet Sounds (Japan, 7243 5 21241 2 1)	p.190	July 7th, 1999	Toshiba-EMI	TOCP-65255
Pet Sounds (Japan, 7243 5 26266 2 5)	p.190	June 19th, 2002	Toshiba-EMI	TOCP-66031
Pet Sounds (Japan, 7243 8 37666 2 8 Mini LP)	p.187	July 23rd, 1998	Toshiba-EMI	TOCP-50859
Pet Sounds (Japan, CDP 7 48421 2)	p.191	Oct. 17th, 1997	Toshiba-EMI	TOCP-3322
Pet Sounds (mono + stereo HCDC 24 bit)	p.81	2001	Capitol	7243 5 26266 2 5
Pet Sounds (mono + stereo)	p.79	999	Capitol	CDP 521241
Pet Sounds (US Sampler)	p.75	1996	Capitol	DPRO 11241
Pet Sounds Sessions (Box Set, all disks)	*p.77*	*1997*	*Capitol*	*7243 8 37662 2 2*
Pet Sounds Sessions (disk #1)	*p.77*	*1997*	*Capitol*	*7243 8 37663 2*
Pet Sounds Sessions (disk #2)	*p.77*	*1997*	*Capitol*	*7243 8 37664 2*
Pet Sounds Sessions (disk #3)	*p.77*	*1997*	*Capitol*	*7243 8 37665 2*
Pet Sounds Sessions (disk #4)	*p.77*	*1997*	*Capitol*	*7243 8 37663 2*
Pet Sounds	p.25/72	1990	BMG	D 100513
Pet Sounds	p.25/72	1990	Capitol	CDP 548421
Pet Sounds	p.73	1993	Fame	CDP 7 48421 2
Rarities (Japan - Coolprice)	p.185	Oct., 1997	Toshiba-EMI	TOCP-3329
Rarities Vol. 1 – The Beach Boys 1962-1968	p.229	2001	Dumb Angel	DA 002
Rarities Vol. 10 – The Beach Boys Live Wash. DC	p.233	2001	Dumb Angel	DA 011
Rarities Vol. 11 – The Beach Boys Live, London	p.234	2001	Dumb Angel	DA 012
Rarities Vol. 12 – The Beach Boys Live	p.234	2001	Dumb Angel	DA 013
Rarities Vol. 13 – Brian Wilson 1976-2000	p.235	2001	Dumb Angel	DA 014
Rarities Vol. 14 – Dennis Wilson, Bamboo +	p.235	2001	Dumb Angel	DA 015
Rarities Vol. 15 – Sweet Insanity + Bonus	p.236	2001	Dumb Angel	DA 016
Rarities Vol. 16 – Brian Wilson Prod. (1962-1963)	p.236	2001	Dumb Angel	DA 017
Rarities Vol. 17 – Brian Wilson Prod. (1963-1964)	p.237	2001	Dumb Angel	DA 018
Rarities Vol. 18 – Brian Wilson Prod. (1964-1965)	p.238	2001	Dumb Angel	DA 019
Rarities Vol. 2 – Land/The Beach Boys 1969-1971	p.229	2001	Dumb Angel	DA 003
Rarities Vol. 3 – BW Demos/The BB's 1972-1976	p.230	2001	Dumb Angel	DA 004
Rarities Vol. 4 – Adult Child/ The BB's 1976-1977	p.230	2001	Dumb Angel	DA 005

The Beach Boys on CD: Appendices

Appendix III

CD Discography (alpha order)

CD Title	Page	Release Date	Label	CD Ref No
Rarities Vol. 5 - The Beach Boys 1978	p.231	2001	Dumb Angel	DA 006
Rarities Vol. 6 - The Beach Boys 1978-1983	p.231	2001	Dumb Angel	DA 007
Rarities Vol. 7 - The Beach Boys 1984-1989	p.232	2001	Dumb Angel	DA 008
Rarities Vol. 8 - The Beach Boys 1990-1998	p.232	2001	Dumb Angel	DA 009
Rarities Vol. 9 - The Beach Boys 1962-1972	p.233	2001	Dumb Angel	DA 010
Salute NASCAR	p.267	1998	Tosko Mrktng.	none
Seaside Dreams	p.155	1995	A PRIORI	CD 791314
Shut Down Vol.2 (Japan - Coolprice)	p.185	Sept., 1997	Toshiba-EMI	TOCP-3316
Shut Down Vol.2 (Japan - Mini LP series)	p.187	1998 & 2000	Toshiba-EMI	TOCP-50853
Shut Down Vol.2 (Japan - PastMasters)	p.196	June, 1990	Toshiba-EMI	CP21-6005
Shut Down Vol.2 (Japan + bonus tracks)	p.198	June 16th, 2001	Toshiba-EMI	TOCP-53165
Shut Down Vol.2	p.18	June 28th, 1994	Capitol	CDP 724382962922
SMILE	p.90	unknown	Odeon	ST-9002
SMILE disk #1 VIGO #1	p.88	1999	Vigotone	VIGO 110
SMILE disk #1	p.89	August, 2003	AB-outback	AB-xxxx1
SMILE disk #2 VIGO #2	p.88	1999	Vigotone	VIGO 111
SMILE disk #2	p.89	August, 2003	AB-outback	AB-xxxx2
Smiley Smile (France + bonus tracks)	App.6	Sept, 1998	Magic Records	4975762
Smiley Smile (Japan - Coolprice)	p.185	Oct., 1997	Toshiba-EMI	TOCP-3323
Smiley Smile (Japan - Mini LP series)	p.187	1998 & 2000	Toshiba-EMI	TOCP-50860
Smiley Smile (Japan - PastMasters)	p.183	June, 1990	Toshiba-EMI	CP21-6012
Smiley Smile (Japan + bonus tracks)	p.198	June 27th, 2001	Toshiba-EMI	TOCP-53171
Smiley Smile	p.26	July 26th, 1994	Capitol	CDP 724382963523
Smiley Smile/Wild Honey	p.68	2001	BMG	D 1400654
Smiley Smile/Wild Honey (Canada)	p.67	1990	Capitol	C2 ?????
Smiley Smile/Wild Honey (UK)	p.66	1990	Capitol	CZ 326
Smiley Smile/Wild Honey	p.181	Dec. 12th, 1990	Toshiba-EMI	TOCP-6516
Smiley Smile/Wild Honey	p.58	2001	Capitol	724353186227
Smiley Smile/Wild Honey	p.65	1990	Capitol	CDP 7 93696 2
Smiley Smile/Wild Honey	p.68	1990	BMG	D ?????
Sound of the Summer Singles (Promo)	p.177	2003	Capitol	7243 5 90000 2 2
Sounds of Summer	p.127	2003	Capitol	724358271027
Spirit of America (Japan - Mini LP series)	p.187	1998 & 2000	Toshiba-EMI	TOCP-50867
Spirit of America	p.99	1988	Capitol	CDP 7466182
Spirit of America	p.99	1991	DCC	GZS-1089
Spirit of the 60's	p.152	1991	Time Life	TL 531/11
Stack-O-Tracks (Japan - Coolprice)	p.185	Oct., 1997	Toshiba-EMI	TOCP-3326
Stack-O-Tracks (Japan - Mini LP series)	p.187	1998 & 2000	Toshiba-EMI	TOCP-50863
Stack-O-Tracks (Japan + bonus tracks)	p.199	June 27th, 2001	Toshiba-EMI	TOCP-53174
Stack-O-Tracks	p.29	July 26th, 1994	Capitol	CDP 724382964124
Stars and Stripes Vol. 1	p.49	1996	River North	751416120522
Still Cruisin' (Japan)	p.201	Oct. 17th, 1997	Toshiba-EMI	TOCP-3330
Still Cruisin'	p.43	1989	BMG	D 144379
Still Cruisin'	p.43	Aug., 1989	Capitol	92639
Studio Sessions '61-'62	p.48	2000	Burning airlines	038894001266
Summer Cruisin' (Mike Love/Bruce Johnston)	p.267	2001	EMI Canada	none
Summer Crush (Special Markets)	p.139	2001	EMI/Hear music	CDP 7243 5 33311 2 2
Summer Days (ASN) (Japan - Coolprice)	p.185	Sept., 1997	Toshiba-EMI	TOCP-3320
Summer Days (ASN) (Japan - Mini LP series)	p.187	1998 & 2000	Toshiba-EMI	TOCP-50857
Summer Days (ASN) (Japan - PastMasters)	p.183	June, 1990	Toshiba-EMI	CP21-6009
Summer Days (ASN) (Japan + bonus tracks)	p.197	June 27th, 2001	Toshiba-EMI	TOCP-53169
Summer Days (ASN)	p.23	June 28th, 1994	Capitol	CDP 724382963325
Summer Dreams	p.103	July, 1990	Capitol	CDP 7946202
Summer in Paradise (UK)	p.44	May, 1993	EMI	0777781036
Summer in Paradise (US)	p.44	Aug., 1992	BRI	BBR727-2
Sunflower (UK)	p.32	unknown	Caribou	EPC 4678362
Sunflower (US)	p.32	Oct. 23rd, 1990	Caribou	ZK 46950
Sunflower	p.199	Aug. 30th, 2000	Toshiba-EMI	TOCP-65565
Sunflower/Surf's Up	p.60	July 18th 2000	Capitol	724352569229
Sunflower/Surf's Up	p.68	2000	BMG	D 1407196
Sunny Times	p.160	1995	A PRIORI	CD 791304
Super Hits	p.158	unknown	Evergreen	2690842
Super Now (The Beach Boys)	p.206	Dec. 10th, 1997	Toshiba-EMI	TOCP-51001

Appendix III

CD Discography (alpha order)

CD Title	Page	Release Date	Label	CD Ref No
Surf Dance Fun	p.156	1995	Back Biter	BB 61052
Surf in the USA	p.166	1994	Music Reflextion	1402.2043-2
Surf's Up	p.199	Aug. 30th, 2000	Toshiba-EMI	TOCP-65566
Surf's Up (UK)	p.33	unknown	Caribou	EPC 4678352
Surf's Up (US)	p.33	Oct. 23rd, 1990	Caribou	ZK 46951
Surfer Girl (Germany)	App.6			
Surfer Girl (Japan - CoolPrice)	p.185	Sept., 1997	Toshiba-EMI	TOCP-3314
Surfer Girl (Japan - Mini LP series)	p.187	1998 & 2000	Toshiba-EMI	TOCP-50851
Surfer Girl (Japan - PastMasters)	p.183	June, 1990	Toshiba-EMI	CP21-6003
Surfer Girl (Japan + bonus tracks)	p.196	June 16th, 2001	Toshiba-EMI	TOCP-53163
Surfer Girl	p.16	June 28th, 1994	Capitol	CDP 724382962823
Surfer Girl/Shut Down Vol. 2 (Canada)	p.67	1990	Capitol	C2 ?????
Surfer Girl/Shut Down Vol. 2 (UK)	p.75	1990	Capitol	CZ 313
Surfer Girl/Shut Down Vol. 2	p.181	Dec. 12th, 1990	Toshiba-EMI	TOCP-6512
Surfer Girl/Shut Down Vol. 2	p.53	2001	Capitol	724353151522
Surfer Girl/Shut Down Vol. 2	p.68	1990	BMG	D 100447
Surfer Girl/Shut Down Vol. 2	p.68	2001	BMG	D 1387786
Surfer Girl/Shut Down Volume 2	p.65	1990	Capitol	CDP 7 93692 2
Surfer's Moon	p.155	1995	Back Biter	BB 61070
Surfin U.S.A./Surfer Girl	p.69	June 9th, 1989	MFSL	UDCD 521
Surfin' Safari (Japan - Coolprice)	p.185	Sept., 1997	Toshiba-EMI	TOCP-3311
Surfin' Safari (Japan - Mini LP series)	p.187	1998 & 2000	Toshiba-EMI	TOCP-50849
Surfin' Safari (Japan - PastMasters)	p.183	June, 1990	Toshiba-EMI	CP21-6001
Surfin' Safari (Japan + bonus tracks)	p.196	June 16th, 2001	Toshiba-EMI	TOCP-53161
Surfin' Safari	p.14	June 28th, 1994	Capitol	CDP 724382966128
Surfin' Safari/Surfin' U.S.A. (Canada)	p.67	1990	Capitol	C2 ?????
Surfin' Safari/Surfin' U.S.A. (UK)	p.66	1990	Capitol	CZ 312
Surfin' Safari/Surfin' U.S.A.	p.181	Dec. 12th, 1990	Toshiba-EMI	TOCP-6511
Surfin' Safari/Surfin' U.S.A.	p.52	2001	Capitol	724353151720
Surfin' Safari/Surfin' U.S.A.	p.65	1990	Capitol	CDP 7 93691 2
Surfin' Safari/Surfin' U.S.A.	p.68	1990	BMG	D 100448
Surfin' Safari/Surfin' U.S.A.	p.68	2001	BMG	D 1387794
Surfin' U.S.A. (Japan - Coolprice)	p.185	Sept., 1997	Toshiba-EMI	TOCP-3312
Surfin' U.S.A. (Japan - Mini LP series)	p.187	1998 & 2000	Toshiba-EMI	TOCP-50850
Surfin' U.S.A. (Japan - PastMasters)	p.183	June, 1990	Toshiba-EMI	CP21-6002
Surfin' U.S.A. (Japan + bonus tracks)	p.196	June 16th, 2001	Toshiba-EMI	TOCP-53162
Surfin' U.S.A.	p.15	June 28th, 1994	Capitol	CDP 077774842228
Surfin'	p.158	1988	Telstar	TRCD 1001
Surfin'	p.162	2000	Varese Sand.	302 066 085 2
Sweet Insanity (bootleg)	p.268	1993	Vigotone	VIGO 112
Tears in The Morning (Dutch Singles Promo)	p.176	1998	EMI	7243 8 86082 2 0
Ten Years of Harmony (Digitally remastered)	p.101	1990	Sony	Sony 465670-2
Ten Years of Harmony	p.101	1987	Caribou	465670-2
The Beach Boys (14 Track Sampler Promo)	p.173	1990	Capitol	DPRO 76168
The Beach Boys (Memory Pop)	p.42	1990	Caribou	CRB 462530 2
The Beach Boys (UK)	p.42	unknown	Caribou	CRB 465013 2
The Beach Boys (US)	p.42	May 1985	Caribou	ZK 39946
The Beach Boys Best Collection	p.165	unknown	Jasrac	R 250065
The Beach Boys Best	p.164	1985	Jasrac	R 950101
The Beach Boys Christmas album	p.169	Oct. 10th, 2000	Disky	CH 884092
The Beach Boys Greatest	p.206	Mar. 30th, 1998	Toshiba-EMI	TOCP-51076
The Beach Boys Surf's Up (Special Markets)	p.134	1989	EMI Music Can.	S21 57240
The Beach Boys Surfin' Hits	p.153	1993	Aloha	AL 10-004
The Beach Boys	p.153	1992	Dynamic	ST 52083
The Beach Boys	p.201	Sept. 27th, 2000	Toshiba-EMI	TOCP-65575
The Beach Boys' Golden Stars	p.133	1990	Capitol (Club)	65 424 4
The Best of The Beach Boys (1966)	p.95	1988	BMG	D 123946
The Best of The Beach Boys (Broth. Years AL)	p.177	2000	Capitol	7243 5 24511 2 BV
The Best of The Beach Boys (Special Markets)	p.137	1997	EMI/Capitol SM	CDP 7243 8 19702 2 0
The Best of The Beach Boys (Special Markets)	p.142	2003	EMI/Capitol SM	CDP 7243 8 19707 2 0
The Best of The Beach Boys Vol.1 (Australia)	p.109	1995	EMI Australia	unknown
The Best of The Beach Boys Vol.2 (Australia)	p.109	1995	EMI Australia	8329102
The Best of The Beach Boys Vol.3 (Australia 1988)	App.6	1988	AXIS/EMI	CDAX 701413

Appendix III

CD Discography (alpha order)

CD Title	Page	Release Date		Label	CD Ref No
The Best of The beach Boys Vol.3 (Australia)	p.109	1995	■	EMI Australia	8329112
The Best of The Beach Boys	p.110	1995	■	Capitol	72483447220
The Best of The Beach Boys	p.112	1996	■	EMI-Australasia	1572092
The Best of The Beach Boys	p.95	1988	■	Capitol	CDP 7 91318 2
The Capitol Years (Australia Box Set disk #1)	*p.131*	*2000*	■	*EMI/Capitol*	*CDAX 791029*
The Capitol Years (Australia Box Set disk #2)	*p.131*	*2000*	■	*EMI/Capitol*	*CDAX 791030*
The Capitol Years (Australia Box Set disk #3)	*p.131*	*2000*	■	*EMI/Capitol*	*CDAX 791031*
The Capitol Years (Australia Box Set disk #4)	*p.131*	*2000*	■	*EMI/Capitol*	*CDAX 791032*
The Capitol Years (Australia Box Set)	*p.131*	*2000*	■	*EMI/Capitol*	*CD CAP 6*
The Capitol Years Japan (disk #1)	*p.131*	*1991*	■	*Toshiba-EMI*	*TOCP-6151*
The Capitol Years Japan (disk #2)	*p.131*	*1991*	■	*Toshiba-EMI*	*TOCP-6152*
The Capitol Years Japan (disk #3)	*p.131*	*1991*	■	*Toshiba-EMI*	*TOCP-6153*
The Capitol Years Japan (disk #4)	*p.131*	*1991*	■	*Toshiba-EMI*	*TOCP-6154*
The Capitol Years Japan (disk #5)	*p.131*	*1991*	■	*Toshiba-EMI*	*TOCP-6155*
The Capitol Years Japan (disk #6)	*p.131*	*1991*	■	*Toshiba-EMI*	*TOCP-6156*
The Capitol Years Japan (disk #7)	*p.131*	*1991*	■	*Toshiba-EMI*	*TOCP-6157*
The Dutch Singles Collection	p.116	1998	■	EMI	724349650725
The Early Years	p.166	1994	■	Mastertone	10027
The Great The Beach Boys	p.162	1993	■	Goldies	GLD 63138
The Little Deuce Coupe (Special Markets)	p.134	1989	■	Capital/EMI SM	CDL 57241
The Magic Collection	p.149	unknown	■	Telstar	MEC 949018
The Originals (box set disk #1, Summer Days...)	*p.48*	*1997*	■	*EMI*	*7243 8 56070 2 8*
The Originals (box set disk #2, TODAY!)	*p.48*	*1997*	■	*EMI*	*7243 8 56072 2 6*
The Originals (box set)	*p.48*	*1997*	■	*EMI*	*7243 8 56069 2 2*
The Very Best of the Beach Boys	p.123	2001	■	EMI/Capitol	724353261528
The Wonderful World of The Beach Boys	p.161	1993	■	Remember	RMB 75634
TODAY! (Japan - Coolprice)	p.185	Sept., 1997	■	Toshiba-EMI	TOCP-3319
TODAY! (Japan - Mini LP series)	p.187	1998 & 2000	■	Toshiba-EMI	TOCP-50856
TODAY! (Japan - PastMasters)	p.183	June, 1990	■	Toshiba-EMI	CP21-6008
TODAY! (Japan + bonus tracks)	p.197	June 16th, 2001	■	Toshiba-EMI	TOCP-53168
TODAY!	p.27	June 28th, 1994	■	Capitol	CDP 724382963226
Today!/Summer Days (and SN's) (Canada)	p.67	1990	■	Capitol	C2 93694
Today!/Summer Days (and Summer Nights)	p.181	Dec. 12th, 1990	■	Toshiba-EMI	TOCP-6514
Today!/Summer Days (and Summer Nights) (UK)	p.66	1990	■	Capitol	CZ 324
Today!/Summer Days (and Summer Nights)	p.56	2001	■	Capitol	724353163921
Today!/Summer Days (and Summer Nights)	p.65	1990	■	Capitol	CDP 7 93694 2
Today!/Summer Days (and Summer Nights)	p.68	1990	■	BMG	D 100449
Today!/Summer Days (and Summer Nights)	p.68	2001	■	BMG	D 1387778
Ultimate Christmas (The Beach Boys)	p.171	Sept, 1998	■	Capitol	7243 4 95734 2 0
Ultimate Christmas	p.197	Nov. 19th, 2002	■	Toshiba-EMI	TOCP-65006
Unsurp. Masters – "The Live Box"	p.227	1998	■	Sea of Tunes	C 9843/44/45
Unsurp. Masters – Alt "Beach Boys Christmas"	p.226	1997	■	Sea of Tunes	C 9708/09/10
Unsurp. Masters "Live in Sacramento 2ND Concert"	p.225	1997	■	Sea of Tunes	C 9702
Unsurp. Masters "Live in Sacramento"	p.225	1997	■	Sea of Tunes	C 9701
Unsurp. Masters Vol. 1 - Alt "Surfin' Safari"	p.208	1997	■	Sea of Tunes	C 9703
Unsurp. Masters Vol. 10 - Alt "Party!"	p.214	1998	■	Sea of Tunes	C 9727/28/29/30
Unsurp. Masters Vol. 11 – 1965	p.215	1998	■	Sea of Tunes	C 9731/32
Unsurp. Masters Vol. 12 – Sloop John B. +	p.216	1998	■	Sea of Tunes	C 9733/34
Unsurp. Masters Vol. 13 - Alt "Pet Sounds" Vol.1	p.217	1998	■	Sea of Tunes	C 9735/36/37/38
Unsurp. Masters Vol. 14 – Alt "Pet Sounds" Vol.2	p.218	1998	■	Sea of Tunes	C 9739/40/41/42
Unsurp. Masters Vol. 15 – Good Vibrations	p.219	1999	■	Sea of Tunes	C 9946/47/48
Unsurp. Masters Vol. 16, SMILE	p.220	1999	■	Sea of Tunes	C9949
Unsurp. Masters Vol. 17, disk #1 SMILE sessions	p.221	1999	■	Sea of Tunes	C9950
Unsurp. Masters Vol. 17, disk #2 SMILE sessions	p.221	1999	■	Sea of Tunes	C9951
Unsurp. Masters Vol. 17, disk #3 SMILE sessions	p.221	1999	■	Sea of Tunes	C9952
Unsurp. Masters Vol. 18 - Alt "Smiley Smile"	p.222	1999	■	Sea of Tunes	C 9953
Unsurp. Masters Vol. 19 - Alt "Wild Honey"	p.223	1999	■	Sea of Tunes	C 9954/9955
Unsurp. Masters Vol. 2 - Alt "Surfin' USA"	p.208	1997	■	Sea of Tunes	C 9704
Unsurp. Masters Vol. 20 – Odds & Ends	p.224	1999	■	Sea of Tunes	C 9956/9957
Unsurp. Masters Vol. 21 – "TODAY/Summer Days"	p.228	1999	■	Sea of Tunes	C 9958
Unsurp. Masters Vol. 3 – Alt "Surfer Girl"	p.209	1997	■	Sea of Tunes	C 9705
Unsurp. Masters Vol. 4 – Miscellaneous Trax	p.209	1997	■	Sea of Tunes	C 9706/9707
Unsurp. Masters Vol. 5 – Miscellaneous Trax, Vol. 2	p.210	1997	■	Sea of Tunes	C 9711

Appendix III

CD Discography (alpha order)

CD Title	Page	Release Date		Label	CD Ref No
Unsurp. Masters Vol. 6 – Alt "All Summer Long"	p.210	1998	■	Sea of Tunes	C 9712/13/14/15
Unsurp. Masters Vol. 7 – Alt "TODAY!"	p.211	1998	■	Sea of Tunes	C 9715/16/17/18
Unsurp. Masters Vol. 8 – Alt "TODAY!" Vol.2	p.212	1998	■	Sea of Tunes	C 9719/20/21/22
Unsurp. Masters Vol. 9 – Alt "Summer Days"	p.213	1998	■	Sea of Tunes	C 9723/24/25/26
Wild Honey (Japan - Coolprice)	p.185	Oct., 1997	■	Toshiba-EMI	TOCP-3324
Wild Honey (Japan - Mini LP series)	p.187	1998 & 2000	■	Toshiba-EMI	TOCP-50861
Wild Honey (Japan - PastMasters)	p.183	June, 1990	■	Toshiba-EMI	CP21-6013
Wild Honey (Japan + bonus tracks)	p.198	June 27th, 2001	■	Toshiba-EMI	TOCP-53172
Wild Honey	p.27	July 26th, 1994	■	Capitol	CDP 724382963622
Youngblood (Carl Wilson solo)	p.261	1983	▪	SONY	SRCS6103
Your Imagination (BW promo)	p.178	1988	▪	Giant/Paladin	PRO CD 9280

Appendix III

CD Discography (alpha order)

CD Title	Page	Release Date	Label	CD Ref No

The Beach Boys on CD: The Beach Boys

Appendix IV
Song Listing (alphabetic order)

The following list includes titles recorded in all of the Beach Boys albums, solo albums and the best known bootlegs of un-released albums (SMiLE (Odeon version), LandLocked (Odeon version) and Bamboo. Some of the recording on the bootlegs have now been officially released on the Good Vibrations box set. The album 'Stack-O-Tracks' is not included. I have also included complete songs which appeared exclusively on certain compilations. Finally, the additional tracks (additional to the original Christmas album) on Ultimate Christmas are also included. Only one song from the Mike Love solo album is included. Alternative mixes, vocal only's, instrument only's on the various box sets and compilations will be set out in the second edition of this book and are not included here.

Song Title	Composer	Album/CD
A "Wonderful" insert	B. Wilson/V.D. Parks	Smile
A casual look	E. Wells	15 Big Ones
A day in the life of a tree	B. Wilson/J. Rieley	Surf's Up
A thing or two	B. Wilson/M. Love	Wild Honey
A young man is gone	B. Troup	L.D. Coupe
Add some music to your day	B. Wilson/M. Love/J. Knott	L'at the Roxy
Add some music to your day	B. Wilson	Sunflower
Airplane	B. Wilson	Love You
All alone	D. Wilson	Bamboo
All dressed up for school	B. Wilson	ASL twofer
All I wanna do	B. Wilson/M. Love	Sunflower
All I want to do	D. Wilson	20/20
All summer long	B. Wilson/M. Love	A.S. Long
All summer long	B. Wilson/M. Love	L'at the Roxy
All this is that	A. Jardine/C. Wilson/M. Love	Carl & TP
Alley oop	D. Frazier	Party!
Amusement parks, U.S.A	B. Wilson/M. Love	Summer Days+
And your dreams come true	B. Wilson/M. Love	Summer Days+
Angel come home	C. Wilson/G. Cushing-Murray	L.A. Light
Anna Lee, the healer	M. Love/B. Wilson	Friends
Aren't you glad	B. Wilson/M. Love	London '69
Aren't you glad	B. Wilson/M. Love	Wild Honey
At my window	A. Jardine/B. Wilson	Sunflower
Auld lang syne (bonus)	Trad. Arr. B. Wilson	Xmas album
Auld lang syne	Trad.	Xmas album
Awake (1970)	B. Wilson	Landlocked
Baby blue eyes	D. Wilson	Bamboo
Baby Blue	D. Wilson/K. Lamm/G. Jakobson	L.A. Light
Baby let your hair grow long	B. Wilson	Brian Wilson
Back home	B. Wilson/N.R Burton	L'at the Roxy
Back home	B. Wilson/N.R. Burton	15 Big Ones
Ballad of ole' Betsy	B. Wilson/R. Christian	L.D. Coupe
Barbara Ann	F. Fassert	L'at the Roxy
Barbara Ann	F. Fassert	London '69
Barbara Ann	F. Fassert	Party!
Barbara	D. Wilson	Bamboo
Barbie	B. Morgan	Lost & Found
Barnyard	B. Wilson	Smile
Be my baby	E. Greenwich/P. Spector/J. Barry	L'at the Roxy
Be still	D. Wilson/S. Kalinich	Friends
Be there in the morning	B. Wilson/C. Wilson/D. Wilson/A. Jardine/M. Love	Friends
Be true to your school (single version)	B. Wilson/M. Love	ASL twofer
Be true to your school	B. Wilson/M. Love	L.D. Coupe
Be with me	D. Wilson	20/20
Beach boys stomp	C. Wilson	Lost & Found
Being with the one you love	B. Wilson	Brian Wilson
Belles of Paris	B. Wilson/M. Love/R. Altbach	M.I.U. album
Bells of Christmas	A. Jardine/R. Altbach/M. Love	Ultimate Xmas
Better get back in bed	B. Wilson	Mt. Vernon EP
Bicycle rider theme	B. Wilson	Smile
Big Sur (4/4 time)	M. Love - The Monterey Saga	Landlocked
Blue Christmas	B. Hayes/J. Johnson	Xmas album
Blueberry hill	Lewis/Stock/Rose	15 Big Ones
Bluebirds over the mountain	E. Hickey	20/20
Bluebirds over the mountains	E. Hickey	London '69
Boogie woodie	Trad. Arr. B. Wilson	Surfer Girl
Break away	B. Wilson/R. Dunbar (Murry Wilson)	20/20 twofer
Bright Lights	C. Wilson/M. Smith	Carl Wilson
Bull session with "Big Daddy"	B. Wilson/C. Wilson/D. Wilson/M. Love/A. Jardine	TODAY!
Busy doin' nothin'	B. Wilson	Friends

Appendix IV
Song Listing (alphabetic order)

Song Title	Composer	Album/CD
Cabinessence	B. Wilson/V.D. Parks	20/20
Cabinessence	B. Wilson/V.D. Parks	Smile
Cabinesssence (backing track)	B. Wilson/V.D. Parks	Smile
California calling	A. Jardine/B. Wilson	The Beach B's
California dreamin'	J. Phillips	Made in USA
Summertime Music	M. Love	S'time Cruisin'
California Girls	B. Wilson/M. Love	In Concert
California girls	B. Wilson/M. Love	L'at the Roxy
California Girls	B. Wilson/M. Love	London '69
California girls	B. Wilson/M. Love	Still Cruisin'
California girls	B. Wilson/M. Love	Summer Days+
California saga/Big Sur	M. Love	Holland
California saga/California	A. Jardine	Holland
California saga/The beaks of eagles	A. Jardine/L. Jardine/R. Jeffers	Holland
Camp California	M. Love	S'time Cruisin'
California feelin'	B. Wilson	Classics BW
Can't wait too long	B. Wilson	Smile
Can't wait too long	B. Wilson	Smiley twofer
Car crazy cutie	B. Wilson/R. Christian	L.D. Coupe
Carl's big chance	B. Wilson/C. Wilson	A.S. Long
Caroline, No	B. Wilson/T. Asher	L'at the Roxy
Caroline, no	B. Wilson/T. Asher	IJWMFT times
Caroline, no	B. Wilson/T. Asher	In Concert
Caroline, no	B. Wilson/T. Asher	Pet Snds Live
Caroline, no	B. Wilson/T. Asher	Pet Sounds
Carry me home	D. Wilson	Bamboo
Catch a wave	B. Wilson/M. Love	Surfer Girl
Celebrate the news	D. Wilson/G. Jakobson	20/20 twofer
Chapel of love	P. Spector/E. Grenwich/J. Barry	15 Big Ones
Cherry, Cherry Coupe	B. Wilson/R. Christian	L.D. Coupe
Child is the father of the man	B. Wilson	Smile
Child of winter	B. Wilson/S. Kalinich	Ultimate Xmas
Christmas day	B. Wilson	Xmas album
Christmas time is here again	B. Holly/J. Allison/N. Petty/A. Jardine (lyrics)	Ultimate Xmas
Chug/a/lug	B. Wilson/G. Usher/M. Love	Surfin' Safari
Cindy, oh Cindy	B. Barons/B. Long	Surfin' twofer
Come go with me	Quick	M.I.U. album
Companion	D. Wilson	Bamboo
Cool, cool water	B. Wilson/M. Love	Sunflower
Cotton Fields (The cotton song)	H. Ledbetter	20/20
Country air	B. Wilson/M. Love	Wild Honey
County fair	B. Wilson/G. Usher	Surfin' Safari
Crack at your window	B. Wilson/A. Jardine	The Beach B's
Cry	B. Wilson	Imagination
Cuckoo clock	B. Wilson/G. Usher	Surfin' Safari
Cuddle up	D. Wilson/D. Dragon	Carl & TP
Custom machine	B. Wilson/M. Love	L.D. Coupe
Dance, dance, dance	B. Wilson/C. Wilson/M. Love	TODAY twofer
Dance, dance, dance	B. Wilson/C. Wilson/M. Love	TODAY!
Darlin'	B. Wilson/M. Love	In Concert
Darlin'	B. Wilson/M. Love	L'at the Roxy
Darlin'	B. Wilson/M. Love	London '69
Darlin'	B. Wilson/M. Love	Wild Honey
Deirdre	B. Johnston/B. Wilson	Sunflower
Denny's drums	D. Wilson	Shut Down V.2
Devoted to you	B. Bryant	Party!
Diamond head	B. Wilson/Vescozo/Ritz/Ackley	Friends
Ding dang	B. Wilson/R. McGuinn	Love You
Disney Girls (1957)	B. Johnston	Surf's Up
Do it again	B. Wilson/M. Love	L'at the Roxy
Do it again	B. Wilson/M. Love	Friends
Do it again	B. Wilson/M. Love	IJWMFT times
Do it again	B. Wilson/M. Love	London '69
Do you like worms	B. Wilson	Smile
Do you remember?	B. Wilson/M. Love	A.S. Long
Do you wanna dance	B. Freeman	TODAY!
Don't back down	B. Wilson/M. Love	A.S. Long
Don't back down	B. Wilson/M. Love	ASL twofer
Don't go near the water	A. Jardine/M. Love	Surf's Up

Appendix IV
Song Listing (alphabetic order)

Song Title	Composer	Album/CD
Don't hurt my little sister	B. Wilson/M. Love	TODAY!
Don't talk (put your head...)	B. Wilson/T. Asher	Pet Sounds
Don't worry baby	B. Wilson/R. Christian	Concert 2'fer
Don't worry baby	B. Wilson/R. Christian	In Concert
Don't worry baby	B. Wilson/R. Christian	L'at the Roxy
Don't worry baby	B. Wilson/R. Christian	Shut Down V.2
Dream Angel	B. Wilson/J. Thomas/J. Peterik	Imagination
Dreamer	D. Wilson/G. Jakobson	P.O. Blue
Drive/in	B. Wilson/M. Love	A.S. Long
End of the show	D. Wilson/G. Jakobson	P.O. Blue
Endless Harmony	B. Johnston	KTS Alive
Everyone's in love with you	M. Love	15 Big Ones
Fall break and back to Winter	B. Wilson	Smiley Smile
Farewell my friend	D. Wilson/G. Jakobson	P.O. Blue
Farmer's daughter	B. Wilson/M. Love	Surfin' USA
Feel Flows	C. Wilson/J. Rieley	Surf's Up
Finders keeprs	B. Wilson/M. Love	Surfin' USA
Forever	D. Wilson/G. Jakobsen	S'in Paradise
Forever	D. Wilson/G. Jakobson	Sunflower
Fourth of July	D. Wilson/J. Rieley	30 Year Box
Fourth of July	D. Wilson/J. Rieley	Landlocked
Friday night	B. Wilson	Smile
Friday night	D. Wilson/G. Jakobson	P.O. Blue
Friends	B. Wilson/C. Wilson/D. Wilson/A. Jardine	Friends
Frosty the snowman	S. Nelson/J. Rollins	Xmas album
Full Sail	C. Wilson/G. Cushing-Murray	L.A. Light
Fun, fun, fun (single version)	B. Wilson/M. Love	S.Down twofer
Fun, fun, fun	B. Wilson/M. Love	Concert
Fun, fun, fun	B. Wilson/M. Love	In Concert
Fun, fun, fun	B. Wilson/M. Love	Shut Down V.2
Funky pretty	B. Wilson/ M. Love/J. Rieley	In Concert
Funky Pretty	B. Wilson/ M. Love/J. Rieley	Holland
Games two can play	B. Wilson	30 Year Box I just
got my pay	B. Wilson/M. Love	30 Year Box
Games two can play	B. Wilson	Landlocked
George fell into his French horn	Not-credited	Smile
Getcha back	M. Love/T. Melcher	The Beach B's
Getting' hungry	B. Wilson/M. Love	Smiley Smile
Girl don't tell me	B. Wilson	Summer Days+
Girls on the beach	B. Wilson	A.S. Long
Givin' you up	C. Wilson/M. Smith/J. Schilling	Youngblood
God only knows	B. Wilson/T. Asher	L'at the Roxy
God only knows	B. Wilson/T. Asher	London '69
God only knows	B. Wilson/T. Asher	Pet Snds Live
God only knows	B. Wilson/T. Asher	Pet Sounds
Goin' on	B. Wilson/M. Love	KTS Alive
Goin' South	C. Wilson/G. Cushing-Murray	L.A. Light
Good time	B. Wilson/A. Jardine	Landlocked
Good time	B. Wilson/A. Jardine	Love You
Good Timin'	B. Wilson/C. Wilson	L.A. Light
Good to my baby	B. Wilson/M. Love	TODAY!
Good Vibrations (Early take)	B. Wilson/M. Love	Smiley twofer
Good Vibrations (Various sessions)	B. Wilson/M. Love	Smiley twofer
Good vibrations	B. Wilson/M. Love	In Concert
Good vibrations	B. Wilson/M. Love	L'at the Roxy
Good vibrations	B. Wilson/M. Love	London '69
Good Vibrations	B. Wilson/M. Love	Smiley Smile
Good Vibrations' closing bit	B. Wilson/M. Love	Smile
Got to know the woman	D. Wilson	Sunflower
Graduation day (studio version)	J. Sherman/N. Sherman	TODAY twofer
Graduation day	J. Sherman/N. Sherman	Concert
H & V/ I'm in great shape/Barnyard	B. Wilson/V.D. Parks	Smile
H.E.L.P is on the way	B. Wilson/M. Love	30 Year Box
H.E.L.P is on the way	B. Wilson/M. Love	Landlocked
Had to phone ya	B. Wilson/M. Love	15 Big Ones
Hang onto your ego	B. Wilson/T. Asher	Pet Sounds
Happy days	B. Wilson	Imagination
Hawaii	B. Wilson/M. Love	Concert
Hawaii	B. Wilson/M. Love	Surfer Girl

Appendix IV
Song Listing (alphabetic order)

Song Title	Composer	Album/CD
He come down	A. Jardine/B. Wilson/M. Love	Carl & TP
He couldn't get his old body moving	B. Wilson/L. Buckingham	Brian Wilson
He's a bum	D. Wilson	Bamboo
Head you win, tails I lose	B. Wilson/G. Usher	Surfin' Safari
Heaven	C. Wilson/M. Smith/M. Sun	Carl Wilson
Help me, Rhonda (single version)	B. Wilson/M. Love	Summer Days+
Help me, Rhonda	B. Wilson/M. Love	In Concert
Help me, Rhonda	B. Wilson/M. Love	L'at the Roxy
Help me, Ronda (LP version)	B. Wilson/M. Love	TODAY!
Here comes the night	B. Wilson/M. Love	L.A. Light
Here comes the night	B. Wilson/M. Love	Wild Honey
Here she comes	R. Fataar/B. Chaplin	Carl & TP
Here today	B. Wilson/T. Asher	Pet Snds Live
Here today	B. Wilson/T. Asher	Pet Sounds
Heroes and Villains (alternate take)	B. Wilson/V.D. Parks	Smiley twofer
Heroes and Villains	B. Wilson/V.D. Parks	Concert 2'fer
Heroes and Villains	B. Wilson/V.D. Parks	In Concert
Heroes and villains	B. Wilson/V.D. Parks	Smile
Heroes and Villains	B. Wilson/V.D. Parks	Smiley Smile
Hey little tomboy	B. Wilson	M.I.U. album
Hold me	C. Wilson/M. Smith	Carl Wilson
Hold on dear brother	R. Fataar/B. Chaplin	Carl & TP
Holidays	B. Wilson	Smile
Holy evening	D. Wilson	Bamboo
Holy, Holy (Morning Christmas)	D. Wilson	Landlocked
Honkin' down the highway	B. Wilson	Love You
Honky tonk	Doggett/Scott/Butler/Sheper/Glover	Surfin' USA
How she boogalooed	M. Love/B. Johnston/A. Jardine/C. Wilson	Wild Honey
Hully gully	F. Smith/C. Goldsmith	Party!
Hurry love	C. Wilson/M. Smith	Carl Wilson
Hushabye	D. Pomus/M. Shuman	A.S. Long
I can hear music	Barry/Greenwich/Spector	20/20
I do love you	S. Wonder	The Beach B's
I do	B. Wilson	S.Down twofer
I get around	B. Wilson/M. Love	A.S. Long
I get around	B. Wilson/M. Love	Concert
I get around	B. Wilson/M. Love	L'at the Roxy
I get around	B. Wilson/M. Love	Still Cruisin'
I just wasn't made for these times	B. Wilson/T. Asher	Pet Snds Live
I just wasn't made for these times	B. Wilson/T. Asher	Pet Sounds
I know there's an answer	B. Wilson/T. Sashen	Pet Snds Live
I know there's an answer	B. Wilson/T. Sashen	Pet Sounds
I love to say da da	B. Wilson	Smile
I should have known better	J. Lennon/P. McCartney	Party!
I wanna pick you up	B. Wilson	Love you
I was made to love her	Cosby/Hardaway/May/Wonder	Wild Honey
I went to sleep	B. Wilson/C. Wilson	20/20
I'd love just once to see you	B. Wilson/M. Love	Wild Honey
I'll be home for Christmas	W. Kent/K. Gannon	Xmas album
I'll bet he nice	B. Wilson	Love You
I'm bugged at my ol' man	B. Wilson	Summer Days+
I'm so lonely	B. Wilson/E. Landy	The Beach B's
I'm so young (alternative take)	W.H. Tyrus Jr.	TODAY twofer
I'm so young	W.H. Tyrus Jr.	TODAY!
I'm the pied piper	B. Wilson/C. Wilson	Mt. Vernon EP
I'm the pied piper/instrumental	B. Wilson/C. Wilson	Mt. Vernon EP
I'm waiting for the day	B. Wilson/M. Love	Pet Snds Live
I'm waiting for the day	B. Wilson/M. Love	Pet Sounds
If I could talk to love	C. Wilson/M. Smith	Youngblood
In my car	B. Wilson/E. Landy/Morgan	Still Cruisin'
In my room (German version)	B. Wilson/G. Usher	S.Down twofer
In my room	B. Wilson/G. Usher	Concert
In my room	B. Wilson/G. Usher	Surfer Girl
In the back of my mind	B. Wilson/M. Love	TODAY!
In the parkin' lot	B. Wilson/R. Christian	Shut Down V.2
In the still of the night	F. Parris	15 Big Ones
Island fever	T. Melcher/M. Love	S'in Paradise
Island girl	A. Jardine	Still Cruisin'

Appendix IV
Song Listing (alphabetic order)

Song Title	Composer	Album/CD
It's a beautiful day	A. Jardine/M. Love	10 Years OH San
Miguel	D. Wilson/G. Jakobson	10 Years OH
It's about time	D. Wilson/B. Burchman/A. Jardine	Sunflower
It's getting late	C. Wilson/Smith Shilling/R. White Johnson	The Beach B's
It's just a matter of time	B. Wilson/E. Landy	The Beach B's
It's not too long	D. Wilson	Bamboo
It's OK	B. Wilson/M. Love	15 Big Ones
It's over now	B. Wilson	30 Year Box Hot fun
in the summertime	S. Stone	S'in Paradise
Surfin'	B. Wilson/M. Love	S'in Paradise
Johnny B. Goode	C. Berry	Concert
Johnny Carson	B. Wilson	Love You
Judy	B. Wilson	Lost & Found
Just got my pay	B. Wilson/M. Love	Landlocked
Just once in my life	P. Spector/C. King/G. Goffin	15 Big Ones
Keep an eye on Summer	B. Wilson/B. Norman	Imagination
Keep an eye on summer	B. Wilson/B. Norman	Shut Down V.2
Keepin' the Summer alive	C. Wilson/R. Bachman	KTS Alive
Kiss me baby	B. Wilson/M. Love	L'at the Roxy
Kiss me, baby	B. Wilson/M. Love	TODAY!
Kokomo	J. Phillips/M. Love/T. Melcher/McKenzie	Still Cruisin'
Kona coast	A. Jardine/M. Love	M.I.U. album
Lady (Fallin' in Love)	D. Wilson	Landlocked
Lady Linda	A. Jardine/Allback	L.A. Light
Lahina aloha	T. Melcher/M. Love	S'in Paradise
Lana	B. Wilson	Surfin' USA
Land ahoy	B. Wilson	Surfin' twofer
Lavender	D. Morgan	Lost & Found
Lay down burden	B. Wilson/J. Thomas	Imagination
Lay down burden	B. Wilson/J. Thomas	L'at the Roxy
Leaving this town	R. Fataar/C. Wilson/B. Chaplin/M. Love	Holland
Leaving this town	R. Fataar/C. Wilson/B. Chaplin/M. Love	In Concert
Let him run wild	B. Wilson/M. Love	Imagination
Let him run wild	B. Wilson/M. Love	Summer Days+
Let him run wild	B. Wilson/M. Love	TODAY twofer
Let it shine	B. Wilson/J. Lynne	Brian Wilson
Let the wind blow	B. Wilson/M. Love	IJWMFT times
Let the wind blow	B. Wilson/M. Love	In Concert
Let the wind blow	B. Wilson/M. Love	Wild Honey
Let us go this way	B. Wilson/M. Love	Love You
Let's go away for a while	B. Wilson	L'at the Roxy
Let's go away for a while	B. Wilson	Pet Snds Live
Let's go away for a while	B. Wilson	Pet Sounds
Let's go to heaven in my car	B. Wilson/G, Usher	Brian Wilson
Let's go trippin'	D. Dale	Concert
Let's go trippin'	D. Dale	Surfin' USA
Let's put our hearts together	B. Wilson	Love You
Little bird	D. Wilson/S. Kalinich	Friends
Little children (demo)	B. Wilson	Brian Wilson
Little children	B. Wilson	Brian Wilson
Little deuce coupe	B. Wilson/R. Christian	Concert
Little Deuce Coupe	B. Wilson/R. Christian	L.D. Coupe
Little deuce Coupe	B. Wilson/R. Christian	Surfer Girl
Little Girl (You're my miss America)	Catalono/H. Alpert	Surfin' Safari
Little Honda	B. Wilson/M. Love	A.S. Long
Little Honda (alternate take)	B. Wilson/M. Love	ASL twofer
Little pad	B. Wilson	Smiley Smile
Little Saint Nick (alternate take)	B. Wilson	Xmas album
Little Saint Nick (single version)	Trad. Arr. B. Wilson	Xmas album
Little Saint Nick	B. Wilson	Xmas album
Little surfer girl	B. Wilson	30 Year Box
Livin' with a heartache	C. Wilson/R. Bachman	KTS Alive
Lonely sea	B. Wilson/G. Usher	Surfin' USA
Long promised road	C. Wilson/J. Rieley	Surf's Up
Long Tall Texan	H. Strezlecki	Concert
Look	B. Wilson	Smile
Lookin' at tomorrow	A. Jardine/G. Winfrey	Surf's Up
Looking down the Coast	B. Wilson - The Monterey Saga	Landlocked
Loop de loop (original version)	A. Jardine/B. Wilson	Landlocked

Appendix IV
Song Listing (alphabetic order)

Song Title	Composer	Album/CD
Louie, Louie	R. Berry	Shut Down V.2
Love and mercy	B. Wilson	Brian Wilson
Love and mercy	B. Wilson	L'at the Roxy
Love and mercy	B. Wilson/E. Landy	IJWMFT times
Love is a woman	B. Wilson	Love You
Love surrounds me	C. Wilson/G. Cushing-Murray	L.A. Light
Love surrounds me	D. Wilson	Bamboo
Luau	B. Wilson	Lost & Found
Magic transistor radio	B. Wilson	Mt. Vernon EP
Make it big	T. Melcher/House/M. Love	Still Cruisin'
Make it good	D. Wilson/D. Dragon	Carl & TP
Male ego	B. Wilson/M. Love/E. Landy	The Beach B's
Mama says	B. Wilson/M. Love	Wild Honey
Marcella	B. Wilson/ T. Almer/J. Rieley	In Concert
Marcella	B. Wilson/T. Almer/J. Rieley	Carl & TP
Match point of our love	B. Wilson/M. Love	M.I.U. album
Maybe I don't know	C. Wilson/Smith Shilling/Levine/Lindsey	The Beach B's
Meant for You	B. Wilson/M. Love	Friends
Meant for you	B. Wilson/M. Love	IJWMFT times
Medley (I get around/little Deuce coupe)	B. Wilson/M. Love/R. Christian	Party!
Meet me in my dreams tonight	B. Wilson/A, Paley/A. Dean	Brian Wilson
Melekalikimaka	A. Jardine/M. Love	Ultimate Xmas
Melt away (early version)	B. Wilson	Brian Wilson
Melt away	B. Wilson	Brian Wilson
Melt away	B. Wilson/E. Landy	IJWMFT times
Misirlou	Roubanis/Wise/Leeds/Russell	Surfin' USA
Mona	B. Wilson	Love You
Monster mash	B. Pickett/L. Copizzi	Concert
Moon dawg	D. Weaver	Surfin' Safari
Moonlight	D. Wilson	Bamboo
Moonshine	D. Wilson/G. Jakobson	P.O. Blue
Morning Christmas (Holy, Holy)	D. Wilson	Ultimate Xmas
Mountain of love	H. Dorman	Party!
Mrs. O'Leary's cow	B. Wilson	Smile
Mt. Vernon & Fairway/theme	B. Wilson	Mt. Vernon EP
My Diane	B. Wilson	M.I.U. album
My Solution (1970; creepy)	B. Wilson	Landlocked
Never learn not to love	D. Wilson	20/20
New Orleans	D. Wilson	Bamboo
Night bloomin' jasmine	B. Wilson	Brian Wilson
Night time (instrumental)	B. Wilson/A. Paley	Brian Wilson
Night time	B. Wilson/A. Paley	Brian Wilson
No/Go showboat	B. Wilson/R. Christian	L.D. Coupe
Noble surfer	B. Wilson/M. Love	Surfin' USA
Of these times	C. Wilson/M. Smith	Youngblood
Oh Darlin'	B. Wilson/M. Love	KTS Alive
Old folks at home/Ol' man river	S. Foster	20/20 twofer
One for the boys	B. Wilson	Brian Wilson
One more night alone	B. Hinche	Youngblood
Only with You (Carl Wilson live)	D. Wilson/M. Love	Landlocked
Only with you	D. Wilson/M. Love	Holland
Our car club	B. Wilson/M. Love	L.D. Coupe
Our car club	B. Wilson/M. Love	Surfer Girl
Our favourite recording sessions	The Beach Boys	A.S. Long
Our prayer	B. Wilson	20/20
Our Prayer	B. Wilson	Smile
Our sweet love	B. Wilson/C. Wilson/A. Jardine	Sunflower
Out in the country		Landlocked
Over the waves	B. Wilson	Landlocked
Pacific ocean blues	D. Wilson/M. Love	P.O. Blue
Palisades Park	C. Barris	15 Big Ones
Pap-omm-mow-mow	Frazer/White/Harris/Wilson Jr.	Concert
Pap-omm-mow-mow	Frazer/White/Harris/Wilson Jr.	Party!
Paradise Found	M. Love/J. Studer	LBW Love
Passing by	B. Wilson	Friends
Passing friend	G. O'Dowd/Hay	The Beach B's
Peggy Sue	Allison/Petty/B. Holly	M.I.U. album
Pet sounds	B. Wilson	L'at the Roxy
Pet Sounds	B. Wilson	Pet Snds Live

Appendix IV
Song Listing (alphabetic order)

Song Title	Composer	Album/CD
Pet Sounds	B. Wilson	Pet Sounds
Pitter patter	B. Wilson/A. Jardine/M. Love	M.I.U. album
Please let me wonder	B. Wilson/M. Love	L'at the Roxy
Please let me wonder	B. Wilson/M. Love	TODAY!
Pom pom play girl	B. Wilson/G. Usher	Shut Down V.2
Punchline	B. Wilson	30 Year Box
Radio King Dom	B. Wilson	Mt. Vernon EP
Rainbows	D. Wilson/C. Wilson/S. Kalanich	P.O. Blue
Remember walking in the sand	Morton	S'in Paradise
Rio Grande (early version)	B. Wilson/A. Paley	Brian Wilson
Rio Grande	B. Wilson/A. Paley	Brian Wilson
River song	D. Wilson	Bamboo
River Song	D. Wilson/C. Wilson	P.O. Blue
Rock and Roll music	C. Berry	15 Big Ones
Rock'N'Roll to the rescue	M. Love/T. Melcher	Made in USA
Rockin' all over the world	J.C. Fogerty	Youngblood
Roller skating child	B. Wilson	Love You
Ruby Baby	J. Leiber/M. Stoller	30 Year Box
Sail on, Sailor (arrangement)	B. Wilson/T. Almer/V.D. Parks/J. Rieley/R. Kennedy	Landlocked
Sail on, sailor	B. Wilson/T. Almer/V.D. Parks/J. Rieley/R. Kennedy	Holland
Sail on, sailor	B. Wilson/T. Almer/V.D. Parks/J. Rieley/R. Kennedy	In Concert
Salt lake City	B. Wilson/M. Love	Summer Days+
San Miguel	D. Wilson/G. Jakobson	Landlocked
Santa Ana winds	B. Wilson/A. Jardine - The Monterey Saga	Landlocked
Santa Ana winds	B. Wilson/A. Jardine	KTS Alive
Santa Claus is comin' to town	J.F. Coots/H. Gillespie	Xmas album
Santa's Beard	B. Wilson	Xmas album
Santa's got an airplane	A. Jardine/B. Wilson/M. Love	Ultimate Xmas
School day (ring, ring goes the bell)	C. Berry	KTS Alive
School girl	D. Wilson	Bamboo
Sea Cruise	Smith	10 Years OH
Sea Cruise	Smith	Bamboo
Seems so long ago	C. Wilson/M. Smith	Carl Wilson
She believes in love again	B. Johnston	The Beach B's
She knows me too well	B. Wilson/M. Love	TODAY!
She says that she needs me	B. Wilson/R. Titelman/C.B. Sager	Imagination
She's goin' bald	B. Wilson/V.D. Parks/M. Love	Smiley Smile
She's got rhythm	B. Wilson/M. Love/R. Altbach	M.I.U. album
She's mine	C. Wilson/M. Smith	Youngblood
Shortenin' bread	Trad. Arr. B. Wilson	L.A. Light
Shut down, America	B. Wilson/R. Christian	L.D. Coupe Spirit of
Shut down	B. Wilson/R. Christian	L.D. Coupe
Shut down	B. Wilson/R. Christian	Surfin' USA
Shut down, part II	C. Wilson	Shut Down V.2
Slip on through	D. Wilson	Sunflower
Sloop john B	Trad. Arr. B. Wilson	L'at the Roxy
Sloop John B.	Trad. Arr. B. Wilson	In Concert
Sloop John B.	Trad. Arr. B. Wilson	London '69
Sloop John B.	Trad. Arr. B. Wilson	Pet Snds Live
Sloop John B.	Trad. Arr. B. Wilson	Pet Sounds
Slow summer dancing (one summer night)	B. Johnston/J. Webb	S'in Paradise
Smile promo advert	Un-credited	Smile
Solar System	B. Wilson	Love You
Some of your love	B. Wilson/M. Love	KTS Alive
Somewhere near Japan	J. Phillips/T. Melcher/M. Love/B. Johnston	Still Cruisin'
Soulful old man sunshine	B. Wilson/R. Henn	Landlocked
Sound of the free	D. Wilson/D. Dragon	Landlocked
South America	B. Wilson/J. Thomas/J. Buffett	Imagination
South bay surfer	B. Wilson/D. Wilson/A. Jardine	Surfer Girl
Steamboat	B. Wilson/J. Rieley	Holland
Still Cruisin'	T. Melcher/M. Love	Still Cruisin'
Still I dream of it	B. Wilson	IJWMFT times
Still Surfin'	M. Love/T. Melcher	S'in Paradise
Stoked	B. Wilson	Surfin' USA
Strange things happen	T. Melcher/M. Love	S'in Paradise
Student demonstration time	J. Leiber/M. Stoller/M. Love (lyric)	Surf's Up
Sumahama	M. Love	L.A. Light
Summer in Paradise	M. Love/T. Melcher/Fall	S'in Paradise
Summer means new love	B. Wilson	Summer Days+

Appendix IV
Song Listing (alphabetic order)

Song Title	Composer	Album/CD
Summer of love	M. Love/T. Melcher	S'in Paradise
Summertime Blues	E. Cochran/J. Capehart	Surfin' Safari
Sunshine	B. Wilson/J. Thomas	Imagination
Sunshine	B. Wilson/M. Love	KTS Alive
Surf jam	C. Wilson	Surfin' USA
Surf's Up	B. Wilson/V.D. Parks	Smile
Surf's Up	B. Wilson/V.D. Parks	Surf's Up
Surfer girl	B. Wilson	In Concert
Surfer girl	B. Wilson	L'at the Roxy
Surfer girl	B. Wilson	Lost & Found
Surfer girl	B. Wilson	Surfer Girl
Surfer's rule	B. Wilson/M. Love	Surfer Girl
Surfin' Safari	B. Wilson/M. Love	Lost & Found
Surfin' safari	B. Wilson/M. Love	Surfin' Safari
Surfin' USA	C. Berry	Surfin' USA
Surfin' USA	C. Berry/B. Wilson	In Concert
Surfin'	B. Wilson/M. Love	Lost & Found
Surfin'	B. Wilson/M. Love	Surfin' Safari
Susie Cincinnati	A. Jardine	15 Big Ones
Sweet Sunday	B. Wilson/M. Love	M.I.U. album
T M Song	B. Wilson	15 Big Ones
Take a load of your feet	A. Jardine/G. Winfrey	Surf's Up
Talk to me	J. Seneca	15 Big Ones
Tears in the Morning	B. Johnston	Sunflower
Tell me why	J. Lennon/P. McCartney	Party!
Ten little indians	B. Wilson/G. Usher	Surfin' Safari
That same song	B. Wilson/M. Love	15 Big Ones
That's not me	B. Wilson/T. Asher	Pet Snds Live Don't
talk (put your head...)	B. Wilson/T. Asher	Pet Snds Live
That's not me	B. Wilson/T. Asher	Pet Sounds
The baker man	B. Wilson	Surfin' twofer
The first time	B. Wilson	L'at the Roxy
The girl from New York city	B. Wilson/M. Love	Summer Days+
The Grammy	C. Wilson/M. Smith	Carl Wilson
The letter	Carson	Rarities (Jap)
The little girl I once knew (single)	B. Wilson	TODAY twofer
The little girl I once knew	B. Wilson	L'at the Roxy
The little old lady from Pasadena	A. Allfield/R. Christian	Concert
The Lord's prayer	A. B. Malotte	Xmas album
The man with all the toys	B. Wilson	Xmas album
The nearest faraway place	B. Johnston	20/20
The night was so young	B. Wilson	Love You
The old master painter	B. Wilson	Smile
The right lane	C. Wilson/M. Smith	Carl Wilson
The rocking surfer	Trad. Arr. B. Wilson	Surfer Girl
The shift	B. Wilson/M. Love	Surfin' Safari
The surfer moon	B. Wilson	Surfer Girl
The times they are a-changin'	B. Dylan	Party!
The Trader	C. Wilson/J. Rieley	Holland
The Trader	C. Wilson/J. Rieley	In Concert
The wanderer	E. Maresca	Concert
The warmth of the sun	B. Wilson/M. Love	IJWMFT times
The warmth of the sun	B. Wilson/M. Love	Shut Down V.2
Their hearts were full of Spring	B. Troup	London '69
Their hearts were full of Spring	B. Troup	Smiley twofer
Then I kissed her	P. Spector/E. Grenwich/J. Barry	Summer Days+
There's no other (Like my baby)	P. Spector/L. Bates	Party!
There's so many (demo)	B. Wilson	Brian Wilson
There's so many	B. Wilson	Brian Wilson
Things we did last summer	Styne/Cahn	30 Year Box
This car of mine	B. Wilson/M. Love	Shut Down V.2
This isn't love	B. Wilson/T. Asher	L'at the Roxy
This whole world	B. Wilson	IJWMFT times
This whole world	B. Wilson	L'at the Roxy
This whole world	B. Wilson	Sunflower
Thoughts of you	D. Wilson/J. Dutch	P.O. Blue
Three blind mice	Trad. Arr. B. Wilson	Smile
Time to get alone	B. Wilson	20/20
Time	C. Wilson/M. Smith	Youngblood

Appendix IV
Song Listing (alphabetic order)

Song Title	Composer	Album/CD
Time	D. Wilson/M. Smith	P.O. Blue
Too early to tell	C. Wilson/M. Smith/J. Daly	Youngblood
Too much sugar	B. Wilson	Brian Wilson
Transcendental meditation	B. Wilson/M. Love/A. Jardine	Friends
Trombone Dixie	B. Wilson	Pet Sounds
Under the boardwalk	Resnick/Young + Love (lyrics)	S'in Paradise
Vega-Tables	B. Wilson/V.D. Parks	Smile
Vegetables	B. Wilson/V.D. Parks	Smiley Smile
Wake the world	B. Wilson/A. Jardine	Friends
Wake the world	B. Wilson/A. Jardine	London '69
Walk on by	B. Bacharach/H. David	20/20 twofer
Walkin' the line (demo)	B. Wilson/N Laird-Clowes	Brian Wilson
Walkin' the line	B. Wilson/N Laird-Clowes	Brian Wilson
Water/ Cool, cool water	B. Wilson	Smile
We got love (studio version)	R. Fataar/B. Chaplin/M. Love	Landlocked
We got love	R. Fataar/B. Chaplin/M. Love	In Concert
We three Kings of Orient are	J. Hopkins	Xmas album
We'll run away	B. Wilson/G. Usher	A.S. Long
We're together again	B. Wilson/D. Wilson	20/20 twofer
Wendy	B. Wilson/M. Love	A.S. Long
What is a young girl made of	B. Morgan	Lost & Found
What more can I say	C. Wilson/M. Smith	Youngblood
What you do to me	J. Hall/J. Hall	Youngblood
What you gonna do about me	C. Wilson/M. Smith	Carl Wilson
What's wrong	D. Wilson/G. Jakobson/M Horn	P.O. Blue
When a man needs a woman	B. Wilson/C. Wilson/D. Wilson/A. Jardine/V.D. Parks/S. Korthof	Friends
When girls get together	B. Wilson/M. Love	KTS Alive
When girls get together	B. Wilson/M. Love	Landlocked
When I grow up (to be a man)	B. Wilson/M. Love	TODAY!
Where has love been	B. Wilson/A. Paley/J.D. Souther	Imagination
Where I belong	C. Wilson/R. White Johnson	The Beach B's
Whistle in	B. Wilson	Smiley Smile
White Christmas	I. Berlin	Xmas album
Why do fools fall in love	F. Lymon/M. Levy	Shut Down V.2
Wild honey	B. Wilson/M. Love	Wild Honey
Wild situation	D. Wilson	Bamboo
Wind chimes (alternate ending)	B. Wilson	Smile
Wind chimes	B. Wilson	Smile
Wind chimes	B. Wilson	Smiley Smile
Winds of change	R. Altback/Tulleja	M.I.U. album
Winter Symphony	B. Wilson	Landlocked
Winter Symphony	B. Wilson	Ultimate Xmas
Wipe our	The Surfaris	Still Cruisin'
With a little help from my friends	J. Lennon/P. McCartney	Rarities (Jap)
With me tonight	B. Wilson	Smile
With me tonight	B. Wilson	Smiley Smile
Woncha come out tonight	B. Wilson/M. Love	M.I.U. album
Wonderful	B. Wilson/V.D. Parks	IJWMFT times
Wonderful	B. Wilson/V.D. Parks	Smile
Wonderful	B. Wilson/V.D. Parks	Smiley Smile
Wouldn't it be nice	B. Wilson/T. Asher	In Concert
Wouldn't it be nice	B. Wilson/T. Asher	L'at the Roxy
Wouldn't it be nice	B. Wilson/T. Asher	Pet Snds Live
Wouldn't it be nice	B. Wilson/T. Asher	Pet Sounds
Wouldn't it be nice	B. Wilson/T. Asher	Still Cruisin'
Wouldn't it be nice	B. Wilson/T. Asher/M. Love	London '69
You and I	D. Wilson/K. Lamm-Wilson/G. Jakobson	P.O. Blue
You need a mess of help to stand alone	B. Wilson/J. Rieley	Carl & TP
You still believe in me	B. Wilson/T. Asher	In Concert
You still believe in me	B. Wilson/T. Asher	Pet Snds Live
You still believe in me	B. Wilson/T. Asher	Pet Sounds
You're so good to me	B. Wilson/M. Love	Summer Days+
You're Welcome	B. Wilson	Smile
You're welcome	B. Wilson	Smiley twofer
You've got to hide your love away	J. Lennon/P. McCartney	Party!
Youngblood	J. Leiber/M. Stoller/Doc Pomus	Youngblood
Your imagination	B. Wilson/J. Thomas/S.R. Dahl	Imagination
Your summer dream	B. Wilson/B. Norberg	Surfer Girl
(I saw Santa) Rockin' around the Xmas…	B. Wilson/A. Jardine (instrumental)	Ultimate Xmas

Appendix IV
Song Listing (alphabetic order)

Song Title	Composer	Album/CD
'Til I die	B. Wilson	IJWMFT times
'Til I die	B. Wilson	L'at the Roxy
'Til I die	B. Wilson	Surf's Up
"Cassius" Love vs "Sonny" Wilson	M. Love/B. Wilson	Shut Down V.2
409	B. Wilson/G. Usher/M. Love	Surfin' Safari
409	B. Wilson/M. Love/G. Usher	L.D. Coupe

The Beach Boys on CD: Appendices

Appendix V

The Rogues Gallery

  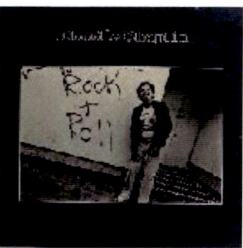 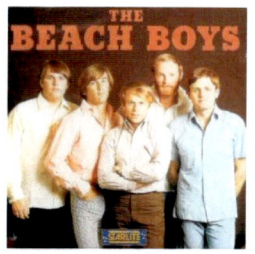

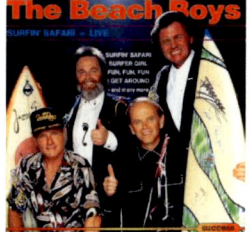 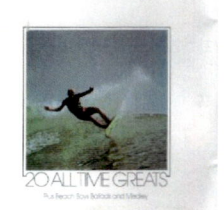  

  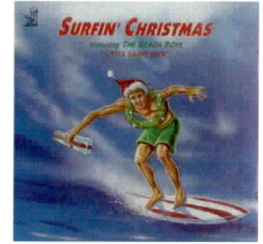 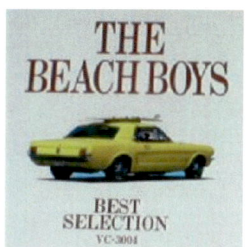

  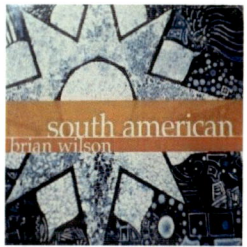

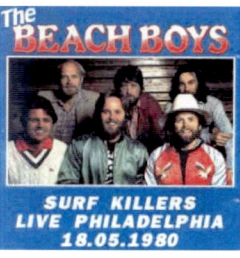 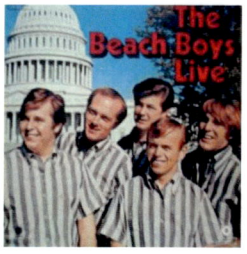

The Beach Boys on CD: Appendices

Appendix V

The Rogues Gallery

Although I have general information on most, the following CD's have escaped my grasp. If you recognise and own any of these CD covers, please contact me. If possible you might provide the following information:-

Release date/Track Listing/CD Serial No./ No of Discs/JPG images

rathmich@gofree.indigo.ie

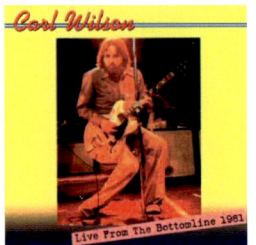

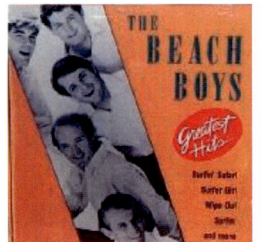

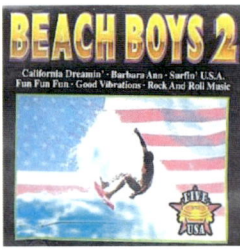

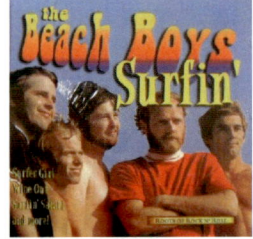

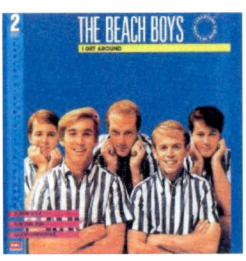
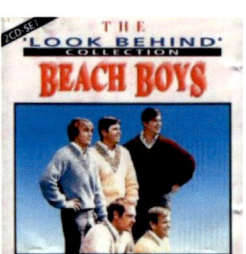

Appendix VI

STOP!! The presses

The following CD's have just dropped into my lap, I'm not going to re-number the pages!

Title: Surfer Girl
Artist:
Released:
Label:
CD Ref. No:
Country:
No. of Disks: 1
Format: Audio CD
Audio: mono/stereo

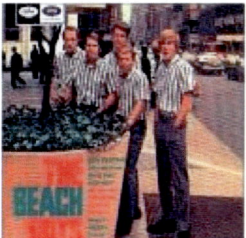
Title: Smiley Smile+
Artist: The Beach Boys
Released: Sept, 1988
Label: EMI/Magic (Fr)
CD Ref. No: 4975762
Country: France
No. of Disks: 1
Format: Audio CD
Audio: mono/stereo

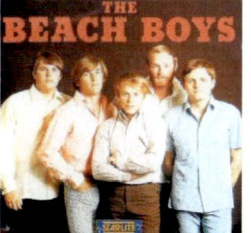
Title: Greatest Hits
Artist: The Beach Boys
Released:
Label: Starlight
CD Ref. No:
Country: Germany
No. of Disks: 1
Format: Audio CD
Audio: mono/stereo

Title: 20 All Time Greats
Artist: The Beach Boys
Released: 1991
Label: Capitol/EMI
CD Ref. No: CDP-791013
Country: Australia
No. of Disks: 1
Format: Audio CD
Audio: mono/stereo

Title: Best Vol. 3
Artist: The Beach Boys
Released: 1988
Label: Axis/EMI
CD Ref. No: CDAX 260104
Country: Australia
No. of Disks: 1
Format: Audio CD
Audio: mono/stereo

Title: Christmas album
Artist: The Beach Boys
Released: 1990's
Label: Axis/EMI
CD Ref. No: CDAX701413
Country: Australia
No. of Disks: 1
Format: Audio CD
Audio: mono/stereo

Title: Imagination (promo)
Artist: Brian Wilson
Released: 1988
Label: Giant
CD Ref. No: 27703
Country: US
No. of Disks: 1
Format: Audio CD
Audio: stereo

Appendix VII

Book references & Internet addresses (URL's)

The following is a list of books, periodicals and Internet references that the reader may find interesting and will provide further information about the Beach Boys. I have repeated certain references previously provide within the book

Bach To The Beach:- Kingsley Abbott
Pub: Helter Skelter, ISBN 1-900924-46-3

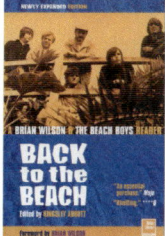

Endless Summer (Periodical):- Dave Beard (editor)

Heroes & Villains:- Steven Gains
Pub: DA CAPA Press, ISBN 0-306-80647-9

How Deep Is The Ocean: - P. Williams
Pub: Omnibus Press, ISBN 0-7119-6197-2

Look, Listen, Vibrate, Smile (Dominic Priore)
Pub: Small Press Distribution, ISBN 0867194170

The Beach Boys (Guide to the Music of): Andrew G. Doe/John Tobler
Pub: Omnibus Press, ISBN 0-7119-5595-6 (Out of Print)

The Beach Boys Pet Sounds:- Kingsley Abbott
Pub: Helter Skelter, ISBN 1-9000924-30-7

The Beach Boys:- David Leaf
Pub: Courage Books,
ISBN, 0-89471-412-0(OOP)

The Beach Boys:- John Tobler
Pub: Phoebus Publishing (OOP)

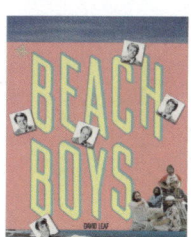

Wouldn't It Be Nice (My own story):- Brian Wilson/Todd Gold
Pub: Bloomsbury, ISBN, 0-7475-3145-5

Appendix VII

Book references & Internet addresses (URL's)

Wouldn't It Be Nice (Beach Boys Pet Sounds):- Charles L. Granata
Pub: Chicago Review Press, ISBN, 1-55652-507-9

The Nearest Faraway Place:- Timothy White
Pub: Henry Holt & Co., ISBN 0-8050-2266-X

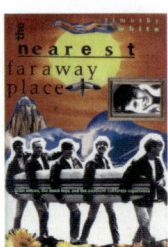

Add Some Music To Your Day:-
Don Cunningham & Jeff Bleiel
Pub: Tiny Ripple Books:
ISBN, 0-9675973-0-72266-X

Denny Remembered:- Edward Wincentsen
Pub: Wynn Publishing: ISBN, 0-9642808-3-3

Dumb Angel:- Adam Webb
Pub: Creation Books: ISBN, 1-84068-015-2

The Beach Boys (in their own words):- Nick Wise
Pub: Omnibus Press: ISBN, 0-7119-3940-3

Appendix VII

Book references & Internet addresses (URL's)

http://eil.com/
Another UK site with a large selection of Beach Boys CD's and LP's etc., Very expensive!!

http://www.musicstack.com/
Fantastic resource for 2nd hand Beach Boys CD's. Seller from all over the world, not always up to date though

http://www.musicexp.com/beachboy/bb1.htm
Michael Murphy's great Beach Boys CD resource. I have bought numerous CD's here. The service is superb.

Internet URL's (Beach Boys Reference sites)

http://www.angelfire.com/la/Beachboysbritain/
The best Beach Boys site in the world. Unequalled site for facts, history etc., etc.,

http://www.cabinessence.com
The 2nd best Beach Boys site in the world. Great resource for bootleg information and links to Beach Boys articles.

http://www.beachboys.com/
A very good Beach Boys site.

http://toshiba-emi.co.jp/
Information on the current Japanese Beach Boys CD catalogue

http://thebeachboys.com/
The official Capitol Record Beach Boys site.

http://www.toshiba-emi.co.jp/international/release/index_j199801.htm
Toshiba-EMI site detailing the release dates of all Beach Boys CD's since 1997. You have to know what 'kanji' for Beach Boys is though...here it is   _____

Appendix VII

Book references & Internet addresses (URL's)

Internet URL's (CD sales and information)

http://www.allmusic.com/
General Music resource (Track listings/Biographies/release dates etc.,)

http://www.bestwebbuys.com/music/index.html
Guide to sites selling Beach Boys CD's (Amazon, eBay etc.,)

http://www.cduniverse.com/
Online Music Store

http://half.ebay.com/index.jsp
Cut down prices at Ebay (not an auction site, available to US/Canada residents)

http://www.ebay.com/
http://www.ebay.co.uk
http://www.ebay.de
Ebay, your source for inexpensive Beach Boys catalogue (be patient though). The best sites are the US/UK/Germany/Australia

http://www.amazon.com
http://www.amazon.co.uk
CD sales, be warned though, they seldom have the rare ones

http://www.djangos.com/
A superb US site for 2nd hand Beach Boys CD's, but be aware, they can send the wrong CD's and the post to Europe is just too slow.

http://www.cdjapan.co.jp/
Buy all your Beach Boys Japanese CD here. An absolutely fantastic service and not too expensive

http://www.101cd.com/Home/
A UK site boasting a huge selection of rare Beach Boys CD's. I have only used their services once, very slow